Face to Face

Early Quaker Encounters
with the Bible

by T. Vail Palmer, Jr.

BARCLAY PRESS
Newberg, OR 97132

Face to Face
Early Quaker Encounters with the Bible
©2016 by T. Vail Palmer, Jr.

BARCLAY PRESS
Newberg, Oregon
www.barclaypress.com
www.barclaypress.com/vailpalmer

Unless otherwise noted, scripture quotations are taken from
The New Revised Standard Version, copyright 1989, 1995 by the
Division of Christian Education of the National Council of
the Churches of Christ in the United States of America.
Used by permission. All rights reserved.

Printed in the United States of America

COVER DESIGN BY DARRYL BROWN

ISBN 978-1-59498-037-4

To my beloved and devoted wife

Izzy

Your urging and backing got me started on this book.

Your continuing support and encouragement have made it easy for me

to persist in the project through thick and thin for all these years.

Contents

Introduction

Through most of our history, Friends have taken the Bible seriously and have looked to it for guidance. Friends have been leaders in testifying against war and working for peace, in recognizing the equality of women and men in Christian ministry, in working against slavery and advocating for social justice.

Yet we find in the Bible words such as these:

- Women should be silent in the churches. For they are not permitted to speak, but should be subordinate (1 Corinthians 14:34).

- Thus says the Lord of hosts, . . . "Go and attack Amalek, and utterly destroy all that they have; do not spare them, but kill both man and woman, child and infant" (1 Samuel 15:2-3).

- You will always have the poor with you (Matthew 26:11).

- Proclaim this among the nations: Prepare war. . . . Beat your plowshares into swords, and your pruning hooks into spears; let the weakling say, "I am a warrior" (Joel 3:9-10).

- Tell slaves to be submissive to their masters and to give satisfaction in every respect (Titus 2:9).

The earliest Friends constantly quoted the Bible—and it is clear that their pioneering positions on matters such as war, women's ministry, and justice derive from their understanding of the Bible.

How can this be? How did they make sense of the diversity within the Bible? Did they have consistent principles of interpretation to help them understand the Bible and to apply it to their own life and history?

Let's start with Robert Barclay, a widely respected Quaker theologian. He claimed that what Quakers believe about the authority of the Bible is that it is but a secondary rule:

> Because [the Scriptures] are only a declaration of the fountain, and not the fountain itself, therefore they are not to be esteemed the principal ground of all truth and knowledge, nor yet the adequate primary rule of faith and manners. Yet because they give a true and faithful testimony of the first foundation, they are and may be esteemed a secondary rule, subordinate to the Spirit, from which they have all their excellency and certainty: for as by the inward testimony of the Spirit we do alone truly know them, so they testify, That the Spirit is that Guide by which the saints are led into all Truth; therefore, according to the scriptures, the Spirit is the first and principal leader.[1]

But as the centuries rolled on, Friends took radically different paths in drawing out the implications of what Barclay had written. When leading Gurneyite Friends gathered in Richmond, Indiana, in 1887 and wrote a Declaration of Faith, they insisted: "whatsoever any one says or does, contrary to the Scriptures, though under the profession of the immediate guidance of the Holy Spirit, must be reckoned and accounted a mere delusion." They maintained "that the Holy Scriptures of the Old and New Testament were given by inspiration of God; that, therefore, there can be no appeal from them to any other authority whatsoever."[2]

In contrast, Lucretia Mott, a radical nineteenth-century Hicksite Friend had this to say about the Bible: "I have now no difficulty in deciding upon the human and ignorant origin of such parts as conflict with the known and eternal laws of Deity in the Physical creation."[3] "The great error of Christendom is, in regarding these scriptures taken as a whole as the plenary inspiration of God, and their authority as supreme."[4] "How satisfactory then are the . . . testimonies of Scripture but not more so than the testimonies of many other servants of God. . . . Are there not equal testimonies born to the truth that are not bound in this volume?"[5]

My great-grandfather, George Lamborn, was a Hicksite Quaker farmer in Lancaster County, Pennsylvania. Many of his neighbors were Bible-loving Mennonite farmers. Lancaster County's climate and red clay soil were ideal for growing tobacco. Those nineteenth-century Quakers and Mennonites all believed that smoking was a vice. The Mennonite farmers had no problem with growing and selling tobacco therefore becoming prosperous. George Lamborn believed it was as sinful to enable others to smoke tobacco as it was for him to smoke; but growing other crops was less lucrative, and he struggled financially. He refused to let his children read the Bible, arguing that those who read the Bible were morally no better than those who didn't.

In my high school days and first year of college I was a wistful agnostic, even as I attended meeting regularly and took part in Young Friends activities. Through reading Thomas Kelly's *A Testament of Devotion* I came to a lively experience of and belief in God; I resonated to his words: "With urgent hunger we read the Scriptures, . . . in order to find more friends for the soul."[6] I thrilled as I read Kenneth Boulding's lecture, "The Practice of the Love of God," into which several deep biblical passages naturally found their way—up to his conclusion: the ringing affirmation that "neither death, nor life, nor angels, nor principalities, nor powers, nor things present, nor things to come, nor height, nor depth, nor any other creature, shall be able to separate us from the love of God."[7] In my religion classes at George School I had discovered biblical criticism, and I knew that however much I might love portions of the Bible, I could not sacrifice my intellect and unquestioningly accept everything in the Bible as literally true. And in my college days I assumed that becoming a Christian would mean swallowing biblical literalism.

When I eventually discovered that this assumption was not correct, I was well on the way to declaring myself a Christian. I had already adopted the practice of reading the Bible regularly, using a weekly lectionary put out by the Kirkridge (Pennsylvania) retreat center. I was committed to "taking the Bible seriously but not literally." I was also committed, in regard to ethical practice, to what I eventually affirmed as "the position that the thought and practice of the first generation of Quakers is somehow normative."[8] It would take me years to work out the implications and interconnections of these two commitments.

My studies during my year at Oberlin College's Graduate School of Theology included basic courses in Old Testament and New Testament. Several years later I resumed my graduate study at the University of Chicago Divinity School. At a retreat for entering students, Old Testament professor J. Coert Rylaarsdam caught my attention when he challenged us to make it our goal to learn to "think Hebrew!" I was eventually able to pass the required exams in biblical studies without taking any further courses, but I did read a number of books on biblical theology during my years at Chicago. Some of these biblical theologians set forth the goal of biblical scholarship in terms that more fully spelled out Rylaarsdam's dictum. Bernhard W. Anderson wrote:

> Our task, then, is to try to understand the biblical message in its dynamic context of culture, politics, and geography. We shall seek to enter into the concrete life-situations out of which the various writings have come, and to understand what the writers were saying to their times, . . . to enter sympathetically and imaginatively into this community and to relive its sacred history.[9]

He urged in another book that the approach to Bible study "is one in which together we shall attempt to stand within the Bible and to look out at the world through the window of biblical faith."[10] And G. Ernest Wright wrote: "Biblical theology is first and foremost a theology of recital. The worshiper listens to the recital and by means of historical memory and identification he participates, so to speak, in the original events."[11]

After I completed my studies at Chicago, I taught philosophy and religion for thirteen years at two colleges, in Kentucky and in Ohio. My teaching included introductory classes in Old Testament and New Testament. Each year I insisted to my Bible students what I had learned from these biblical theologians: The basic aim of biblical criticism is *empathy*: to be able to feel ourselves into the position of the writers and first readers of the Old Testament and New Testament writings; to get into the same drama in which these people were involved. And yet, as important as reading the Bible with empathy had become as my goal, I had not figured out what connection this might have with the Quaker faith and heritage, which were equally important to me.

Making that connection was a long time in coming. In 1979 I left my college position and moved to Portland, Oregon, in order to attend and become active at Reedwood Friends Church. For much of the next dozen years I served as clerk of the board for the Center for Christian Studies (CCS) at Reedwood. Early in 1991, I offered to teach a CCS course in which I would survey various interpretations of what early Quakerism was all about. Others felt strongly that it was time for CCS to offer a Bible course. Eventually, it was agreed that I would teach a course in how early Friends used the Bible. This was not a topic that I had ever seriously studied.

I began with the obvious: the earliest Friends were constantly quoting the Bible—and it was clear that their pioneering positions on such matters as war, women's ministry, and justice derived from their understanding of the Bible. What I needed to do was to investigate the ways in which these Friends used the Bible if I was to understand how Friends came to be—Friends.

In this CCS course on early Friends and the Bible, I looked intensively at a few brief writings and brief sections of longer writings to see if I could discover by close examination just *how* the earliest Friends used the Bible in these writings. I began with one short epistle by George Fox and the opening pages of a long epistle by Edward Burrough. Both were packed full of biblical quotations and references in a very flowing, almost breathless style. They never gave chapter and verse numbers; I had to do my homework with a concordance to come up with that information. It seemed clear that Fox and Burrough did not appeal to quotations and citations as external resources or as the authority which they asked Friends to accept as final. Neither did they appear to utilize Bible references to confirm claims that had come to them from some other source. Their biblical references seemed to be a natural part of the flow of their writing.

My "aha" moment was when I realized that Fox and Burrough expressed and embodied the very empathy that the biblical theologians recognized as the goal of biblical scholarship. They expected and assumed that their Quaker readers would also stand within the Bible—within the thought- and life-world of the earliest Christians—and look out at the world through the window of biblical faith.

I turned to Margaret Fell's pamphlet, *Womens Speaking Justified*. I found that she, too, eloquently demonstrated her love for and empathy with women in the Bible who spoke out for God and Christ. She showed examples of how Paul and the other apostles supported and encouraged women who worked to promote the gospel:

> If the Apostle would have had Womens speaking stopt, and did not allow of them, why did he entreat his true Yoak-Fellow to help those Women who laboured with him in the Gospel? Phil. 4.3. And why did the Apostles joyn together in Prayer and Supplication with the Women, and Mary the Mother of Jesus, and with his Brethren, Acts 1.14. if they had not allowed, and had union and fellowship with the Spirit of God, wherever it was revealed in Women as well as others?[12]

Here Fell was reading the Bible in personal, rather than legalistic, terms.

Perhaps most Christian theologians, ministers, and moralists have looked to the Bible as a handbook, a collection of resources and guidelines for salvation and Christian living—a set of propositions from which a theological or ethical system can be deduced and built up. Or maybe better, they regarded the Bible as a legal constitution, not subject to amendment as the American constitution is. George Fox, Edward Burrough, and Margaret Fell turned that approach upside down.

For example, concerning women's place in the church, John Calvin based his argument on these biblical statements: "Let your women keep silence in the churches: for it is not permitted unto them to speak; but they are commanded to be under obedience. . . . It is a shame for women to speak in the church" (1 Corinthians 14:34-35 KJV), and "Let the woman learn in silence with all subjection. But I suffer not a woman to teach, nor to usurp authority over the man, but to be in silence" (1 Timothy 2:11-12 KJV). From these rules Calvin deduced, arguing that "common sense tells us that the rule of women is improper and defective,"[13] that women have no right to exercise any authority in the church—and particularly not to teach or to preach the gospel.

Calvin's education as a lawyer clearly showed. But George Fox and Margaret Fell were pioneers of narrative theology. In Fell's *Womens Speaking Justified* and Fox's earlier tract, *The Woman Learning in Silence*, they made their point, that women had the full right to teach, preach, and exercise authority in the church, by retelling stories about women in the Bible:

> Philip had four daughters that did prophesy, which the apostle did not forbid; and saith the apostle, despise not prophesying.[14]

> Anna the prophetess, . . . spake of Christ, to all them that looked for redemption in Jerusalem. Here was a large testimony borne of Jesus by Anna the prophetess.[15]

It was Mary Magdalen that was sent to declare his resurrection, and she was to tell the brethren (the disciples) whither Christ was to go. . . . It was Mary that first declared Christ after he was risen.[16]

It was Mary Magdalene, and Joanna, and Mary the Mother of James, and the other Women that were with them, which told these things to the Apostles. . . . Mark this, you that despise and oppose the Message of the Lord God that he sends by Women; what had become of the Redemption of the whole Body of Man-kind, if they had not believed the Message that the Lord Jesus sent by these Women, of and concerning his Resurrection? And if these Women had not thus, out of their tenderness and bowels of love, who had received Mercy, and Grace, and forgiveness of sins, and Virtue, and Healing from him; which many men also had received the like, if their hearts had not been so united and knit unto him in love, that they could not depart as the men did, but sat watching, and waiting, and weeping about the Sepulchre until the time of his Resurrection, and so were ready to carry his Message, as is manifested; else how should his Disciples have known, who were not there?[17]

This was Elizabeths Sermon concerning Christ, which at this day stands upon Record: and then Mary said, My Soul doth magnifie the Lord, and my Spirit rejoyceth in God my Saviour; . . . he hath put down the mighty from their Seats, and exalted them of low degree; he hath filled the hungry with good things, and the rich he hath sent empty away; he hath holpen his Servant Israel, in remembrance of his mercy, as he spake to his Father, to Abraham, and to his Seed for ever. Are you not here beholding to the Woman for her Sermon, to use her words to put into your Common Prayer? and yet you forbid Womens Speaking. Now here you may see how these two Women prophesied of Christ, and Preached better then all the blind Priests did in that Age, and better then this Age also.[18]

Understanding that the starting place of Fox and the early Friends was their reading of the Bible with empathy also gives us fresh insight into some of the strange and bizarre actions of these first Quakers. For instance, two biblical prophets had proclaimed, as the word of the Lord: "Woe to the bloody city!" For Nahum (Nahum 3:1 KJV) the "bloody city" was Nineveh, the capital of the conquering Assyrian empire. For Ezekiel (Ezekiel 24:6, 9 KJV) it was Jerusalem. When George Fox came to the city of Lichfield, these very words were given to him: "The word of the Lord came unto me again to cry, 'Woe unto the bloody city of Lichfield!'"[19]

Sometimes Friends felt called by God to repeat precisely the actions of some biblical character. For example, the prophet Isaiah reported: "At the same time spake the LORD by Isaiah the son of Amoz, saying, Go and loose the sackcloth from off thy loins, and put off thy shoe from thy foot. And he did so, walking naked and barefoot. And the LORD said, . . . My servant Isaiah hath walked naked and barefoot three years for a sign and wonder upon Egypt and upon Ethiopia" (Isaiah 20:2-3 KJV). Several Friends, including Robert Barclay, identified themselves so closely with Isaiah that they, too, heard and obeyed a call from the Lord to walk naked as a sign. When I visited the "Quaker country" in northwest England, I remember seeing in one town a seventeenth-century pub with a sign in front—Ye naked man—named for a Quaker who had walked naked in that street.

Perhaps the strangest instance of empathetic identification with people of the Bible came in connection with James Nayler's notorious ride into Bristol. In Mark's account of Jesus' entry into Jerusalem, "They brought the colt to Jesus, and cast their garments on him; and he sat upon him. And many spread their garments in the way" (Mark 11:7-8 KJV). Just so, Nayler's follower Dorcas Erbury took off her clothes and spread them on the road ahead of his donkey.

Robert Barclay did show some awareness of the way in which the first Friends used the Bible. In discussing the value of the scriptures, he wrote:

> God hath seen meet that herein we should, as in a looking-glass, see the conditions and experiences of the saints of old; that finding our experience answer to theirs, we might thereby be the more confirmed and comforted, and our hope of attaining the same end strengthened; that observing the providences attending them, seeing the snares they were liable to, and beholding their deliverances, we may thereby be made wise unto salvation.[20]

If later generations of Friends had taken this as Barclay's defining statement on the scriptures, rather than the one I quoted at the outset, we might possibly have been spared some of the brutal arguments they got into over the authority of the Bible and of the Spirit. At the very least, we might not have forgotten what the Bible really meant to the earliest Friends.

When I taught a follow-up class in 1999 on Friends and the Bible, I stated flatly that Fox's, Fell's, and Burrough's empathetic way of reading and understanding the Bible had disappeared after the first generation of Quakerism. In 2003, Michael Birkel, professor of religion at Earlham College, published an essay, "Preparing the Heart for Sympathy: John Woolman Reading Scripture," and a book, *A Near Sympathy: The Timeless Quaker Wisdom of John Woolman*. When I read these, I discovered a major exception: John Woolman had read the Bible with deep empathy, and this reading had remarkable consequences for his sensitivity to the conditions of people in all walks of life in his own day.

Birkel showed that Woolman even went beyond the earliest Friends in his empathetic reading of scripture. Woolman expressed a connection to Moses: "I had a near sympathy with the prophet in the time of his weakness, when he said, 'If thou deal thus with me, kill me I pray thee out of hand, if I have found favour in thy sight' (Numbers 11:15)."[21] Unlike Fox and Burrough, Woolman here showed conscious awareness that he was reading the Bible with empathy. And then Woolman went a step further: he also made clear his "near sympathy" in his remarkable ability "to identify with the oppressed of his day."[22] Woolman wrote, during his visit to the Delaware Indians at Wyalusing,

> I was led to meditate on the manifold difficulties of these Indians, . . . and a near sympathy with them was raised in me; and my heart being enlarged in the love of Christ, I thought that the affectionate care of a good man for his only brother in affliction does not exceed what I then felt for that people.[23]

Birkel argued convincingly that it was Woolman's "near sympathy" with the biblical prophets that opened the way to his "near sympathy" with Native Americans and black slaves.

However, Woolman's use of the Bible was very different in his essays against slavery. In these essays he appealed to natural reason as well as to scripture, and he argued rationally from scriptural principles. And even in his *Journal* he used the phrase "near sympathy" or "nearer sympathy" only three times. I have concluded that, while an empathetic reading of the Bible was an important aspect of John Woolman's spirituality, it was not the center or linchpin of his understanding of Quakerism or of the Christian faith. It was, rather, a grace note that enriched his theology and spirituality, sweetened the austerity of his lifestyle, and deepened his remarkable sensitivity to persons of all conditions and walks of life.

Aside from Woolman, I have found no evidence that any Friends, from the late seventeenth century until well into the twentieth century, either took an empathetic approach to the Bible themselves or recognized that the earliest Friends had done so. In the twentieth century, I find that a few Friends have taken steps back toward an empathic reading of scripture. In *Reality of the Spiritual World* Thomas Kelly wrote of

> the Fellowship and Communion of the Saints, the Blessed Community. We find a group answer in the Scriptures. For now we know, from within, some of the Gospel writers, and the prophets, and the singers of songs, or Psalms. For they are now seen to be singing our song, or we can sing their song, or the same song of the Eternal Love is sung through us all, and out into the world. In mad joy we re-read the Scriptures, for they have become new. They are . . . a disclosure of kindred souls who have known a like visitation of God.[24]

In the October 1991 issue of *Quaker Religious Thought*, entitled "Fox Loved the Apostle Paul," Alan Kolp concluded,

> Fox loved the Apostle Paul . . . because the apostle opened up and articulated reality as Fox experienced it and understood it. It is at this level today we can best appreciate both Paul and Fox. . . . It is . . . important in our own way to know that God is at work in this world bringing a new heaven and a new earth. Both Paul and Fox knew this divine plan and participated in it. Their call was and still is our call—we, too, can plan to participate in God's triumphal transformation.[25]

I first published my findings, that the earliest Friends were reading the Bible with empathy, in the March 1993 issue of *Quaker Religious Thought*. Since that time, a number of Friends have connected in print with the idea of reading the Bible with empathy. *The Quaker Bible Reader* is a collection of essays by Quakers on how to read the Bible. In one of these essays Lonnie Valentine, professor of peace and justice studies at Earlham School of Religion, wrote,

> Even those biblical characters and events we do not like can become fellow sufferers with us. More importantly, by engaging the text deeply, we might find we have some friends to join us in the walk towards a more peaceful world. . . . We can empathize with all these ancient voices who, like us, wrestled with the question of what

God was doing and tried, within the limits of language, to present what they found. The Bible itself recognizes that there are conflicting voices, and presents them for us to engage.[26]

In another of the essays (on the Letter to the Hebrews), John Punshon, now retired from teaching at Woodbrooke and at Earlham School of Religion, wrote, "The Letter to the Hebrews draws its significance from an underlying narrative it assumes and partially articulates. I pray and think the way I do because I place myself in this story. I . . . read . . . as one who participates in the reality it describes."[27]

In her book, *Holiness: The Soul of Quakerism*, Carole Spencer (now teaching at Earlham School of Religion) asserted:

> Quakers lived, breathed and were infused by the words of Scripture. It was foundational to all their theology and spirituality. . . . Their understanding and use of Scripture has stronger affinity with the spiritual interpretation practiced by the early Greek Fathers such as Origen and John Chrysostom than the Reformers had.[28]

She clarified this point in a footnote: "Karen Torjesen describes Origen's biblical hermeneutic as a process of the reader being placed within the text and its meaning written on the soul."[29]

Gerard Guiton, an Australian Quaker scholar, published *The Early Quakers and the 'Kingdom of God'* in 2012. In this book he wrote:

> The early Friends had a comprehensive and penetrating knowledge of the Bible through which they forged an intimate relationship with the Hebrew prophets, with Jesus and the apostles—messengers all of the Light's [God's] sovereignty, the Light being their final authority. At times the relationship was so intimate it was as if they were the prophets, they were Jesus and the apostles. As such, the Quakers saw themselves as living the Kingdom experience of the primitive Jesus Way and at a portentous moment in history when the "Day of the Lord"—that moment of conviction, the Kingdom of God itself—was ushering in the End-time.[30]

Two Friends, Michael Birkel and Daniel Smith-Christopher, have devoted more attention and detail to spelling out and developing their understanding of reading the Bible with empathy.

Before he portrayed John Woolman's "near sympathy" with biblical writers, Michael Birkel had published an article in the September 2001 issue of *Quaker Religious Thought* entitled "Reading Scripture with Dorothy White." He devoted this article to a 1662 writing by early Quaker Dorothy White, *A Trumpet Sounded out of the Holy City*. Birkel noted that in this writing "we see a poetic, imaginative reading of Scripture."[31] In particular, he affirmed that

> Dorothy White here identifies herself as an heir to the biblical prophets. . . . She saw external parallels between their days and her own: outward oppression and hope for liberation. She found parallels in the inward life: the movement from interior bondage to freedom. . . . Her reading of Scripture shaped her understanding of events in her personal life, and her personal experiences in turn gave shape to her reading of Scripture. The relationship was rich and complex.[32]

In his 2005 book, *Engaging Scripture: Reading the Bible with Early Friends*, Michael Birkel set forth as his focus that early Friends "did not simply read the scriptures. They lived them. For them, reading the Bible was not just an exercise in information. It was an invitation to transformation."[33] In his exposition of Robert Barclay's "looking-glass" passage about the scriptures, Birkel explained:

> The life experiences of biblical characters are comparable to our own; their spiritual conditions are ours. . . . To read scripture is to realize that we are participants in the great ongoing story of God's people. This suggests a great richness of the inward life and a profound sense of connectedness. The lives of our forebears continue in us, offering us wisdom.[34]

In his commentary on an epistle by George Fox, Birkel concluded: "His epistle invites us to look within and discover just how vast the interior geography is. The story in the Bible is our own story. It is relived in our own lives."[35]

The main part of Michael Birkel's book is a series of suggested guidelines, exercises, or methods for "meditative reading," as a way to attain the empathy with biblical people that the early Friends and John Woolman had achieved. Birkel summarized this process:

> The sense of connectedness that we may come to feel with biblical stories and figures through meditative reading can grow to be applied to wider life. As we come to see that the biblical story is our

personal story, we may also come to see that others' stories can in some sense become our own story.[36]

Daniel Smith-Christopher is still a member of Northwest Yearly Meeting of Friends Church, even though he has been a faculty member for the past twenty-five years at a Jesuit university, Loyola Marymount, in Los Angeles. His approach to learning how to read the Bible with empathy is radically different from Michael Birkel's. In *The Religion of the Landless* (1989) he sought insights into understanding the Hebrew community in Babylonian exile by comparing their situation with that of recent and contemporary "minority" or "exile" groups: Bantus in South Africa under apartheid; African American slaves; Japanese Americans interned during World War II; Bikini Islanders relocated in order to allow United States' testing of nuclear weapons. In a lecture series at Reedwood and New York Yearly Meeting, "A Theology for Living in Babylon: The Hebrew Exile and Our Exile," he suggested that our survival as Friends—or even as Christians—in the contemporary world may depend on regaining a similar minority consciousness. And he proposed that recapturing and remembering our Quaker past (as a "peculiar people"), particularly by telling the stories of our heroes of the faith and by developing new rituals of separation from the surrounding society, might be strategies that would help us to regain our empathy and identification with the early Quaker community and beyond it, with the early Christian community.

In his 2002 book, *A Biblical Theology of Exile*, Daniel Smith-Christopher made his standpoint clear:

> In writing about the exile, I chose to write from the perspective of an empathy, if not open sympathy, with the attempts of refugee Hebrews to rebuild a social life from the pieces left by the Chaldean militias of the sixth century, the Persian militias of the fifth and fourth centuries, the Hellenistic phalanxes of the third and second centuries, and so on.[37]

In 2007 Daniel Smith-Christopher published *Jonah, Jesus, and Other Good Coyotes*. At the outset he stated one point sharply: "The Bible does not always speak with one voice on all issues of interest to modern readers."[38] Through much of the book he follows an argument that persisted and developed through centuries of Hebrew, Jewish, and early Christian history: "This is a good experiment, then, for learning to listen to other 'voices' in the Bible."[39] In the process he shows that some of the Old Testament passages that many Friends have found problematic or even offensive actually express "the language of anguish and anger." And he challenges us: "Can we read these ventings of emotions—even the horrific imagery used—with historical appreciation of the realities of suffering that give rise to such emotion?"[40] A call indeed to empathetic reading.

What would empathetic reading of the Bible look like today? It can involve an exercise of the imagination:

Were you there when they crucified my Lord? . . .
Sometimes it causes me to tremble, tremble, tremble.

Put ourselves in the place of Mary, the mother of Jesus—or of John, the beloved disciple. We are standing there, looking on, shivering in the darkness—the darkness at noon. Even God seems to have forsaken him. Sobs of grief rack our bodies.

In our empathy we do more than share the emotions of John and Mary. Our perceptions, dispositions, and intentions will be affected. Entering into the life of these biblical persons becomes an exercise in character formation. As we identify ourselves with Mary, with apostles like John and Paul, with the great Old Testament prophets—even with Jesus himself—we share their compassion for the poor, for persons not protected by the structures of their society, for foreigners. We empathize with these waifs and strays and cross boundaries into the fellowship of outsiders—"strangers and foreigners on the earth" (Hebrews 11:13).

A power comes into our lives as we identify with the ancient prophets and apostles. We can even say that we live in the same Spirit that they lived in. And that power, that Spirit, transforms our lives into resurrection glory.

Were you there when He rose from the tomb? . . .
Sometimes I feel like shouting glory, glory, glory!
Were you there when He rose from the tomb?

A powerful tool for learning to read the Bible with empathy is word study. There are some excellent, easy-to-read word studies: Howard Macy's pamphlet, *The Shalom of God*; Eugene Roop's study of the Hebrew words *mishpat* and *sedeqah* in his 1977 *Quaker Religious Thought* essay, "Justice in the Biblical Tradition"; William Barclay's little books, *A New Testament Wordbook* and *More New Testament Words*. Becoming familiar with the rich variety of meanings of words in the original Hebrew and Greek can help us ease our way into the thinking of the writers of the books of the Old and New Testaments.

Many biblical scholars have noted that some passages or writings are not compatible with others in the Bible; the Bible just does not speak with a single voice on many issues. Reading empathetically helps us recognize ongoing dialogues within the Bible, sometimes continuing and developing over many centuries. One example will set forth clearly the type of situation that we face:

In the gospel of Mark, Jesus said,

> Whoever divorces his wife and marries another commits adultery against her; and if she divorces her husband and marries another, she commits adultery (Mark 10:11-12).

The gospel of Matthew reported Jesus as saying,

> Anyone who divorces his wife, except on the ground of unchastity, causes her to commit adultery (Matthew 5:32).

Paul wrote, in his first letter to the Corinthians,

> If any believer has a wife who is an unbeliever, and she consents to live with him, he should not divorce her. And if any woman has a husband who is an unbeliever, and he consents to live with her, she should not divorce him. . . . But if the unbelieving partner separates, let it be so; in such a case the brother or sister is not bound (1 Corinthians 7:12-13, 15).

For those who use the Bible as legal constitution, there is a problem. In one text, remarriage after divorce is forbidden in all cases; each of the other texts allows for a single type of exception, but the exceptions are quite different. The problem—here and elsewhere—becomes one of trying to harmonize the discrepancies, usually in quite ingenious and involved ways.

Now let us take a case. A woman, a member of our meeting or church, is married to a husband who frequently subjects her to physical abuse or extreme verbal and emotional abuse. Experience indicates that, if she remains in the marriage, she is in danger of suffering serious injury or even death. What do we counsel? Using the Bible as legal constitution, we would advise her to remain married—or, if she does get a divorce, not to remarry while the husband lives. No biblical text lists physical or emotional abuse as an exception. What if we look at the Bible empathetically? We would try to understand Jesus in his own historical context, the Jewish community. Jewish scripture had made provision for husbands to divorce their wives; one school of scribes permitted divorce even if she burnt the beans; no provision was made for wives to initiate divorce. In this first-century patriarchal society, there was no ready way for a divorced woman to make her way financially. Jesus is pictured in the gospels as showing special concern for women. Could not his prohibition of divorce be rooted in his care for women's rights and welfare? Wouldn't this perspective lead us to give very different advice to the woman in our congregation?

On to the big picture. We will be guided in our ethical choices and in the overall direction of our lives by some of the rich words and ideas in the Bible – *mishpat, sedeqah* (justice), *hesed* (covenant love), *shalom* (peace, wholeness). But there are strands in the Bible that stand in tension or even opposition to this larger vision. We have to pick and choose. We find good precedent, even in the Bible, for making these hard choices. When Peter came to Antioch, Paul "opposed him to his face, because he was clearly in the wrong" (Galatians 2:11 NEB).

When God spoke to Elijah in the "still, small voice" at Mount Horeb, he commanded Elijah to anoint Hazael as king of Aram (Syria), Jehu as king of Israel, and Elisha as prophet: "Whoever escapes from the sword of Hazael, Jehu shall kill; and whoever escapes from the sword of Jehu, Elisha shall kill" (1 Kings 19:17). When Elisha eventually carried out the anointing of Jehu, he gave these orders from God: "Strike down the house of . . . Ahab. . . . The whole house of Ahab shall perish. . . . I will cut off from Ahab every male, bond or free, in Israel" (2 Kings 9:7-8). And Jehu "killed all who were left of the house of Ahab in Jezreel" (2 Kings 10:11)—seventy sons of Ahab, and many others. A century later, when Jehu's great-grandson was king of Israel, a son was born to the prophet Hosea and his wife, "And the LORD said to him, 'Name him Jezreel; for in a little while I will punish the house of Jehu for the blood of Jezreel, and I will put an end to the kingdom of the house of Israel'" (Hosea 1:4). Was Jehu's blood-bath at Jezreel God's command or his own great sin? Which prophet(s) truly heard the word of God—Elijah and Elisha, or Hosea? We must decide.

In making our decision, dare we do less than to look to Jesus for our primary clue as to who God really is? Would we not then find God's word and purpose in the texts that portray justice as restorative justice—ensuring that everyone's needs are met rather than striving to give people what they deserve; responding to crime by meeting the needs of perpetrator, victim, and the community rather than seeking closure by punishing the offender? Would we not see peace and covenant love personified in the one who met evil with nonviolence and reached out across boundaries and broke down the walls that divide? We recognize indeed that

> Love is patient; love is kind; love is not envious or boastful or arrogant or rude. It does not insist on its own way; it is not irritable or resentful; it does not rejoice in wrongdoing, but rejoices in the truth. It bears all things, believes all things, hope all things, endures all things (1 Corinthians 13:4-7).

Is it not true empathy to recognize that "there is no longer Jew or Greek, there is no longer slave or free, there is no longer male and female; for all of you are one in Christ Jesus"? (Galatians 3:28). The great mission of the church, the people of God, is to be an ever-widening covenant community in which all hostile groups come together—Jew and Gentile, black and white, gay and straight, American and Middle Eastern—because

> Christ Jesus . . . is our peace; in his flesh he has made both groups into one and has broken down the dividing wall, that is, the hostility between us, . . . that he might create in himself one new humanity in place of the two, thus making peace, and might reconcile both groups to God in one body through the cross. . . . You are no longer strangers and aliens, but you are citizens with the saints and also members of the household of God (Ephesians 2:13-16, 19).

We are indeed playing our destined part in God's history, "according to [God's] good pleasure that he set forth in Christ, as a plan for the fullness of time, to gather up all things in him, things in heaven and things on earth" (Ephesians 1:9-10).

1

George Fox Meets the Seekers: A Mighty Act of God?

After the 1952 Friends World Conference at Oxford, several hundred Friends from all over the world made a pilgrimage to the northwestern part of England. There, for a week, in busload-sized groups, we took turns visiting locations in Westmoreland, Lancashire, and western Yorkshire, including Pendle Hill, Firbank Fell, Swarthmoor Hall, Briggflatts Meeting House, and Lancaster Prison.

The organizers of this pilgrimage had publicized it as a celebration of the tercentenary of the founding of the Religious Society of Friends. They argued that a series of events in June 1652 marked the beginning of Quakerism as a large-scale, dynamic movement. Although a few small groups of Quakers already existed, when George Fox preached to large bodies of Seekers at Sedbergh, Firbank Fell, Preston Patrick, and Underbarrow, large numbers of these Seekers were convinced of the truth of Fox's preaching and became large Quaker communities. From this beginning, Quakerism spread rapidly during the next few years through England and Wales. Much of this growth was spearheaded by the work of traveling Quaker preachers known today as the "Valiant Sixty," many of whom were Seekers who became Friends during those few days in June 1652.

What actually happened at Sedbergh and Firbank Fell? Just what was the importance and meaning of those events? What causes led up to them, and what were their long-term consequences?

To try to answer such questions, I will begin with a recent controversy between two Quaker historians, Larry Ingle and Doug Gwyn. Ingle sharply criticized Gwyn as being one of a succession of Quaker historians who have proposed theological interpretations of George Fox and the early Friends instead of concentrating on a careful examination of the social, political, and economic context of the movement. Ingle argued that "people like Gwyn are so enthralled by their quest for the holy grail of theological truth . . . that they are simply unable or unwilling to submit themselves to the lowly and pedestrian discipline of simply trying to make sense about what happened."[1] Gwyn responded that "Ingle's viewpoint is just as ideologically conditioned and interested as is a theological position. His pose . . . holds that the historian, using scientific methods of research, can overcome all partisanship and become value-free, detached in presenting and interpreting the data. There is no such position on earth!"[2] Gwyn insists that Ingle, too, as "an honest self-aware scholar must put his or her position of engagement out front to the reader and not pose as an impartial oracle, testifying to 'what happened.'"[3]

I am in complete agreement with Doug Gwyn on this point. No historian, no scholar, no observer of any event is capable of having a completely objective, value-free view of what is happening or has happened. We inevitably interpret what we perceive and how we understand the experiences of others, and our interpretations are colored by our personal temperaments, life-experiences, and values. As philosopher Alfred North Whitehead so aptly wrote, "If we desire a record of uninterpreted experience, we must ask a stone to record its autobiography."[4] Paul grasped this point nearly two thousand years ago: "We see in a mirror, dimly" (1 Corinthians 13:12)—or, in the evocative words of the King James translation, "through a glass, darkly." Even in physics, we now know that we cannot achieve absolutely precise knowledge; at the quantum level the very act of observation makes an impact on the position and momentum of the objects being observed.

This does not mean, as some relativists or extreme post-modernists would have it, that there is only your truth and my truth, but no ultimate truth behind and beyond what we see and understand. We can never in this world attain to a complete and perfect knowledge of "what really happened," but we can reach toward a converging grasp of it as we bring our contrasting interpretations into dialogue with one another. This dialogue can be open and honest only if we first become as self-aware as possible about our own interpretive biases and values, and then become as open and up-front as possible with one another in our mutual quest for truth. *This* is the "holy grail" that historians and theologians alike are seeking. Is this search folly or a worthy quest?

Folly enters in when the human scientists—historians, sociologists, economists, psychologists—are tempted to approximate the relative precision and objectivity that the physicists and the chemists expect to achieve. In the physical world it makes sense to speak of objective truth, but not in the human world. Martin Buber wisely reminded us that our understanding of other persons does not come through an objective, I/it, relationship. It must be I/thou. The ultimate truth, in all interpersonal and social relationships, is not objective but intersubjective. We will come closer to this truth not through objective detachment but through empathy. None of us, of course, attains to complete empathy with everyone here and now, or in the past. All of us empathize more readily with some people than with others. Yet the better we can put ourselves inside the skin of the people we are seeking to understand and explain, the closer we will come to the full truth about them and their place in society and in history.

And so it is time for me to be upfront about my own stance—about the starting points of my own outlook on life and history.

As I have developed the values and refined the worldview through which I understand society and history, I have been inspired by two movements: the Quaker movement of the mid-seventeenth century, and the Biblical Theology Movement of the mid-twentieth century. As a child I was thrilled by the courage and powerful steadfastness of the first generation of Friends. Their devotion to integrity, peace, tolerance, and justice was a beacon to me in a world that was struggling through economic hard times and hurtling toward war. As a teenager I learned from Friends, guided by Rufus Jones and Howard Brinton, that these first Quakers were mystics—steeped in a vivid experience of the presence of God and committed to an optimistic belief in that of God in every person. Since I myself had not experienced God's presence, I remained an agnostic, albeit a wistful one. I was a seeker, longing

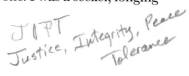

JIPT
Justice, Integrity, Peace, Tolerance

for an experience of God's reality and hoping that such an experience would give me the power to live up to the ideals that I saw as having become reality in the lives of the early Friends.

During my undergraduate years at the University of Pennsylvania, I took part in many activities organized by Philadelphia Yearly Meeting's Young Friends movement. Early on, I was in a small group that met regularly to read and discuss William Penn's *Rise and Progress of the People Called Quakers*. This was my first direct encounter with anything written by a seventeenth-century Friend. I was confounded. Penn's message was strongly Christ-centered; he quoted the Bible freely. He wrote of "the benighted state of man after his fall"[5] and of "the sins and trespasses in which they were dead."[6] I was aghast when our beloved pioneer of religious toleration wrote of Roman Catholicism: "The false church sprang up. . . . In truth she was mystery Babylon, the mother of harlots."[7] He scoffed at the Baptists: "They rested also too much upon their watery dispensation."[8] Where was the mystical, Spirit-centered, optimistic, tolerant, early Quaker that I was expecting to find?

One day I went to a meeting of that group—but no one else showed up. A slender book, written by a Quaker, was lying on a table. I picked it up and started reading. The book was *A Testament of Devotion*, by Thomas Kelly. His words seemed to sing. I was swept up into an overwhelming experience of God's presence and love. I was finally convinced that God was real. I wanted more.

One of the adult advisors to the Young Friends movement was Jean Toomer, a sweet-spirited, mystical poet. I turned to him for advice on other books to read that could move me further along the path of devotion to God, which I was determined to follow. He recommended the *Letters of Isaac Penington* (a leading seventeenth-century Friend) and Aldous Huxley's *The Perennial Philosophy*, an anthology of writings by mystics from various religious traditions including Christianity, Islam, Buddhism, Hinduism. As I read these books, Penington's *Letters* indeed warmed and thrilled me, much as had Kelly's writings. Most of what I read in Huxley's book left me cold. I wondered to myself: why the difference?

Shortly before my graduation, I attended a seminar led by a Friend named Lewis Benson who had written a pamphlet titled *Prophetic Quakerism*. He believed that Rufus Jones had been wrong about early Friends: Quakerism began not as a philosophical, mystical movement centering on "that of God in everyone," but as a prophetic, Christ-centered movement focusing on the claim that "Christ has come to teach his people himself."

To me, this interpretation made a lot more sense of the writings of George Fox and William Penn. Too often the mystical interpreters had dismissed the strongly biblical and Christ-centered writings of early Friends as simply speaking in language that their contemporaries would understand. But I had some difficulty with accepting a Christ-centered understanding of Quakerism. I thought that, in order to be a Christian, a person had to be a biblical literalist—to put aside the critical intellect in one's approach to the Bible. That was a sacrifice I was not able or willing to make. And I did not understand how Jesus could be at the same time both a human being and divine (at least in any unique sense).

After my graduation I went to work on a cooperative farm in California. The United States government passed a peacetime conscription law, and although I openly refused to register for the draft, I was ignored by the authorities. After two years I returned to the East Coast, planning to enroll in the Graduate School of Theology at Oberlin College, but on the day that I arrived at my parents' home in Pennsylvania, war broke out in Korea. I was soon arrested by the FBI for my refusal to register.

While waiting to appear in federal court, I read an article in *The Christian Century* by Charles Clayton Morrison. He explained how Christ-centered "neo-orthodox" thinkers, including Karl Barth and Reinhold Niebuhr, accepted liberalism's methods of biblical criticism, but carried these methods out so thoroughly that they came to conclusions about issues such as sin, grace, and the nature of Christ, which differed sharply from the conclusions of most religious liberals. This article removed one of my major problems in accepting Christianity as the truth; it is indeed possible to be a Christian without being a biblical literalist.

At my first court appearance I pled *nolo contendere*, but was not immediately sentenced. I took up residence at Quaker study center Pendle Hill while awaiting sentence. I checked out a book from Swarthmore College library, *God Was In Christ* by D. M. Baillie. Donald Baillie led me through a careful series of arguments showing how the Christian faith involves a number of paradoxes, including the central paradox of grace—my experience that the good which I do is entirely my own responsibility and also wholly the work of God's grace in me. From this it was a small leap to the paradox of the Incarnation—of Jesus being both God and human: "The Man in whom God was incarnate would claim nothing for Himself as a Man, but ascribed all glory to God."[9] With Donald Baillie's help, I was finally able to accept the Christian faith as true.

In the nine and a half months that I spent in prison for my refusal to register, I had plenty of time for reading. For me, the most significant book I read during that period was *The Quest of the Historical Jesus*, by Albert Schweitzer. The story Schweitzer told, of attempts through the nineteenth century to get behind the text of the gospels and recover the actual life and message of the historical Jesus was fascinating. The final chapters, in which he presented his own conclusions about Jesus were shocking—all the more so because I was completely convinced by his reasoning.

Schweitzer called his interpretation of Jesus "thoroughgoing eschatology." He showed that Jesus completely accepted the apocalyptic tradition that had crystallized in Judaism with the book of Daniel—that Jesus expected history to come to an end in dramatic fashion, in a very short time—and that this expectation was, of course, mistaken. Jesus' worldview was incomprehensible to our modern outlook on life: "He comes to us as One unknown."[10] I had long since accepted the importance of critical study of the Bible: nothing in the Bible was infallible, but the words of the historical Jesus himself, if we could just fight back to them through the presuppositions of the early Christians, would be the firm, trustworthy bedrock. And now I discovered that the whole message of Jesus, whom I had only recently recognized as fully God and fully human, was grounded on a colossal mistake. I had come up against my first major crisis of faith.

During the next dozen years the question of eschatology in the Bible, in the teachings of Jesus—and even in early Quaker thought—became a central issue in my own intellectual quest. In my year at Oberlin, just after my release from federal prison, I became acquainted with the work of British Bible scholar C. H. Dodd. Dodd pointed out that there is a second strand of thought in the teachings of Jesus: that the kingdom of God had already begun to arrive in the work that Jesus himself was doing on earth. Dodd called this strand "realized eschatology." Dodd's evidence was strong, but I recognized that he had at most pointed to a tension in Jesus' eschatology—between the "now" and the "not quite yet."

After I finished one year at Oberlin, it was five years before I resumed my graduate studies at the University of Chicago Divinity School. In my first weekend at the Divinity School, I attended a retreat for entering students. I recall vividly the words of Old Testament professor J. Coert Rylaarsdam at that retreat; he affirmed that our goal as students and scholars should be to learn to "think Hebrew."

Since I had taken basic Old Testament and New Testament courses at Oberlin and was concentrating in a different area (ethics and society) at Chicago, I took no more formal Bible courses. Nevertheless, in order to clarify my own basic theological stance, over the next few years I studied books by a number of biblical scholars, including Oscar Cullmann, Walther Eichrodt, G. Ernest Wright, Bernhard W. Anderson. These scholars were representative of what can be termed the Biblical Theology Movement. As I read their works, I kept finding myself moving back to the great theological pioneer of that movement, Karl Barth. Although I have not read anywhere near all of Barth's works, I have read enough to appreciate enormously his contributions to contemporary thinking about God and the Bible.

Nineteenth- and early twentieth-century biblical scholars had concentrated on analysis, on objectively understanding the historical and literary context of biblical writings, on breaking down traditional understandings of the Bible and its meaning. By the middle of the twentieth century, Barth and his followers in the Biblical Theology Movement had taken the next step and were attempting a new synthesis, a fresh understanding of the message of the biblical authors. The goal of their scholarship was to recover the theology of the biblical writers to the extent that they—and we—could feel themselves into the position of the writers and first readers of the biblical books. Coert Rylaarsdam summarized this goal in a single phrase; Karl Barth and Bernhard Anderson spelled it out in a little more detail:

> The commentator is thus presented with a clear "Either-Or." The question is whether or no he is to place himself in a relation to his author of utter loyalty. Is he to read him, determined to follow him to the very last word, wholly aware of what he is doing, and assuming that the author also knew what he was doing? . . . Anything short of utter loyalty means a commentary *on* Paul's Epistle to the Romans, not a commentary so far as possible *with* him—even to his last word.[11]

Our task, then, is to try to understand the biblical message in its dynamic context of culture, politics, and geography. We shall seek to enter into the concrete life-situations out of which the various writings have come, and to understand what the writers were saying to their times, . . . to enter sympathetically and imaginatively into this community and to relive its sacred history.[12]

The approach to Bible study that Anderson urged "is one in which together we shall attempt to *stand within* the Bible and to look out at the world through the window of biblical faith."[13]

I have come to agree that our aim is to enter into the same drama in which the Hebrews and early Christians were involved—to examine the Old Testament and the New Testament from within. In a word, the goal of our biblical study is *empathy.*

I can go a step further. When G. Ernest Wright wrote, "Biblical theology is first and foremost a theology of recital. The worshiper listens to the recital and by means of historical memory and identification he participates, so to speak, in the original events,"[14] he was affirming that biblical theology itself is an exercise in empathy.

What do we find when we enter with empathy into the world of the Bible? We find first, as Karl Barth admitted, that "within the Bible there is a strange, new world."[15] The Bible does contain history, morality, religion, but at its depth we do not find only these; we find God. "We have found in the Bible a new world, God, God's sovereignty, God's glory, God's incomprehensible love. Not the history of man but the history of God! . . . Not human standpoints but the standpoint of God!"[16] And who is the God whom we discover in the Bible? "The redeemer of my brothers and sisters. . . . The redeemer of a humanity gone astray. . . . The redeemer of the groaning creation about us."[17] God is the One who "makes a new heaven and a new earth, and, therefore, new men, new families, new relationships, new politics."[18]

Within the Biblical Theology Movement we recognize that the writers of the biblical books present us with a variety of different world views and theologies, but we discern some basic underlying themes that run consistently through these differing outlooks. The *foundational* theme is expressed in the metaphor of God as king. God is more than a loving parent and a beloved friend; God is the awesome, almighty majesty in whose service we discover our true selves and our greatest freedom. God communicates with humanity primarily through a series of events in history in which he both reveals himself to us—his nature, his will, his purpose—and establishes his purpose, his kingship, his reign on earth. These events make up *heilsgeschichte*—"salvation history" or "holy history."

We call these events the "mighty acts of God." Two of these events are primary: the Exodus (the escape of the Hebrew slaves from Egypt) and the ministry of Jesus Christ, culminating in his crucifixion and resurrection. Other mighty acts are recognized by the eye of faith: God's promise to Abraham, the victorious reign of king David, the exile of Judah to Babylon and the return from exile, the first Christian mission to the Gentiles. In these events God enters in person into history; calls a people to himself; establishes the beginning of his reign, his kingdom and power, on earth; wins decisive victory over the forces that oppose him. And many of the biblical writers also look forward to another final, mighty act of God, in which his rule over the world is fully established and his victory becomes complete. They use a variety of phrases to refer to this expected event: the day of the Lord, that day, the kingdom of God, the new Jerusalem, the coming of the Lord.

The next major theme of biblical theology is the *covenant*. The mighty acts of God are covenant-making events. In them the sovereign God has elected a people to be his own, established with them a compact of mutual faithfulness, and set forth the terms under which this compact is to be fulfilled. God takes the initiative in establishing covenant with a community, a people, not simply with separate individuals. But the covenant community is a community, which itself gives meaning to the individual. Within the community, each individual is addressed directly by God; thus no totalitarian rule by any human monarch, no oppression of even the poorest and weakest member of the community is permitted.

The original covenant between God and Israel was initiated by God in bringing the Hebrew slaves out of Egypt and was ratified at Mount Sinai, when God set forth the terms by which the people were to respond to this initiative—the Ten Commandments—and affirmed his promise: "If you obey my voice and keep my covenant, you shall be my treasured possession out of all the peoples. . . . You shall be for me a priestly kingdom and a holy nation" (Exodus 19:5-6). The biblical writers read the covenant-concept back into history before Moses: two accounts of a covenant that God made with Abraham and his descendants, and an account of a covenant that God made with Noah and his descendants (all of the human race since Noah).

Within this understanding of God and the people, sin and unrighteousness are fundamentally a breaking of the covenant relationship: ingratitude or mistrust toward God, injustice or arrogance toward other members of the community. The people constantly rebel and break the covenant. The good news is that, even then, God does not forsake his people, but time and again restores the covenant or even creates a new covenant. The greater news—grasped at first by Second Isaiah (a scholarly designation for Isaiah 40-55) and the authors of Ruth and Jonah; in the story of Noah; and then fully and decisively by Jesus, Peter, and Paul—is that God's covenant with a small group of people, the Hebrews, is in God's full purpose the first step toward a universal covenant with all peoples.

While I was a student at Chicago, several Friends got together and organized the Quaker Theological Discussion Group. These Friends, sobered by two world wars, world-wide economic collapse, and the horrors of Nazism and the Holocaust, had come to question Protestant and Quaker liberalism's optimistic faith in human progress; they were also questioning Rufus Jones's and Howard Brinton's interpretation of early Quakerism as a mystical movement centered on an optimistic belief in "that of God in everyone." They wanted to establish a forum for discussing theological issues and understandings of Quakerism with one another, as well as with any liberal or evangelical Friends willing to enter the dialogue. They also envisaged founding a journal in which the fruits of this dialogue could be published.

I attended the first conference of the Quaker Theological Discussion Group and found it to be a place where I could sharpen my own understanding of what Quakerism was all about. I became a regular attender of the group's conferences and soon of its executive committee meetings, and eventually served for several years as editor of its journal, *Quaker Religious Thought*. During my college teaching years, when I was remote from any Friends meeting or church, the Discussion Group became my de facto spiritual home.

The Quaker Theological Discussion Group afforded a context in which I could clarify my own understanding of what Quakerism is all about. In one paper that I read at a conference of the Discussion Group, I affirmed my basic position: "The thought and practice of the first generation of Quakers is somehow normative. . . . We cannot go back to a literal repetition or imitation of seventeenth-century Quakerism, but the insights of that generation will form the basis for any meaningful reconstruction or renewal of Quaker Christianity."[19] My fundamental quest was to tease out that "somehow": just what was the central insight of early Quakerism—what Melvin Endy has more recently termed "the linchpin of the [Quaker] movement"?[20]

Colleagues in the Quaker Theological Discussion Group made noteworthy contributions to my understanding of major themes in the thought and work of early Friends. Hugh Barbour and T. Canby Jones showed how George Fox, James Nayler, and Edward Burrough distilled the picture of the Lamb's War out of the profuse imagery of the book of Revelation. These early Friends understood that they were engaged in an intense, yet always nonviolent, struggle against the powers of evil within themselves and in the social and political structures of their world. I was particularly inspired by Canby Jones's insistence that the Lamb's War provides the basis for Quaker testimonies and action in the world today:

> Just as the early Friends expected to win the Lamb's war and then see his victory in England so must we. The arena of the present day conflict is on every level of existence wherever evil is found.
>
> We are called to overcome ignorance, poverty, disease, secularism, racism and war; all social ills; the depths of sin and the deepest spiritual needs of men. All of these are the arena of the conflict. Wherever they are being overcome the power of the conquering Lamb is already at work. . . .
>
> This is a new kind of war that restores instead of kills.[21]

My thinking was stretched by Rob Tucker's expansion of the social and political implications of the Lamb's War in his seminal essay, "Revolutionary Faithfulness." He summed up his analysis of the Lamb's War in these words: "The first Friends stormed the Kingdom as though it were the Bastille. New Christian behavioral patterns, new social and political and economic insights were spun off as a by-product. . . . The central principle was and should be faithfulness, private and corporate, and its corollary, an openness to the unexpected."[22] He clarified how different was the meaning of Christian language for early Friends from the use of that language by modern evangelical or liberal Christians and Friends:

> When early Friends spoke of Christ's saving grace and the need to respond to it, they meant not only that individuals should be reborn, but that Christian community should be reborn to perform a revolutionary function in history, through day-to-day immediate corporate faithfulness to its divine Leader. . . .
>
> Our problem is complicated by the fact that early Quaker thinking about community was aborted.[23]

Rob Tucker reminds us:

early Quakerism was "prophetic, catholic, and revolutionary." . . .

It is not easy to focus upon the revolutionary aspects of early Quakerism. Because George Fox was relatively successful in his ecclesiastical and theological aims, and unsuccessful in his social aims, we naturally tend to see his program in the former terms.[24]

I find it essential to recognize that the first Quakers were a people, a community called by God, not simply a gathering of God-inspired individuals. More specifically, they were a covenant community. These thoughts have also been emphasized more recently by Douglas Gwyn in his book, *The Covenant Crucified*. Doug made it clear that the Lamb's War was, indeed, "based on the image of the Lamb, the Risen Lord, in the book of Revelation, waging cosmic war against the forces of religious, economic, and political repression," but it was also "a covenantal conflict."[25] Beyond this, he spelled out in considerable detail how the failure of the Lamb's War to make any significant impact on British society led Friends to rethink their social and political ideas. When they finally had opportunity to put their views into practice with the founding of Pennsylvania in 1682, we do not find William Penn writing about this "holy experiment" in terms of the Lamb's War or the biblical covenant. Instead, he appealed to such ideas as natural rights and the social contract—key phrases in the political philosophy of Penn's friend John Locke.

One question on which Friends in the Quaker Theological Discussion Group have held varying views is the question of the place of early Quakerism in the manifold spectrum of churches, denominations, and movements that constitute Christianity. Rufus Jones had positioned Friends in a long tradition of mystical movements, within both Roman Catholicism and heretical sects, stretching back to the Greek philosopher Plato. Hugh Barbour placed Quakerism squarely in the Protestant camp: "Historically and theologically, Friends are Protestants."[26] Lewis Benson, for a period in his life, felt that early Quakers belonged together with sixteenth-century Anabaptists as examples of "Spiritual Reformation" or perhaps "churches of the Cross"; later in life he backed away from this association with the Anabaptists and emphasized the absolute uniqueness of George Fox's vision of Christian faith and community.

To me it has seemed clear that the early Quaker vision of Christianity had much in common with the positions of the fourteenth-century Lollards in England and the sixteenth-century Anabaptists in Switzerland, Germany, and the Netherlands (particularly the strands that became the Mennonites, the Amish, and the Hutterites). I found my views supported and clarified in an essay by Maurice Creasey, "Radical Christianity and Christian Radicalism." In this essay, Maurice pointed to "two disastrous weaknesses that have beset the Christian community throughout its history. These are its *theological timidity* and its *ethical insensitivity.*"[27] In contrast, he listed

> many groups and movements which, throughout Christian history, have felt after a quality of spiritual life and have sought to embody a pattern of Christian discipleship closer than anything they saw in the church of their own day to that reflected in the New Testament.[28]

He gave special attention to two such movements, the sixteenth-century "Radical Reformation" (including the Anabaptists) and seventeenth-century Quakerism.

A number of Mennonite scholars were seeking ways of recovering the original Anabaptist vision. I sought and found opportunities to enter into dialogue with them and with some scholars from the Church of the Brethren, in the hope of clarifying my understanding of the original Quaker vision in the context of a broader "radical Christianity and Christian radicalism." One such opportunity came at a "Believers' Church" conference in 1967, which included attendees from a wider variety of denominations. An instructive point of disagreement arose when a couple of persons present argued that, on principle, there could be no "mighty acts of God" after the close of the New Testament period, until the final establishment of God's kingdom on earth. One Friend (was it Canby Jones?) responded that mighty acts of God have indeed occurred at times through the history of the Christian faith, and that we can expect more. I recognized this as a defining point of the Quaker vision; this might well be the true import of the Quaker concept of "continuing revelation." With this in mind, I have even speculated on what events in Christian history might be candidates for consideration as further mighty acts of God. The career of St. Francis of Assisi and the founding of the Franciscan Movement? The attempts to restore primitive Christianity—the church of the cross—by the earliest Anabaptists and the first Quakers? The founding of the Confessing Church in Germany and its struggle against Nazism? The non-violent campaigns of the 1960s civil rights movement in the American South, centered in the leadership of Martin Luther King, Jr.?

A few months after that conference, I was invited to join a small study group, the War-Nation-Church Study Group (WANACH), whose sessions I attended regularly once or twice a year as long as I continued teaching college. Members of that group from whom I gained important insights included Mennonites John Howard Yoder and Paul Peachey, and Lutheran Larry Rasmussen.

The April 1968 meeting of the War-Nation-Church Study Group included a joint session with the Chicago Society for Biblical Research, at which John Howard Yoder read a remarkable paper on "The Possibility of a Messianic Ethic." In this paper he proposed that Jesus was reaffirming the Old Testament vision of the jubilee year as the platform for his own social ethics. (Yoder later published this paper as part of his classic, *The Politics of Jesus*.) I found in this essay and in Rob Tucker's "Revolutionary Faithfulness" a remarkable point of convergence between Mennonite and Quaker scholarship—all the more remarkable because I was able to make certain that neither Yoder nor Tucker was aware at the time of what the other was writing. I made this point of convergence the focus of a paper that I wrote in 1969. In particular, I pointed to the description in John Yoder's paper of the community that Jesus was founding:

> There are thus about the community of disciples those sociological traits most characteristic of those who set about to change society: a visible structured fellowship, a sober decision guaranteeing that the costs of commitment to the fellowship have been consciously accepted, and a clearly defined life style distinct from that of the crowd. This life style is different, not because of arbitrary rules, . . . but because of the exceptionally normal quality of humanness to which the community is committed. The distinctness is . . . a nonconformed quality of ("secular") involvement in the life of the world. It thereby constitutes an unavoidable challenge to the powers that be and the beginning of a new set of social alternatives.[29]

Meanwhile, in "Revolutionary Faithfulness," Rob Tucker gave a description of the early Quaker community as a revolutionary fellowship:

> It is instructive to make a list of specific revolutionary ingredients in original Quakerism:
>
> 1. Early Friends knew that what they were doing really mattered in world history. . . . History *is* God-in-history. To early Friends, *they* were the whole point of history. . . .
>
> 2. They possessed a revolutionary vision. . . . They envisioned a Christian world radically different from the actual world; this was the source of their social creativity. . . .

3. Early Friends were not class-bound. . . . They felt alienated from their society; they were outsiders. . . .

4. Early Friends understood that revolutionists need the support of revolutionary communities. . . .

5. The intense corporateness of early Quakerism is its most alien characteristic to us today. . . .

6. Early Friends had a revolutionary discipline, summarized in the word "faithfulness." . . . Discipline . . . was understood dynamically in terms of loyalty to a leader, rather than statically in terms of obeying rules. . . .

7. Finally, early Friends built a revolutionary apparatus through which to do the work of overturning the old and instituting the new.[30]

I noted in my paper that the similarity between Yoder's and Tucker's insights was at the sociological, descriptive level, and I was left hanging with a theological question: "Even if we have some idea what such a community might look like, how does it actually come into being?"[31]

With this question I conclude my portrayal of the glass through which I view, however darkly, the vast panorama of Quaker history, and through which I now return my focus to George Fox's remarkable encounter with the Seekers at Sedbergh and Firbank Fell.

During the 1640s and early 1650s, England was in turmoil. During the 1550s many Protestant leaders, persecuted by Roman Catholic Queen Mary, had fled to Europe—some of them to Geneva, where they flourished and rejoiced in John Calvin's "school of Christ." On their return to England after Elizabeth I became queen, they were bitterly disappointed at the direction taken by the re-established Church of England. Worship in this church retained many traditional elements from the country's Roman Catholic past, and conformity was enforced by an authoritarian hierarchy of archbishops and bishops. Those who returned from Europe insisted on a more clearly Protestant liturgy and Calvinist creed. Failing in their attempts to "purify" the church, by turning it in a more Protestant and biblical direction, they became known as Puritans.

During the next ninety years, the Puritan party steadily grew in strength and popularity, but faced increasing resistance to change on the part of the bishops and of Kings James I and Charles I. In government, the elected

Parliaments found their powers being steadily eroded by the increasingly authoritarian rule of Charles I. Tensions and hostilities heightened until civil war broke out in 1641.

Puritanism became an increasingly diverse movement. From the 1630s on, more and more Puritans despaired of effecting change within the Church of England and formed Separatist congregations outside of the state church. Some of these Separatists, the General Baptists, rejected the Calvinist theology of predestination. During the Civil War, an even greater variety of religious and political groupings emerged. Gradually, individuals and groups withdrew from all organized churches and became Seekers. Seekers often joined together into a wide variety of amorphous groups. Most of them no longer took part in the sacraments of the church, particularly in the Eucharist or holy communion. Yet, as Doug Gwyn suggests, many of them had much in common; they were "mourning in Babylon, worshiping in penitent silence, waiting for a new revelation that will revive primitive Christianity. This mournful sense of captivity would not simply celebrate the secret glory of an invisible church; it ached for a visible, gathered church."[32]

The Civil War ended when the Puritan forces executed King Charles I in 1649, and Oliver Cromwell, the general who led the victorious Puritan army, became the ruler of England with the title of Lord Protector. The Civil War had become far more than a struggle to purify church government and theology. There was widespread expectation among the diverse Puritan population that the revolutionary changes that were taking place in politics and religion were going to come to a climax with the outbreak of the kingdom of God itself, beginning in England. Many Seekers, of course, shared in this eschatological hope and excitement.

In northwest England there was a large number of Seekers in Westmoreland and nearby portions of Yorkshire and Lancashire. Many of them gathered together for regular meetings under the leadership of ministers such as Francis Howgill, Thomas Taylor, John Audland, and John Camm. These Seekers were evidently among the many who were waiting for the day of the Lord, the coming of the kingdom of God. Francis Howgill referred to his own expectations when he looked back to this time of seeking and waiting, and to the day when this hope was fulfilled:

> There was something revealed in me, that the Lord would teach his
> people himself. And so I waited and many things opened in me of a

time at hand. . . . My mind was turned to the Light, and I had pure openings and prophecies to come, and a belief that I should see the Day. . . .

But all laid down in sorrow when the Day of the Lord was made manifest, for I was overthrown.[33]

George Fox's account meshed closely with Howgill's recollection of the crucial events:

There was a great fair at Sedbergh. . . . I went to the fair and declared through the fair the day of the Lord, and after I had done I went into the steeplehouse yard. . . . There I declared the everlasting Truth of the Lord and the word of life for several hours, and that the Lord Christ Jesus was come to teach his people himself. . . . There stood up a Separate preacher, one Francis Howgill. . . . Then said Francis Howgill, "This man speaks with authority and not as the scribes." . . .

And the next First-day I came to Firbank Chapel where there was a great meeting of the sober people of the country, where Francis Howgill and John Audland had been preaching in the morning. . . .

In the afternoon the people gathered about me with several Separate teachers, where it was judged there were above a thousand people; and all those several Separate teachers were convinced of God's everlasting Truth that day; amongst whom I declared freely and largely God's everlasting Truth and word of life about three hours. . . .

I was made to open to the people that . . . Christ was come.[34]

In another context, Howgill described in dramatic, rapturous language the tremendous impact that Fox's preaching had on this body of Seekers:

God out of his everlasting Love did appear unto us, according to the desire of our hearts, who longed after him; . . . and God out of his everlasting Love, and great Mercy, sent one unto us immediately by his Power, a Man of God, one of Ten Thousand, to instruct us in the Way of God more perfectly; who laid down the sure Foundation, and declared the acceptable Year of the Lord; . . . and the Lord of Heaven and Earth we found to be near at hand; and as we waited upon him in pure Silence, our Minds out of all things, his Dreadful

Power, and Glorious Majesty, and Heavenly Presence appeared in our Assemblies, when there was no Language, Tongue nor Speech from any Creature, and the Kingdom of Heaven did gather us, and catch us all, as in a Net; and his Heavenly Power at one time drew many Hundreds to Land, and we came to know a place to stand in, and what to wait in; and the Lord appeared daily to us, to our Astonishment, Amazement, and great Admiration, insomuch that we often said one unto another, with great joy of Heart, *What, is the Kingdom of God come to be with men? And will he take up his Tabernacle among the Sons of Men, as He did of old?*[35]

These Seekers were clearly convinced that Christ had in truth come again, that the kingdom of God had arrived and was present in their midst. This was perhaps the purest known case of what C. H. Dodd, in the twentieth century, was to call "realized eschatology."

Like the Seekers, George Fox had gone through periods of despair. Unlike them, his quest was a solitary search, and he felt compelled to wander widely around England in search of a solution. What was the ground for his despair? What was he seeking for? Unlike Martin Luther or John Bunyan, he was not weighed down by a sense of his own unworthiness or sinfulness or by a driving need to feel accepted by God:

When I came to eleven years of age, I knew pureness and righteousness. . . . The Lord taught me to be faithful in all things. . . .

As I grew up, . . . I never wronged man or woman in all that time, for the Lord's power was with me and over me, to preserve me. . . . People had generally a love to me for my innocence and honesty.[36]

A popular view of Fox is that he was seeking a vital experience of the presence of God. Elbert Russell, for instance, wrote: "He was seeking, with the mystic's thirst, for direct access to God. He was restless with that restlessness that can only be quieted when the soul finds rest in God. . . . His great release and transformation came"[37] in one grand moment when, in Fox's words,

All my hopes in . . . all men were gone, so that I had nothing outwardly to help me, nor could tell what to do, then, Oh then, I heard a voice which said, "There is one, even Christ Jesus, that can speak to thy condition", and when I heard it my heart did leap for joy. . . . And this I knew experimentally.[38]

But Fox himself has given us important clues that lead me to question this understanding of his search. He recounted a clear experience of God's presence at the very outset of his quest, a dialogue in which he

> cried to the Lord, who said unto me, "Thou seest how young people go together into vanity and old people into the earth; and thou must forsake all, both young and old, and keep out of all, and be as a stranger unto all."
>
> Then, at the command of God, on the 9th day of the Seventh Month 1643, I left my relations and brake off all familiarity or fellowship with young or old.[39]

George Fox's experience of hearing that Christ Jesus could speak to his condition, when his heart leapt for joy, did not provide the answer to his doubts and despair; it was not long after this that "My troubles, my sorrows, and my temptations were so great, that I thought many times I should have despaired, I was so tempted."[40] This sharp alternation of states continued: "At another time I saw the great love of God, and I was filled with admiration at the infiniteness of it."[41] Soon after this, "I was tempted again to despair, as if I had sinned against the Holy Ghost. And I was in great perplexity and trouble for many days."[42] Indeed, Fox was to continue his search, through many ups and downs, for another five years.

On one occasion, soon after he had completed his search and entered into the next stage of his life, Fox downplayed the significance of religious experiences:

> I came up to Swarthmoor again, and there came up four or five priests, and I asked them whether any of them could say they ever had a word from the Lord to go and speak to such or such a people and none of them durst say so. But one of them burst out into a passion and said he could speak his experiences as well as I; but I told him experience was one thing but to go with a message and a word from the Lord as the prophets and the apostles had and did, and as I had done to them, this was another thing.[43]

What was it, then, that George Fox felt so lacking that he spent nine years in such impassioned and determined search? What was it that he had finally found, when he came to his world-shaking encounter with the Westmoreland Seekers? Attempting to answer these questions, I have focused on what was going on at the very beginning and at the completion of his quest.

The day before he left home to begin seeking, George Fox had been at a fair with two professing Christians (one of them being his own cousin). He joined them for a drink of beer, "for I loved any that had a sense of good, or that did seek after the Lord." But when they proposed turning the occasion into a binge-party, "I was grieved that any that made profession of religion should offer to do so."[44] The Lord's response that night—"Thou seest how young people go together into vanity and old people into the earth"—confirmed and justified his distress. What was lacking for George Fox was not in himself but in the society in which he lived: the absence of authentic Christian fellowship and community.

Over the next nine years of searching, George Fox reported receiving quite a few "openings" from God, which clarified his own understanding of the scriptures and of Christian ministry, or pointed out specific directions for his own life and calling. The final two openings seem actually to be two parts of a single great opening. One day in 1652, "I spied a great high hill called Pendle Hill, and . . . I was moved of the Lord to go atop of it." When he had climbed Pendle Hill, "The Lord let me see atop of the hill in what places he had a great people to be gathered."[45] That night or the next morning, at an alehouse near Sedbergh, "The Lord opened to me at that place, and let me see a great people in white raiment by a river's side coming to the Lord."[46] A few days later, in Sedbergh,

> I went to a Separate meeting at Justice Benson's, where the people were generally convinced; this was the place that I had seen a people coming forth in white raiment. A mighty meeting there was and is to this day, near Sedbergh, which I gathered in the name of Jesus.[47]

Within the next week came the great gatherings at the Pentecost fair in Sedbergh and near the chapel on Firbank Fell in which George Fox came together with Francis Howgill and many other Seekers to form the first large, dynamic community of Quakers. This was, in truth, the authentic Christian fellowship and community that Fox had set out in search of nine years earlier.

There is a further dimension to Fox's "opening" at Pendle Hill. He reported that, at the top of the hill, "I was moved to sound the day of the Lord."[48] The exact meaning of this cryptic clause is puzzling, but it clearly places the Lord's assurance of "a great people to be gathered" within an eschatological context. Again, when Fox proclaimed at Sedbergh, "that the Lord Christ Jesus was come," and at Firbank Fell that "Christ was come," he was using the language of realized eschatology. The response of the Seekers, as reported by Francis Howgill—"What, is the kingdom of God come to be with men?"—certainly shows that they grasped that the supreme magnitude of what George Fox was telling them was taking place in their midst.

The characteristic note of George Fox's teaching throughout his ministry is sounded in these words: "Sound the trumpet of the Lord of hosts, whose terrible day is come and coming."[49] "The mighty day of the Lord is come and coming."[50] Such phrases indicate a tension between the realized and the imminent future aspects of the coming of the kingdom of God—reminiscent of the tension that we find in the message of Jesus. As I read the works of Fox more closely, I understand him to be saying that the rapid spread of the Quaker movement was the occasion of God's judgment: men and women were being judged by their response to the faith as embodied in this people of God. To those who had already heard and embraced this gospel, Fox could say that the Day of the Lord "is come." To the rest of the world, that Day is soon "coming": "Now you are come before the bar of the Lamb, and his throne, and the bride, the Lamb's wife is come, the true church which was before and in the days of the apostles."[51] Perhaps Fox resolved this present/future tension too easily.

One of the Westmoreland Seekers who became a Quaker as a result of hearing George Fox's message in June 1652 was eighteen years old at that time. His name was Edward Burrough. He spent the next decade in almost continuous service to the new community and its message. He was a prolific writer of epistles, controversial tracts, and proclamations of the gospel. He suffered imprisonments for his faith, and died in prison in London in 1663. Most of his writings were published in 1672 in a single large volume, whose lengthy title begins, *The memorable Works of a Son of Thunder and Consolation*. . . . In reading these works I had a strong impression that Edward Burrough's thunder and consolation originated primarily in the book of Revelation; I suspect that this was his favorite book in the Bible.

The dominant thrust of Revelation is eschatological; it focuses on the idea that God will bring human history to a dramatic climax and goal. Revelation belongs to a particular subgroup of eschatological writings that are called "apocalyptic." Apocalyptic eschatology emphasizes the dramatic suddenness of the coming of the Day of the Lord, a sharp struggle between the forces of God and of evil, leading up to this final event (often expressed in bizarre symbolism and imagery), and the imminently near—but still future—arrival of the end of history.

Burrough echoed a favorite phrase of George Fox when he wrote: "Now the Day of the Lord is come and coming."[52] We can find passages in Burrough's *Works* that emphasize a futurist eschatology and others that reflect a realized eschatology. His approach to the tension between the "already" and the " not yet" in eschatology differs somewhat from Fox's, largely because of his greater dependence on the book of Revelation. He did not try, as many interpreters of Revelation have done, to fit the events of history into a rigid scheme. He did insist that in his own day the drama portrayed in that book was finally unfolding, that events already in motion would shortly bring in the final Day of the Lord:[53] "The Lord of Heaven and Earth is now turning the World up-side down, all old things shall pass away, all things shall become new by fire."[54] "Now is the time wherein the Lord God of Heaven and Earth is setting up a Kingdom."[55]

There is a major problem with this early Quaker stance, which Pink Dandelion has helpfully summarized as "realising eschatology."[56] We look back and see that history did not come to a dramatic eschatological conclusion in the seventeenth century. As Dandelion noted, within less than a decade and a half,

> Quakers sensed that they . . . were going to have to face a further wait. The *Testimony to the Brethren* of 1666, a forceful instruction to local Meetings as to how to organise themselves and conduct their affairs and the template for the "settling" of the Society, symbolises this move back from a sense of quickly unfolding end time to a longer-term mission.[57]

And so, "In the periods of Quaker history that followed the early enthusiasm of the 1650s, the Friends would need to devise their own meantime theology as evidence of the imminent Second Coming receded."[58]

> Maurice Creasey has stated the problem even more forcefully when he referred to a defective awareness of what is often called the "eschatological tension" between the "now" and the "not yet." . . . Early Friends were so vividly conscious of the reality of the spiritual fellowship into which they had been gathered that they felt they were living fully within "the kingdom." For them, the events of the Incarnation and Pentecost had ushered in the New Age in its fullness—there was nothing further, in principle, to be entered upon. There had, indeed, supervened the "dark night of Apostasy," and Friends did not, I think, sufficiently consider the theological implications of this fact.[59]

The problem is this: since the first Friends were so evidently mistaken in their "realizing eschatology," how can we rely on any of their thought and practice that may depend on this expectation, and accept it as normative? The Lamb's War, in particular, was a theme that they derived from the eschatology of the book of Revelation. It was a struggle that they thought was rapidly heading for the final victory of the Lamb. How, then, can I join with Canby Jones in insisting that the Lamb's War must be basic to our Quaker testimony and action today?

The first step in dealing with this problem—the problem arising from unfulfilled expectations of the present or near future coming of the Day of the Lord—is to remember that the problem is not confined to George Fox and other early Friends.

Two poles of their expectation can be found in the very sayings of Jesus, "Those who are ashamed of me and of my words, of them the Son of Man will be ashamed when he comes in his glory and the glory of the Father and of the holy angels. But truly I tell you, there are some standing here who will not taste death before they see the kingdom of God" (Luke 9:26-27), and "The kingdom of God is not coming with things that can be observed; nor will they say, 'Look, here it is!' or 'There it is!' For, in fact, the kingdom of God is among you" (Luke 17:20-21 [or "the kingdom of God is within you" KJV]). This tension in the words of Jesus could well be summed up in the favorite Quaker phrase: "The day of the Lord is come and coming."

The early Christian church after Jesus, just like the early Friends, had to deal with a fading expectation of the imminent or even "realizing" arrival of the kingdom of God. Outside of the gospels, clear statements that the kingdom of God is already present simply disappear from the rest of the New Testament. Paul, in his earliest letters, appears to have expected Christ's return to earth in his own lifetime:

> We who are alive, who are left until the coming of the Lord, will by no means precede those who have died. For the Lord himself . . . will descend from heaven, and the dead in Christ will rise first. Then we who are alive, who are left, will be caught up in the clouds together with them to meet the Lord in the air; and so we will be with the Lord forever (1 Thessalonians 4:15-17).

In a later prison letter, Paul had come to recognize the likelihood that he would die before the return of Christ:

For to me, living is Christ and dying is gain. If I am to live in the flesh, that means fruitful labor for me; and I do not know which I prefer. I am hard pressed between the two: my desire is to depart and be with Christ, for that is far better; but to remain in the flesh is more necessary for you (Philippians 1:21-24).

By the late first or early second century, the author of 2 Peter had to face questions that were being raised by the delay in the expected return of Christ: "Scoffers will come, . . . saying, 'Where is the promise of his coming? For ever since our ancestors died, all things continue as they were from the beginning of creation!'" (2 Peter 3:3-4), and to provide an explanation to account for this delay:

With the Lord one day is like a thousand years, and a thousand years are like one day. The Lord is not slow about his promise, as some think of slowness, but is patient with you, not wanting any to perish, but all to come to repentance. But the day of the Lord will come like a thief, and then the heavens will pass away with a loud noise, and the elements will be dissolved with fire, and the earth and everything that is done on it will be disclosed (2 Peter 3:8-10).

When King Solomon died in 922 BC the Hebrew kingdom was divided into two monarchies, the kingdom of Israel in the north and the kingdom of Judah in the south. During the period of the Hebrew monarchies, significant religious leadership was provided by a succession of prophets. The prophets were passionate defenders of the covenant relationship between God and the people. They proclaimed God's steadfast love for the people of God but also insisted that God would punish the people when they violated the terms of their covenant with God and with one another.

The Hebrews and their prophets looked back to the mighty act of God, when God rescued them from slavery in Egypt and established the covenant which constituted them as a people. They often looked forward to a future "Day of the Lord," when God would act powerfully again in their midst. Many of the prophets, from Amos (around 750 BC) onward, insisted that the Day of the Lord would be a day when God would act in fearsome judgment upon the people; often they proclaimed that this judgment would come about through their being conquered by one of the powerful empires that surrounded them. Some of the prophets expressed a hope that God would act again after that, perhaps in the distant future, and re-establish his covenant with the Hebrew people.

In the year 721 BC, the Assyrian empire did conquer the kingdom of Israel and carry many of its leading citizens off into exile. The kingdom of Judah managed—barely—to survive. Around that time, a prophet named Isaiah was prominent in Jerusalem, the capital of Judah. At one point, Isaiah stated that the Lord had called him to "bind up the testimony, seal the teaching among my disciples" (Isaiah 8:16). It appears that Isaiah founded a school of prophets, who carried on his tradition long after his death and preserved many of his sayings in written form—the core of what eventually became the book of Isaiah.

In 612 BC the Assyrian empire was defeated and replaced by the equally ruthless and cruel Babylonian empire. A few years later, the kingdom of Judah was conquered by the Babylonians. During the next couple of decades, the prophet Jeremiah argued that the Babylonians were God's unwitting instruments of judgment against the unfaithful kingdom of Judah and that the Jewish people should therefore submit to their Babylonian rulers. Nevertheless, the puppet kings of Judah rebelled twice against Babylonian rule. The Babylonian emperor Nebuchadrezzar II (or Nebuchadnezzar) decisively put down the revolt each time and deported many leading Jewish citizens to Babylonia. The second time, in 587 BC, the Babylonians also destroyed the Jewish temple in Jerusalem and installed a governor in place of the last king of Judah. The Jews in exile in Babylonia suffered oppression so cruel that, according to Daniel Smith-Christopher, it would not be far from the truth to call it imprisonment or slavery.[60]

After Nabonidus became Babylonian emperor in 555 BC, tensions between the emperor and the priests of the Babylonian religion weakened the empire internally. Cyrus became emperor of Persia, to the east; in 546 BC he conquered the kingdom of Lydia (northwest of Babylonia) by which time the Persians were the strongest empire in the Middle East. In 539 BC Cyrus defeated the Babylonian empire and brought it to an end. By 525 BC the Persians had also won control over Egypt.

Some time between 546 and 540 BC, a new prophet arose within the Jewish community in exile in Babylonia and proclaimed a message of hope:

Comfort, O comfort my people,
  says your God.
Speak tenderly to Jerusalem,
  and cry to her
that she has served her term,

that her penalty is paid,
that she has received from the LORD's hand
double for all her sins (Isaiah 40:1-2).

We do not know this prophet's name, or anything about his (or her?) personality. It is likely that he belonged to the school of prophets founded by Isaiah and that the prophets in that school believed that his words deserved to be preserved together with the words of their founder; this prophet's words now make up chapters 40 through 55 of the book of Isaiah. For these reasons, many biblical scholars today simply call him "Second Isaiah."

Second Isaiah assured the Jewish exiles in Babylon that God would soon bring them back to their homeland. This would be another mighty act of God, similar to the Exodus when he had brought their ancestors out from their slavery in Egypt. But he was saying even more than this: biblical scholar Bernhard Anderson has referred to "Second Isaiah's proclamation that the New Age was beginning. . . . In the political ferment of his time he saw the sign of Yahweh's coming to liberate his people, and to inaugurate his kingdom."[61] In language that hinted at the similarity between Second Isaiah's expectation and that of the early church, Anderson wrote of Second Isaiah's confirmation that "Israel stands on the threshold of the new age. The decisive moment has come. The time is fulfilled and the kingdom of God is drawing near."[62] To fully appreciate the dramatic import of Second Isaiah's message, let us listen to the prophet's own words:

I will bring near my deliverance swiftly,
    my salvation has gone out
    and my arms will rule the peoples;
the coastlands wait for me,
    and for my arm they hope.
Lift up your eyes to the heavens,
    and look at the earth beneath;
for the heavens will vanish like smoke,
    the earth will wear out like a garment,
    and those who live on it will die like gnats;
but my salvation will be forever,
    and my deliverance will never be ended (Isaiah 51:5-6).

So the ransomed of the LORD shall return,
    and come to Zion with singing;
everlasting joy shall be upon their heads;

they shall obtain joy and gladness,
and sorrow and sighing shall flee away (Isaiah 51:11).

For you shall go out in joy,
   and be led back in peace;
the mountains and the hills before you
   shall burst into song,
   and all the trees of the field shall clap their hands.

Instead of the thorn shall come up the cypress;
   instead of the brier shall come up the myrtle;
and it shall be to the LORD for a memorial,
   for an everlasting sign that shall not be cut off (Isaiah 55:12-13).

These verses imply a final undoing of the curse uttered by God before he drove Adam and Eve out of the Garden of Eden:

Cursed is the ground because of you;
   in toil you shall eat of it all the days of your life;
thorns and thistles it shall bring forth for you (Genesis 3:17-18).

We also have here a context for one of George Fox's "openings": "Now was I come up in spirit through the flaming sword into the paradise of God. All things were new, and all the creation gave another smell unto me than before. . . . I was come up to the state of Adam which he was in before he fell."[63]

For the mountains may depart
   and the hills be removed,
but my steadfast love shall not depart from you,
   and my covenant of peace shall not be removed,
   says the LORD, who has compassion on you (Isaiah 54:10).

We can say with confidence that Second Isaiah was expecting the final mighty act of God to occur in the near future. God's final victory over evil would be won, and the world would again become the paradise that the biblical writers portrayed as the original condition of humanity and of the whole creation.

In fact, Second Isaiah's hopeful prophecy was fulfilled—but only in part. The Persian emperor, Cyrus, reversed the Assyrian and Babylonian policy of deporting conquered populations from their homes and allowed the peoples in exile to return to their own homelands. He issued a written edict on behalf of the Jewish exiles:

"Thus says King Cyrus of Persia: The LORD, the God of heaven, has given me all the kingdoms of the earth, and he has charged me to build him a house at Jerusalem in Judah. Any of those among you who are of his people—may their God be with them!—are now permitted to go up to Jerusalem in Judah, and rebuild the house of the LORD, the God of Israel" (Ezra 1:2-3).

Cyrus even provided funds for rebuilding the temple: "Let the cost be paid from the royal treasury" (Ezra 6:4). Beginning in 538 BC, several groups of Jewish exiles returned to Judah. They completed the rebuilding of the temple in 515 BC. Seventy years later, Nehemiah returned from the Persian capital to Jerusalem, where he served as governor and led the project of rebuilding Jerusalem's city walls.

But Judah was no paradise. There were tensions between the returning exiles and the Jewish people who had remained behind in Judah—and even more so with the Samaritans just to the north. Famines and plagues of locusts made life precarious. The newly rebuilt temple was far less splendid than the one that had been destroyed: "Who is left among you that saw this house in its former glory? How does it look to you now? Is it not in your sight as nothing?" (Haggai 2:3). Decades later Ezra, religious leader of the Hebrew community, lamented, "We are slaves today, slaves in the country which you gave to our ancestors" (Nehemiah 9:36 NJB). The "everlasting joy" promised by Second Isaiah was receding into the far distant future.

We seem to be facing a problem that has no solution. Second Isaiah foresaw an imminent day of the Lord, fulfilling history and bringing it to an end. His expectation was realized only in a partial way. Jesus of Nazareth foresaw an imminent coming of the kingdom of God, a coming that was already beginning to be realized in his own ministry. The early church soon recognized that this simply was not going to happen in their time. I believe there can be a solution to this problem if we put the eschatological strand of thought, seen in the messages of Second Isaiah and Jesus, into a wider perspective and look at it as but one strand in the whole tapestry of biblical theology.

Historically, we see this strand first in the book of Amos. Amos was responding to an expectation that was already becoming popular in the kingdom of Israel:

> Alas for you who desire the day of the LORD!
>> Why do you want the day of the LORD?
> It is darkness, not light (Amos 5:18).

Israelites, remembering former mighty acts of God—the Exodus, perhaps the reign of David—were hoping for another such event in which God would lead them to victory over foreign enemies. Amos agreed that there would indeed be another mighty act of God; but in light of the people's persistent breaking of God's covenant with them, it would be a day of punishment—military defeat and exile: "Israel shall surely go into exile away from its land" (Amos 7:17). Amos saw the day of the Lord as an event *within* history. He did not yet visualize the *end* of history.

After Amos, the magnitude of the day of the Lord expanded in the thought of the prophets until it became Joel's "great and terrible day of the Lord" (Joel 2:31), and a time described in the grotesque visions of the book of Daniel, coming to a climax in the sublime picture of

> One like a human being
>> coming with the clouds of heaven. . . .
> His dominion is an everlasting dominion
>> that shall not pass away,
> and his kingship is one
>> that shall never be destroyed (Daniel 7:13-14).

Yet the final day of the Lord was still to be a mighty act of God, different in degree but not in essential nature from God's past mighty acts.

When we come to the New Testament, we find a whole range of expectations about the coming mighty act of God from the visions in the book of Revelation—fully as bizarre and world-shaking as those in the book of Daniel—to the gentler picture in Paul's letter to the Ephesians in which "the Church is treated as a kind of preliminary model, on a small and imperfect scale, of what the final state of mankind is to be in God's design."[64] The final state, of course, is referred to "as a plan for the fullness of time, to gather up all things in him, things in heaven and things on earth" (Ephesians 1:10). In the meantime, in face of the deep and implacable hostility between Jews and Gentiles, symbolized by the wall dividing the Court of the Gentiles from the inner courts of the Jewish temple (which was broken down when the Romans destroyed Jerusalem and the temple in AD 70) we see the church's role as a preliminary model:

Remember that at one time you Gentiles . . . were . . . without Christ, being aliens from the commonwealth of Israel, and strangers to the covenants of promise, having no hope and without God in the world. But now in Christ Jesus you who once were far off have been brought near by the blood of Christ. For he is our peace; in his flesh he has made both groups into one and has broken down the dividing wall, that is, the hostility between us. He has abolished the law with its commandments and ordinances, that he might create in himself one new humanity in place of the two, thus making peace, and might reconcile both groups to God in one body through the cross, thus putting to death that hostility through it (Ephesians 2:11-16).

What is common to all of these hopes is the expectation of another mighty act of God, whether through catastrophe, bringing heaven and earth to an end, or through the ongoing, present process of dealing constructively with deep-seated hostilities in the day-to-day work of living together as the people of God.

I have previously stated that the events in history that can be called mighty acts of God include the exile of Judah to Babylon and the return from exile, and the ministry of Christ culminating in his crucifixion and resurrection. Second Isaiah and Jesus may have been mistaken in their belief that they were living in the days of the final mighty act of God, but they were certainly correct in recognizing that a mighty act of God was going to occur in the very near future or was even already in progress.

A mighty act of God is an event in which God both makes himself known to his people and acts to establish his kingship or reign on earth. It would be fair to say that realizing eschatology has been going on for a long time—at least since the days of Moses or even Abraham. Eschatology is not a continuous process, but takes place in a succession of discrete historical events. We have no way of knowing how many such events there will be in the future, or how long they will extend into the future: "But about that day or hour no one knows, neither the angels in heaven, nor the Son, but only the Father" (Mark 13:32).

When we reflect on God's awesome majesty, we can imagine what it must be like to be living in the midst of God's action in history when he makes himself known and exercises his power to bring the world, or even some part of the world, more fully in line with his purposes, and to be aware that this is what is happening. Events must seem momentous, titanic. It must seem that God is turning the world upside down.

> Even the nations are like a drop from a bucket,
>   and are accounted as dust on the scales;
>   see, he takes up the isles like fine dust. . . .
> It is he who sits above the circle of the earth,
>   and its inhabitants are like grasshoppers (Isaiah 40:15, 22).

What God is doing is so far above and beyond our puny understanding; surely these events are so great that God must finally be accomplishing his goals and bringing in his kingdom for good and forever. It is only when time has put some distance after the event that someone can finally recognize "that with the Lord one day is like a thousand years, and a thousand years are like one day. The Lord is not slow about his promise, . . . but is patient with you, not wanting any to perish, but all to come to repentance" (2 Peter 3:8-9).

As long as we remember that God's revelation is present in his acts in history, in which he encounters his people, and that the words of the prophets and of the apostles are reflections (in all their humanness) on God's revelation—so far we will be safe in searching for God's word, purpose, and will within and behind those words. As Karl Barth reminded us, this is the task of theology:

> Its searching of the Scriptures consists in asking the texts whether and to what extent they might witness to him; however, whether and to what extent they reflect and echo, in their complete humanity, the Word of God is completely unknown beforehand. . . . The Word of God itself, as witnessed to in the Bible, is not immediately obvious in any of its chapters or verses. On the contrary, the truth of the Word must be *sought* precisely, in order to be understood in its deep simplicity. Every possible means must be used.[65]

Many have believed a mighty act of God, which occurred in their time—in which they were indeed personally involved—was the final mighty act of God, the arrival of the kingdom of God in all its power. Dare we say that George Fox and Francis Howgill made this mistake? Was the encounter of George Fox with the Seekers also a mighty act of God? If this was so, then we can unashamedly expect to learn more about God and his purpose in history by looking at the way of life and the spirituality that shone forth in the new movement which emerged from that encounter: the early Friends.

I can explore this question by reminding us of two aspects of the meaning of the term, "mighty act of God":

- A mighty act of God is an event in which God establishes his purpose, his reign on earth; God wins decisive victory over the forces of evil.

- A mighty act of God is a covenant-making event; God takes the initiative in establishing or renewing covenant with a community, a people of God.

The first Friends understood themselves to be a covenant people. Edward Burrough reminded Friends that the covenant was what bound them together in love and unity: "Have Love and Unity in the Spirit of the Lord and with one another, that oneness of Heart and Soul and Spirit may be amongst us, being bound up in the holy Covenant of the Father."[66] In *The Covenant Crucified*, Doug Gwyn has clarified the meaning of the covenant for early Friends. Some of his summary points include: "The Quaker Movement was a covenantal initiative of God, breaking into history at a crucial moment of transition."[67] Gwyn emphasized "their *participational* sense of covenant."[68]

It is easy for us as Friends to venerate the founders of our faith and to idealize their accomplishments. Let me turn to an astute outside observer for a judgment that may make greater claim to objectivity. Philosopher William James, in his classical study, *The Varieties of Religious Experience*, wrote of George Fox: "The Quaker religion which he founded is something which is impossible to over-praise. In a day of shams, it was a religion of veracity rooted in spiritual inwardness, and a return to something more like the original gospel truth than men had ever known in England."[69] It is also significant that this movement, started with the encounter between Fox and the Seekers, has survived for more than three hundred fifty years. Quakerism has not only survived, I have heard it said—so many times and from so many sources that it seems to be a cliché—that Friends over these centuries have exercised an influence for good far beyond our numbers. We can think of the contributions that Quaker individuals and groups have made in the areas of religious liberty, abolition of slavery, women's suffrage, prison and mental health reform, business and industry, science. Can we doubt that God has worked through this movement to further the establishment of his rule on earth and to win victories over the forces of evil?

I am strongly drawn to the conclusion that the encounter between

George Fox and the Seekers was in truth a mighty act of God. In the final analysis, of course, no individual has the authority to make such a pronouncement. Mighty acts of God are recognized by the eye of faith, but this must be the eye of faith of the covenant people of God. What I can plead for as a recorded minister, attentive to the word of God, is authority to speak a prophetic message to Friends, to propose that God is calling us to claim our heritage as a people—that our beginning was indeed a mighty act of God.

2

The First Friends

The year was 1991. I had served for several years as clerk of the board that carried on the work of the Center for Christian Studies (CCS), an adult education program at Reedwood Friends Church in Portland, Oregon. I had offered to teach a CCS course in which I would survey various interpretations of what early Quakerism was all about. Others felt strongly that it was time for CCS to offer a Bible course. The attempt to resolve these competing proposals provided an instructive case study in the Quaker business process at work. Eventually, I was led to suggest a change in the focus of the course I proposed to teach: I would teach a course in how early Friends used the Bible. This was not a topic that I had ever seriously studied. Indeed, I did not know of any study, by anyone, that I could turn to as a resource; I would have to start from scratch, going back directly to early Quaker writings if I was to find anything to say on the subject.

The results proved to be surprisingly fruitful. What I discovered, with some help from the Friends who attended the course, was made available to a wider audience as an article in *Quaker Religious Thought.*[1] Several years later, in a series of classes that I taught a number of times in Reedwood's Center for Christian Studies and adult Sunday school, I expanded the subject by tracing some various ways in which Friends have interpreted the Bible throughout our history. What I present here, in this chapter and in the further "Friends and the Bible" chapters, is essentially an expanded and refined version of what I originally set forth in those courses at Reedwood.

Most Friends throughout our history have taken the Bible very seriously and have looked to it for guidance. But we can find all sorts of disturbing things in the Bible, in particular, passages in which women and slaves are told to keep to their inferior places in the social order; passages in which God commands war—war of the most brutal sort; passages that imply acceptance of the status quo of poverty and injustice. Yet Friends have been in the forefront in testifying against war and for the equality of women in Christian ministry, in working against slavery and for social justice. How can this be?

Actually, Friends are not unique. Anyone who wishes to take the Bible seriously and honestly will sooner or later come up against the problem: how to make sense of the diversity in the Bible. It is a truism that you can use the Bible to prove almost anything you want. Is there a responsible way to make sense of the Bible? Are there principles of interpretation that give us ways to use and understand the Bible without simply importing our own biases and prejudices and letting them control what we find in the Bible?

There is a big word that covers these issues—hermeneutics. If we had the time and the intention, we could examine the issue of hermeneutics through the entire history of the Christian church. But I believe that, if we confine ourselves to one small corner of Christian history—the history of Quakerism—we will discover enough insights and pitfalls to give us a good start in dealing with this problem for ourselves, here and now.

The earliest Friends were constantly quoting the Bible, and it is clear that their pioneering positions on war, women's ministry, and justice derived from their understanding of the Bible. We will investigate ways in which these Friends used the Bible in order to understand how Friends came to be—Friends. How did they make sense of the diversity within the Bible? Did they have consistent principles of interpretation to help them understand the Bible and to apply it to their own life and history?

In order to deal with these questions, I had to take a new approach to my study of early Friends. In earlier years, like many students of early Quaker thought, I had gone through the entire published works of George Fox and of Edward Burrough in order to find central themes and emphases in their thought. In my first CCS course on early Friends and the Bible, I made a fresh attempt to answer these questions about early Quaker hermeneutics. This time, I looked intensively at a few brief writings and brief sections of longer writings to see if I could discover by close examination just *how* the earliest Friends used the Bible in these writings.

I began by looking at two works addressed to Friends in the first years of the Quaker movement. One of these was George Fox's Epistle II, written in 1650:

> Friends, The children of the devil, how expert are they in evil, in all deceit in his kingdom; and yet they may speak of the things of God: but no vulturous eye or venomous beast ever trod in the steps of the just, though they may talk of the way. For who have their conversation in this world, and only mind the things of this world, in vain do they profess godliness.
>
> But the children of God, who are conceived and begotten of him, are not of this world, neither do they mind only the things of this world, but the things which are eternal. But the children of this world do mostly mind the external things, and their love is in them, and the other live by faith; the one is sanctified by the word, the other painted with the words. The children of God are pure in heart, not looking only at the outside. The favour of the world and friendship thereof is enmity to God, man may soon be stained with it. Oh! love the stranger, and be as strangers in the world, and to the world! For they that followed Christ in his cross, they were strangers in the world, and wonders to the world, and condemned by the world; and the world knew him not, neither doth it them that follow him now. So, marvel not if the world hate you; for the world lieth in hatred and wickedness. Who love this world, are enemies to Christ; and who love the Lord Jesus Christ, and have him for their Lord over them, they are redeemed out of the world. The world would have a Christ, but not to rule over them; the nature of the world is above Christ in man, until Christ hath subdued that nature in man. While the nature of the world doth rule in man, Oh! the deaf ears and blind eyes, and the understandings, that are all shut up amongst them, with which they judge! But who love the Lord Jesus Christ, do not mind the world's judgment, nor are troubled at it; but consider all our brethren, who have gone before us.

When ye think ye are past all crosses, when the trial doth come, ye will find a cross to that will which doth meddle with the things of God presumptuously; that man may live in joy, but the spirit is in bondage. Rejoice not in the flesh, but in the spirit, which crucifieth all fleshly boastings: if the fleshly will be fed, then carelessness cometh up, and they fall into flatness, (from the spirit,) and are mindless of the Lord God; such are soon up and down. The serpent tempted Eve to eat of the forbidden fruit, and she took and gave to her husband, and so they fell under the serpent's power, and the creatures, out of the power of God, which would have kept them in dominion. And so, Adam and Eve, and the serpent, all went out of truth. And Eve eating of the tree of knowledge, she had knowledge and wisdom after the fall, but not in the dominion, in the power of God. But the seed Christ, which was in the beginning, bruiseth the serpent's head, and he is the wisdom of God.[2]

My first impression was that this epistle was packed full of biblical references, in a very flowing style. Just how many biblical quotations or citations are there here? (By "citation" I mean a paraphrase of a Bible passage, close enough to the actual wording that Fox must certainly have had that passage in mind.) To answer that question, I went to work with a concordance. In addition, I asked the members of the CCS class to do some homework and see how many biblical references they could find. Between us, we came up with the following:

children of the devil (1 John 3:10; Acts 13:10)

things of this world (1 John 2:15)

profess godliness (Titus 1:16)

begotten of him (1 John 5:18)

not of this world (John 17:16)

things which are eternal (2 Corinthians 4:18)

children of this world (Luke 16:8)

live by faith (Galatians 3:11)

sanctified by the word (1 Timothy 4:5)

pure in heart (Matthew 5:8)

looking at the outside (1 Samuel 16:7)

friendship thereof is enmity to God (James 4:4)

love the stranger (Deuteronomy 10:19)

strangers in the world (Hebrews 11:13)

followed Christ in his cross (Mark 8:34)

the world knew him not (John 1:10)

neither doth it them that follow him (1 John 3:1)

marvel not if the world hate you (1 John 3:13)

the world lieth in hatred and wickedness (1 John 5:19)

who love the world, are enemies to Christ (Philippians 3:18)

deaf ears and blind eyes, and the understandings (Mark 8:17-18)

when the trial doth come (1 Peter 1:7; 4:12)

rejoice not in the flesh, but in the spirit (1 Corinthians 13:6)

crucifieth all fleshly boastings (Galatians 5:24)

fleshly will (John 1:13)

serpent tempted Eve to eat of the forbidden fruit, and she took and gave to her husband (Genesis 3:1-6)

tree of knowledge (Genesis 2:9)

the seed Christ . . . bruiseth the serpent's head (Genesis 3:15)

which was in the beginning (John 1:2)

the wisdom of God (1 Corinthians 1:24)

Two notes: First, I cannot guarantee that we identified *all* of the biblical references in this epistle. Second, just how closely does the wording have to be to that of a biblical passage to count? That is a judgment call. In this case, I believe it is safe to be conservative on this point.

We can now see how closely Fox packed this letter to Friends with biblical quotations and citations. The epistle took up one page of printed text. We counted thirty biblical references.

The next work I looked at was the opening page and a half of Edward Burrough's "An Epistle to all the Saints whom God hath called," written in 1657:

To all the Children of Light every where, who feareth and loveth
the Lord, who are begotten of God, and unto whom he is known
in the spirit and in the truth; this is a testimony of the Fathers love
unto you, Grace, Mercy, and Peace from him that lives for ever, the
God of Light and Life be multiplyed in you all, that you may day-
lie be renewed in strength, and girded with truth, and armed with
the whole Armour of God, and may be kept by his Power until
the day of Salvation, to walk in the Government and subjection
to Jesus Christ, witnessing the power and presence of God in you,
and amongst you, giving you power to fulfil his will in all things,
and that in all righteousness, and out of all evil you may be led, and
preserved unto the end, and in the end, to shew forth the praises of
God in this generation, as a people called of him, and redeemed by
him for his glories sake; even so Amen, and Amen. Dearly beloved,
be not ignorant, but this know, This is the Message which came unto
you, which is true and faithful, and everlasting, That the true God
is light, and in him is no darkness at all; and this is the Message of
Peace and Reconciliation, and of glad tydings unto all that have
sought the Lord, which we received of him, and you have heard,
and there is not another to be declared; and all that have received
it, are gathered up to God, and are in Covenant with him, and one
with another, and are in that which reconcileth and joyneth unto
Christ Jesus (the Husband) and second *Adam*, who is the Lord from
Heaven, the Prince of Peace, the Saviour and the deliverer, who
is made manifest in Power, and condemneth the Transgressor, and
slayeth the enmity, and raiseth the life out of death; and this is he who
kills and makes alive, even the God who is light, who brings down
one, and sets up another; who makes war against the mighty, and
gives Peace to the poor; and besides him there is none; he searcheth
mans heart, and tryeth the reins, and knows the thoughts, and every
creature is manifest in his sight, who gives to every one according to
his doings; and this is he who standeth in the Congregation of the
righteous, even in the midst of us, & sitteth Judge among the gods,
unto him must all the gods of the earth bow, and the Inhabitants of
the earth must tremble before him, and unto him every Tongue shall
confess, and the light in every man shall answer when he ariseth to
judgement, who is a swift witness to condemn or justifie all the children of men upon the face of the earth.

This is the God of truth whom we worship, and who will be worshipped in spirit and in truth, who is the God of *Abraham* and his seed for ever; and with him there is no change, nor shadow of turning; and he hath made known his Name, and his Power, and his wonderful works in this his day, and hath caused his voice to be heard in the earth, and the dead hath heard and now liveth.

And his Name is exalted on high amongst all that fear him and obey his voice; and he hath given his Son a Covenant of Light, who lighteth every man that cometh into the world with the true Light of Life, or Condemnation, that all who receive him may come to the knowledge of the Father, whom to know is life eternal.

And this is the Christ, the Saviour, in which we have believed, and which we preach, who is the Way, the Truth and the Life, the Foundation of God which cannot be moved, the Word of God is his Name, and there is no other Name given for salvation. This is he that was dead, and is alive, and lives for evermore; and there is no other to be looked for; if any preach any other, let him be accursed; and if any bring any other Message, let them not be received.[3]

The style seems similar to Fox's. I sense a breathlessness in Burrough's letter, as though his thoughts were pouring out faster than he could get them down on paper. Was this epistle packed as full of biblical references as Fox's letter? Using the same process, we came up with the following list:

Children of Light (Luke 16:8; John 12:36; Ephesians 5:8;
   1 Thessalonians 5:5)

begotten of God (1 John 5:18)

in the spirit and in the truth (John 4:23, 24)

Grace, Mercy, and Peace from (1 Timothy 1:2; 2 Timothy 1:2;
   Titus 1:4; 2 John v. 3)

him that lives for ever (Revelation 1:18)

renewed in strength (Isaiah 40:31; Isaiah 41:1)

girded with truth (Ephesians 6:14)

the whole Armour of God (Ephesians 6:11)

kept by his Power (1 Peter 1:5)

the day of Salvation (Isaiah 49:8; 2 Corinthians 6:2)

the power of God (1 Peter 1:5)

presence of God (Psalm 68:8)

in all righteousness (Ephesians 5:9)

out of all evil you may be led (Matthew 6:13; Luke 11:4)

shew forth the praises of God in this generation (Psalm 79:13; Isaiah 60:6; 1 Peter 2:9)

dearly beloved (2 Corinthians 7:1; 12:19; 1 Peter 2:11)

be not ignorant (2 Peter 3:8)

true and faithful (Revelation 21:5)

God is light, and in him is no darkness at all (1 John 1:5)

Message of Reconciliation (2 Corinthians 5:19)

glad tydings (Luke 1:19; 8:1; Acts 13:32; Romans 10:15)

sought the Lord (Psalm 34:4; 77:2)

second *Adam* (1 Corinthians 15:45)

the Lord from Heaven (1 Corinthians 15:47)

Prince of Peace (Isaiah 9:6)

made manifest (John 1:31)

slayeth the enmity (Ephesians 2:16)

kills and makes alive (1 Samuel 2:6)

God is light (1 John 1:5)

makes war against the mighty (Job 12:19; Revelation 19:11)

he searcheth mans heart (Romans 8:27)

and tryeth the reins (Jeremiah 11:20)

knows the thoughts (Psalm 94:11)

every creature is manifest in his sight (Hebrews 4:13)

gives to every one according to his doings (Psalm 28:4)

standeth in the Congregation of the righteous (Psalm 1:5; 82:1)

Judge among the gods (Psalm 82:1)

unto him every Tongue shall confess (Philippians 2:11)

swift witness (Malachi 3:5)

God of truth (Deuteronomy 32:4)

who will be worshipped in spirit and in truth (John 4:23-24)

God of *Abraham* (Exodus 3:6; Matthew 22:32)

and his seed for ever (Psalm 105:6; Luke 1:55)

there is no change, nor shadow of turning (James 1:17)

he hath made known his Name, and his Power, and his wonderful
    works (1 Kings 8:43; Psalm 111:4; Isaiah 64:2)

hath caused his voice to be heard (Isaiah 30:30)

his Name is exalted (Isaiah 12:4)

lighteth every man that cometh into the world (John 1:9)

the Father, whom to know is life eternal (John 17:3)

the Way, the Truth and the Life (John 14:6)

there is no other Name given for salvation (Acts 4:12)

was dead, and is alive (Revelation 2:8)

and lives for evermore (Revelation 1:18)

no other to be looked for (Matthew 11:3; Luke 7:19-20)

if any preach any other, let him be accursed (Galatians 1:8)

if any bring any other Message, let them not be received (2 John v. 10)

The portion I have quoted from Burrough's epistle is only eleven lines
longer than Fox's epistle, yet we found more than fifty-five biblical quotations and citations in it—almost twice as many. Burrough's epistle is even
more tightly packed with Bible references than Fox's.

As I read these two epistles, I was struck by the manner in which these
biblical phrases emerged. Neither Fox nor Burrough gave any chapter and
verse numbers; I had to do my homework with a concordance to come up
with that information. It seems clear that Fox and Burrough were not appealing to these quotations and citations as external resources or as authorities

that they were asking Friends simply to accept as final. Neither did they appear to be coming up with Bible references to confirm claims that had come to them from some other source. Their biblical references seemed to be a natural part of the flow of what they were saying.

As I attempted to understand and appreciate this use that Fox and Burrough were making of the Bible, I was reminded of the goal—indeed, the achievement—of the twentieth-century Biblical Theology Movement: to read the Bible with empathy. I could see that the epistles of Fox and Burrough expressed and embodied precisely this empathy. Although they had a few Old Testament references, their quotations and citations were mainly from the New Testament. As far as possible, Fox and Burrough were actually thinking *with* Paul, John, and Luke. They had entered sympathetically and imaginatively into the New Testament community and were reliving its sacred history. Further, they were expecting and assuming that their Quaker readers were also standing within the Bible—within the thought- and life-world of the earliest Christians—and were looking out at the world through the window of biblical faith.

These two epistles are examples of pastoral writings, written to encourage the faithful in the "Camp of the Lord."[4] The earliest Friends also wrote a great many polemical tracts, addressed to their critics or to those who persecuted them. One such tract was "A Measuring Rule Concerning Liberty and Persecution," by George Fox. This tract was specifically aimed at those who enforced an "act concerning the people of God called Quakers,"[5] which made it a criminal offense for more than three Friends to meet together. Fox quickly established community between Quakers and the first disciples of Jesus in this respect:

Which act, had it been in the days of the apostles, would have taken hold of Christ and his apostles, for he had twelve that often met together; and by this he might have but three, for if there were five, it had been in the transgression, who also had seventy disciples more. . . . Would Christ (and his disciples), the wisdom of God, do you think, have obeyed this act, and not met with his disciples? . . . And also, Christ said to his disciples, "that they should wait together at Jerusalem, and not depart;" and they did meet together, and you know that their meetings were different from the Jews and heathen; and they were to wait together at Jerusalem until they received power from on high.[6]

Fox also found himself and Friends to be in community with many Old
Testament heroes:

> And consider, Daniel and the three children met, and disobeyed the
> king's command; and Mordecai, who would not bow, disobeyed the
> king's command; and the midwives disobeyed Pharaoh's command
> for not putting the children to death. . . . And the apostles disobeyed
> the high priest's and council's command, when they charged them
> that they should speak no more in that name: yet in the thing that
> is good, just and righteous, the righteous always have been, and are
> ever subject to every ordinance of man for the Lord's sake, to such
> as were for the punishment of evildoers, and for the praise of them
> that do well, that they might live a godly and peaceable life.[7]

In the last three lines of this passage, we see how Fox brought in slightly
abbreviated quotations from 1 Peter 2:13-14 and 1 Timothy 2:2 as an inte-
gral, natural part of his narrative. Further on, we find Fox making interesting use of a phrase from Jesus' parable of the fig tree: "Cut it down; why
cumbereth it the ground?" (Luke 13:7 KJV):

> Therefore, cumber not the ground, you adulterers, cumber not the
> earth, you drunkards, cumber not the ground, you swearers, cum-
> ber not the ground, you proud, vain persons, . . . cumber not the
> ground, thou persecutor of the children of the Most High, cumber
> not the ground, ye rich gluttons.[8]

And then, in an interesting twist, Fox turned this identification with
people in the Bible back onto those who persecuted the Quakers:

> And the Philistines grieved the spirit of the Lord, and they were the
> persecutors, and they turned against the just.
>
> And the Sodomites were the persecutors of the just, and the
> Sodomites were such as lived in abundance of idleness and fulness,
> and those that were idle and full persecuted the righteous and the
> just, and the true worshippers. . . .
>
> And the Jews that professed the law, the words of God, and did
> live out of the life of the law of God, such did and do persecute the
> just; and such professors were always, and now are persecutors.
>
> And always such as preached for hire, and divined for money,
> and taught for filthy lucre, and such shepherds, bishops and priests,

that taught for the fleece and the wool, and for handfuls of barley, and for pieces of bread, and were covetous; such were and are persecutors, and false worshippers, and persecutors of the just and the true worshippers of God in the spirit. . . .

Cain, Ham, Nimrod, Ishmael, Esau, Balaam, Sodomites, Philistines, pharisees, chief priests, Babylon; were not these envious, wild, profane, idle, covetous, oppressors, persecutors, false worshippers? and so you that be of the same nature, and of the same birth, was it not, and is it not the first birth? if it be so, know your own kindred, and come out of this kindred.[9]

("For handfuls of barley, and for pieces of bread" is a quotation from Ezekiel 13:19.) Just as George Fox identified Friends with biblical heroes of the faith, so he identified those who persecuted Friends with a whole series of bad actors in the biblical narratives.

One of the outstanding leaders among the earliest Friends was Margaret Fell. She lived at Swarthmoor Hall, near the town of Ulverston in northwestern Lancashire, with her husband, Judge Thomas Fell, and their son and seven daughters. Judge Fell was traveling on his judicial circuit when George Fox visited Swarthmoor and spoke at the church in Ulverston in June 1652. Margaret Fell, her daughters, and several family servants all became Quakers before her husband returned home. Thomas Fell did not join Friends, but used his power as a local judge and member of Parliament to support and protect Friends in northwestern England. Margaret Fell made Swarthmoor Hall in effect the administrative center of the earliest Quaker movement. She entertained traveling Quaker ministers at Swarthmoor Hall, administered the Kendal fund that covered traveling expenses for itinerant ministers, and kept up an extensive correspondence with these early traveling leaders. She also wrote an autobiography and a number of tracts in defense of Quaker principles. One of these tracts, *Womens Speaking Justified*, was published in 1666. Thomas Fell died in 1658; in 1669 Margaret Fell married George Fox.

In *Womens Speaking Justified* we have perhaps an even clearer example of empathy with biblical writers and characters than we have already seen in the writings of Fox and Burrough. Margaret Fell was here defending Quaker practice, in which both men and women fully shared in spoken gospel ministry, against opponents who argued that the Bible did not permit women to preach. She noted that these opponents based their objections on two New

Testament passages: 1 Corinthians 14:34-35 ("Let your women keep silence in the churches: for it is not permitted unto them to speak; but they are commanded to be under obedience, as also saith the law. And if they will learn any thing, let them ask their husbands at home: for it is a shame for women to speak in the church" [KJV].) and 1 Timothy 2:11-12 ("Let the woman learn in silence with all subjection. But I suffer not a woman to teach, nor to usurp authority over the man, but to be in silence" [KJV].)

In her response, we can note Margaret Fell's keen sense of the specific circumstances that Paul was addressing so that she could emphasize the distinction between his general principles of Christian truth and advice that he was offering for specific historical situations:

And now to the Apostles words, which is the ground of the great Objection against Womens Speaking; And first, 1 *Cor.* 14. let the Reader seriously read that Chapter, and see the end and drift of the Apostle in speaking these words: for the Apostle is there exhorting the *Corinthians* unto charity, and to desire Spiritual gifts, and not to speak in an unknown tongue; and not to be Children in understanding, but to be Children in malice, but in understanding to be men; and that the Spirits of the Prophets should be subject to the Prophets; for God is not the Author of Confusion, but of Peace: And then he saith, *Let your Women keep silence in the Church*, etc.

Where it doth plainly appear that the Women, as well as others, that were among them, were in confusion; for he saith, *How is it Brethren? when ye come together, every one of you hath a Psalm, hath a Doctrine, hath a Tongue, hath a Revelation, hath an Interpretation? let all things be done to edifying.* Here was no edifying, but all was in confusion speaking together; Therefore he saith, *If any man speak in an unknown Tongue, let it be by two, or at most by three, and that by course; and let one Interpret; but if there be no Interpreter, let him keep silence in the Church.* Here the Man is commanded to keep silence as well as the Woman, when they are in confusion and out of order.[10]

Margaret Fell went further, and countered her opponents' appeal to Paul's words, by showing examples of how Paul and the other apostles supported and encouraged women who worked to promote the gospel:

If the Apostle would have had Womens speaking stopt, and did not allow of them, why did he entreat his true Yoak-Fellow to help those Women who laboured with him in the Gospel? *Phil.* 4.3. And why did the Apostles joyn together in Prayer and Supplication with the Women, and *Mary* the Mother of Jesus, and with his Brethren, *Acts* 1.14. if they had not allowed, and had union and fellowship with the Spirit of God, wherever it was revealed in Women as well as others?[11]

We begin to see here that Fell read the Bible in personal, rather than legalistic, terms. This becomes even clearer where she portrayed the ways in which Jesus commended the faith and work of women as persons:

Again, Christ Jesus, when he came to the City of *Samaria*, where *Jacobs* Well was, where the Woman of *Samaria* was; you may read, in *John* 4. how he was pleased to preach the Everlasting Gospel to her; and when the Woman said unto him, *I know that when the Messiah cometh*, (which is called Christ) *when he cometh, he will tell us all things;* Jesus saith unto her, *I that speak unto thee am he;* This is more than ever he said in plain words to Man or Woman (that we read of) before he suffered. Also he said unto *Martha*, when she said, she knew that her Brother should rise again in the last day, Jesus said unto her, *I am the Resurrection and the Life: he that believeth on me, though he were dead, yet shall he live; and whosoever liveth and believeth shall never die. Believest thou this?* she answered, *Yea Lord, I believe thou art the Christ, the Son of God.* Here she manifested her true and saving Faith, which few at that day believed so on him, John 11. 25, 26.

Also that Woman that came unto Jesus with an Alabaster Box of very precious Oyntment, and poured it on his Head as he sat at meat; it's manifested that this Woman knew more of the secret Power and Wisdom of God, then his Disciples did, that were filled with indignation against her; and therefore Jesus saith, *Why do ye trouble the Woman? For she hath wrought a good work upon me; Verily, I say unto you, Wheresoever this Gospel shall be preached in the whole World, there shall also this that this Woman hath done, be told for a memorial of her,* Matthew 26. Mark 14. 3.[12]

Thus we see that Jesus owned the Love and Grace that appeared in Women, and did not despise it; and by what is recorded in the Scriptures, he received as much love, kindness, compassion, and tender dealing towards him from Women, as he did from any others, both in his life time, and also after they had exercised their cruelty upon him; for *Mary Magdalene*, and *Mary* the Mother of *Joses*, beheld where he was laid; *And when the Sabbath was past,* Mary Magdalene, *and* Mary *the Mother of* James, *and* Salom, *had brought sweet spices that they might annoint him: And very early in the morning, the first day of the week, they came unto the Sepulchre at the rising of the Sun; And they said among themselves, Who shall roll us away the stone from the door of the Sepulchre? And when they looked, the stone was rolled away, for it was very great;* Mark 16. 1, 2, 3, 4. Luke 24.1,2. *and they went down into the Sepulchre;* and as *Matthew* saith, *The Angel rolled away the stone; and he said unto the Women, Fear not, I know whom ye seek, Jesus which was Crucified; he is not here, he is risen,* Mat. 28. Now *Luke* saith thus, That *there stood two men by them in shining apparel, and as they were perplexed and afraid, the men said unto them, He is not here; remember how he said unto you when he was in* Galilee, *That the Son of Man must be delivered into the hands of sinful men, and be crucified, and the third day rise again; and they remembred his words, and returned from the Sepulchre, and told all these things to the eleven, and to all the rest.*

It was *Mary Magdalene,* and *Joanna,* and *Mary* the Mother of *James,* and the other Women that were with them, which told these things to the Apostles, *And their words seemed unto them as idle tales, and they believed them not.* Mark this, ye despisers of the weakness of Women, and look upon your selves to be so wise; but Christ Jesus doth not so, for he makes use of the weak.[13]

Mark this, you that despise and oppose the Message of the Lord God that he sends by Women; what had become of the Redemption of the whole Body of Man-kind, if they had not believed the Message that the Lord Jesus sent by these Women, of and concerning his Resurrection? And if these Women had not thus, out of their tenderness and bowels of love, who had received Mercy, and Grace, and forgiveness of sins, and Virtue, and Healing from him; which many men also had received the like, if their hearts had not been so united and knit unto him in love, that they could not depart as the men did, but sat watching, and waiting, and weeping about the Sepulchre until the time of his Resurrection, and so were ready to carry his Message, as is manifested; else how should his Disciples have known, who were not there?[14]

We can keep on quoting passages in which Margaret Fell eloquently demonstrated her love for and empathy with women in the Old Testament and the New Testament who spoke out for God and Christ:

More might be added to this purpose, both out of the Old Testament and New, where it is evident that God made no difference, but gave his good Spirit, as it pleased him, both to Man and Woman, as *Deborah, Huldah, & Sarah. . . . And* Anna *the Prophetess, who was a Widow of fourscore and four years of age, which departed not from the Temple, but served God with fastings and prayers night and day, she coming in at that instant,* (when old *Simeon* took the Child Jesus in his arms, and) *she gave thanks unto the Lord, and spake of him to all them who looked for Redemption in* Jerusalem, *Luke* 2.36, 37, 38. And *Philip* the Evangelist, into whose house the Apostle *Paul* entered, who was one of the Seven, *Acts* 6:3. He had four Daughters which were Virgins, that did prophesie, *Acts* 21.[15]

And *Isaiah*, that went to the Prophetess, did not forbid her Speaking or Prophesying, *Isa.* 8. And was it not prophesied in *Joel* 2, that *Hand-maids should Prophesie? . . .* This was *Elizabeths* Sermon concerning Christ, which at this day stands upon Record: And then *Mary* said, *My Soul doth magnifie the Lord, and my Spirit rejoyceth in God my Saviour, for he hath regarded the low estate of his Hand-maid: for behold, from henceforth all Generations shall call me blessed; for he that is mighty, hath done to me great things, and holy is his Name; and his Mercy is on them that fear him, from Generation to Generation; he hath shewed strength with his Arm; he hath scattered the proud in the imaginations of their own hearts; he hath put down the mighty from their Seats, and exalted them of low degree; he hath filled the hungry with good things, and the rich he hath sent empty away; he hath holpen his Servant* Israel, *in remembrance of his mercy, as he spake to his Father, to* Abraham, *and to his Seed for ever.* Are you not here beholding to the Woman for her Sermon, to use her words to put into your Common Prayer? and yet you forbid Womens Speaking. Now here you may see how these two Women prophesied of Christ, and Preached better then all the blind Priests did in that Age, and better then this Age also, who are beholding to Women to make use of their Words.[16]

Even more sharply than George Fox, Margaret Fell had no trouble locating the opponents of Quakerism within the biblical scheme—in the darkest places imaginable:

Those that speak against the Womans speaking, speak against the Church of Christ, and the Seed of the Woman, which Seed is Christ; that is to say, Those that speak against the Power of the Lord, and the Spirit of the Lord speaking in a Woman, simply, by reason of her Sex, or because she is a Woman, not regarding the Seed, and Spirit, and Power that speaks in her; such speak against Christ, and his Church, and are of the Seed of the Serpent, wherein lodgeth the enmity.[17]

All this opposing and gainsaying of Womens Speaking, hath risen out of the bottomless Pit, and spirit of Darkness that hath spoken for these many hundred years together.[18]

As we come to appreciate the extent to which the earliest Friends entered with empathy into the biblical world and the history of the ancient Israelites and the early church, we find new dimensions of meaning in much of the language and activity of these Friends. This must have been what George Fox meant when he wrote of the need to "come . . . into the same power and Spirit that the prophets and apostles were in."[19]

This understanding of where Fox and the early Friends were coming from also gives us fresh insight into some of the strange and bizarre actions of the first Quakers. For instance, two biblical prophets had proclaimed as the word of the Lord: "Woe to the bloody city!" (Ezekiel 24:6-9 KJV; Nahum 3:1 KJV). When George Fox came to the city of Lichfield, these very words were given to him: "The word of the Lord came unto me again to cry, 'Woe unto the bloody city of Lichfield!'"[20]

Sometimes Friends felt called by God to repeat precisely the actions of some biblical character. For example, the prophet Isaiah reported: "At the same time spake the LORD by Isaiah the son of Amoz, saying, Go and loose the sackcloth from off thy loins, and put off thy shoe from thy foot. And he did so, walking naked and barefoot. And the LORD said, . . . my servant Isaiah hath walked naked and barefoot three years for a sign and wonder upon Egypt and upon Ethiopia" (Isaiah 20:2-3 KJV). Several Friends, including Robert Barclay, identified themselves so closely with Isaiah that they, too, heard and obeyed a call from the Lord to walk naked, as a sign. When I visited the "Quaker country" in northwest England, I remember seeing in one town a seventeenth-century pub with a sign in front—"Ye naked man"—named after a Quaker who had walked naked in that street.

Perhaps the strangest instance of empathetic identification with people of the Bible came in connection with James Nayler's notorious ride into Bristol. In Mark's account of Jesus' entry into Jerusalem, "They brought the colt to Jesus, and cast their garments on him; and he sat upon him. And many spread their garment in the way" (Mark 11:7-8 KJV). Just so, Nayler's follower Dorcas Erbury took off her clothes and spread them on the road ahead of his donkey.

The early Quakers' identification with the people of the Bible went far deeper, of course, than simply mimicking specific words or actions of the prophets and apostles. In my first chapter I pointed out the similarity between John Howard Yoder's description of the community that Jesus was founding and Rob Tucker's description of the early Quaker community. In 1969 I was searching for a theological explanation of this similarity: "Even if we have some idea what such a community might look like, how does it actually come into being?" It was to be more than twenty years before I got a clue to any answer to this question. I can now suggest the probable source or origin of the distinctive style of life of the Quaker community: It resembled the community of the first disciples precisely because the early Friends had internalized the life of the early church with such deep empathy, because the history of the first apostles had become their own history. They "were there when they crucified my Lord."

I went on to probe even more deeply into the ways in which early Friends expressed and displayed their empathy with the life of the Bible. At this point I am deeply indebted to Alan Kolp's insight that George Fox's language is "rich in symbols and metaphor."[21] This is true not only of Fox's language but also of the language of the Bible itself. We can think of Jesus' use of gigantic exaggeration, and of his tendency to speak in parables—basically extended similes: "the kingdom of God is like . . . ." Biblical language consists not simply of prose propositions and narratives; much of the biblical literature is poetic and dramatic in form. The biblical writings abound in verbal and visual symbolism.

My question was: To what extent did the early Friends make use of *biblical* metaphors and symbolism in their writings? I returned to the few selections I had already examined, with this question in mind. I readily found, in them, these metaphors:

Fox, Epistle II: children of the devil/children of this world/children of God; strangers in the world; Christ, the wisdom of God; the seed Christ bruiseth the serpent's head.

Burrough, 1657 Epistle: children of light; girded with truth; the whole armour of God; God is light; Christ, the second Adam; God makes war against the mighty; Christ is the Way, the Truth, and the Life.

Fox, "A Measuring Rule": cumber not the ground; taught for the fleece and the wool, and for handfuls of barley, and for pieces of bread.

Fell, *Womens Speaking*: "a Woman clothed with the Sun. . . . the Church of Christ is a Woman";[22] the Seed of the Woman is Christ; I am the Resurrection and the Life; the secret Power and Wisdom of God; their tenderness and bowels of love; God hath shewed strength with his Arm; the imaginations of their own hearts; the Seed of the Serpent.

Writings of early Friends were full of biblical metaphors and symbols. Kolp has pointed out that Fox's was primarily an "affective spirituality,"[23] emotional, spontaneous, imaginative, sensual. For such a spirituality, metaphorical and symbolic language is clearly the most appropriate form of expression. Empathy, of course, is an emotive, affective route into someone else's world.

A contemporary work on the Bible and Christian ethics has emphasized the use of the Bible in

Character Formation. . . . The most effective and crucial impact of the Bible in Christian ethics is that of shaping the moral identity of the Christian and the church. . . . The treatment of those biblical stories, symbols, images, paradigms, and beliefs expressly at the point of their shaping moral character"[24]

needs to receive increased attention. Using specific examples, Birch and Rasmussen encouraged Christians to internalize biblical themes, stories, figures of speech. This comes close to what Fox and the early Friends were doing with their empathetic understanding of biblical history, with their use of biblical metaphors, with their affective biblical spirituality.

In my first chapter, I showed how my own values and worldview have been nurtured and inspired primarily by the earliest Quaker movement and the twentieth-century Biblical Theology Movement. Over many years I have clarified my own understanding of major themes and insights in early Quakerism through dialogue with colleagues in the Quaker Theological Discussion Group. In all this I have been trying to grasp the central thrust or insight—the linchpin—of the thought and spirituality of George Fox and the other Seekers-turned-Quakers. I now believe that I have finally found the linchpin of George Fox's understanding of Quakerism; it was his *hermeneutical method*—his reading of the Bible with empathy, which led to an affective spirituality, grounded in biblical symbolism and metaphor. And his early colleagues, such as Edward Burrough and Margaret Fell, shared this fundamental insight with him.

This hermeneutical method was not unique or even original with Fox and the earliest Friends. I had myself first become acquainted with it when I immersed myself in the writings of the twentieth-century Biblical Theology Movement: scholars such as Karl Barth, Bernhard W. Anderson, and G. Ernest Wright. Carole Spencer has noted that "early Quaker understanding and use of scripture has stronger affinity with the spiritual interpretation practiced by the early Greek fathers. . . . Karen Torjesen [in her book on Origen] describes biblical hermeneutic as a process of the reader being placed within the text and its meaning written on the soul."[25] Paul Bock, in conversation with me, has suggested that my description of Fox's empathetic approach to the Bible seems very similar to Ignatius Loyola's use of scripture. Michael Birkel's understanding of the way early Friends read the Bible is similar to what I have proposed here, with some interesting nuances of difference:

> Early Friends used biblical language to describe their inward experiences. If we pay careful attention to the references to scripture in their writings, we can come to understand their spiritual experiences more fully. We can appreciate the interplay of scripture and experience in their lives. Our focus here is with a way of reading scripture that is reflective, meditative, even poetic. . . .
>
> The relationship that early Friends had with scripture was rich and complex. They read the Bible in terms of their own particular inward experiences, yet they perceived their world in profoundly biblical terms. Their spiritual experiences shaped their reading of the Bible, and the Bible shaped their understanding of their experiences. They did not simply read the scriptures. They lived them. For them, reading the Bible was not just an exercise in information. It was an invitation to transformation.[26]

Birkel also emphasized that early Friends were not the first Christians to read the Bible in this way:

> To read the scriptures is to look in a mirror and find one's own inner life reflected in the lives of spiritual forebears. Reading the scriptures is an experience of growing self-knowledge. The life experiences of

biblical characters are analogous to the reader's. The biblical story is recapitulated in the life of the believing reader. Each has his own exile, her own exodus. . . . *Lectio divina,* or sacred reading, . . . is a meditative and imaginative practice of reading scripture with roots in the medieval monastic tradition. Early Friends developed their own similar approach to reading the Bible as a worshipful act.[27]

How does one discover or come to this empathetic approach to the Bible? One route, followed by the recent Biblical Theology Movement, has been that of serious, disciplined biblical scholarship. But George Fox and the early Friends found their way to such a standpoint without benefit of this sophistication. Indeed, such Friends as Fox, Burrough, and Fell did not even show any conscious awareness that this was what they were doing. Certainly they never mentioned reading the Bible empathetically or making use of biblical metaphors and symbolic language. (And perhaps that was one reason why, as we shall see, this way of reading and understanding the Bible virtually disappeared at the end of the first generation of Quakerism.) Was this discovery by Fox and his contemporaries a matter of sheer religious genius, or was there something in their own historical situation that enabled them to do this?

Studies by Daniel Smith-Christopher and Peter Gomes suggest the latter possibility. Daniel Smith-Christopher's insights into the period of the Babylonian exile of the Jews and their return to Palestine led him to seek patterns that might be echoed in the experience of contemporary "exile" communities. His studies of groups like Japanese Americans during World War II and Native American communities disclosed patterns of behavior that had remarkable parallels with the experience of the Jewish exiles. Since then, in his teaching and in field studies, he has discovered that members of modern minority, "exile" groups, such as African Americans and Native Americans, are readily able to identify with the work, for instance, of Ezra—a leader whom most European and European-American biblical scholars find it staggeringly difficult to appreciate.

And Peter Gomes, who was Plummer Professor of Christian Morals at Harvard when he passed away in 2011, shows how the empathetic approach has come easily to African Americans:

Black preaching, coming out of an oral and aural tradition, is overwhelmingly narrative, and the point of a story is to get into it as quickly and as thoroughly as possible. . . . Black preaching endeavors to remove as many barriers between the thing preached and those to whom it is preached as quickly as possible, so that the "objective" story becomes with very little effort, "our" story, or "my" story. Distinctions between then and now, while possibly of some rhetorical use, more often than not get in the way. Thus, when the black preacher preaches about the exodus of the Jews from Egypt under the leadership of Moses, he does not dwell on the fact that most black people have more in common culturally with the benighted Egyptians than with the Jews. We are the Jews, and their exodus is ours, not by analogy but by participation and experience. . . .

African Americans who read and heard the Bible did not stop to ask if it was literally true, inspired, and inerrant, for they knew that on the authority of their own experience as a people troubled, transformed, and redeemed. The biblical world may be different from the new world to which they had been transported in chains and against their wills, but the view of God was to them the same in both worlds. Hence, what God did for Daniel and the three Hebrew children in the fiery, fiery furnace, God not only would do, but already had done with them. . . . Far more than fact-obsessed white Protestant Christians, the African American believer saw the story whole, saw that it had his face and name on it, and embraced the teller and the tale.[28]

Was there anything in the social or historical situation of early Friends that would have made it easy for them to enter empathetically into the lives of the Hebrews and early Christians? Richard Vann's sociological analysis of early Quakers has offered me some suggestions:

Eldest sons were almost never converted to Quakerism. Its appeal was all but entirely limited to the younger children within a family. . . . Those excluded from inheritance of the family land or business were more susceptible to joining a persecuted religious minority.[29]

I have used the word "movement" to describe the first few years of Quakerism because it . . . seems to catch the essentials of the situation: fluidity and mobility, . . . in the basic sense of moving about the country. . . . The most mobile elements in the population, wholesale traders and former army officers, were the principal carriers of the new religion. It also seems that Quakerism made its greatest appeal to men who had changed their place of residence at least once, and perhaps several times, since their births. Even the gentry converts were not, for the most part, from "established" families, which may be another way of saying that they were at least relative newcomers.[30]

After the long feudal ages in which people's security was founded in the attachment of the same family (whether lord or serf) over many generations to the same piece of land, change came rapidly. The economic, social, and political conditions of the seventeenth century threw many people into sudden geographical mobility. Relatively well educated and articulate, these younger sons of the gentry and mobile soldiers and merchants were well able to express their deep sense of rootlessness and unease.[31] I can see that it was not difficult for these Quakers to identify themselves "as aliens and exiles" (1 Peter 2:11) and to recognize their forebears as "strangers and foreigners on the earth" (Hebrews 11:13).

Early Friends such as George Fox, Margaret Fell, and Edward Burrough found their way to a deeply empathetic reading and understanding of the Bible in spite of their lack of sophistication or training in theology and biblical scholarship. One early Friend, Samuel Fisher, had a degree from Oxford and was a trained biblical scholar before he was converted to Quakerism by Fox in 1655. His longest work, *Rusticus ad Academicos*, written in 1660, was a defense of Quakerism against attacks by contemporary Bible scholars. In spite of his stance as a "rustic" against the academics, he displayed formidable sophistication in his own understanding of the Bible. He dropped a few hints that suggest an empathetic approach to scripture: he criticized a "fleshly wisdom" that "enters no farther into the inside of the Scripture"[32] but concerned itself only with "the bare Letter, and meer outside of the Scriptures."[33] He described the experience of the biblical writers in terms that echoed the life and inspiration of his fellow Quakers:

> The holy men of God, who either wrote their Scripture with their own Hands, or dictated to such as they required to Pen it from their Mouthes, as themselves spake from the Mouth of God, . . . had both then, and long before also an Active concurrence thereof, and such an Active obedience to God as all men are by the Law of God, *i.e.* the Light in the Conscience obliged to, whereby they were made, and became first Holy Men before they were used by God in such an holy work, as Preaching and Writing out his mind to others, and were brought into the thing or life itself they spake and wrote of, and were purged from Lusts and Defilements, and Iniquities.[34]

Aside from these fleeting hints, Samuel Fisher's approach to biblical texts was generally objective. Even though his prose was wordy and sometimes hard to follow, he showed considerable skill in analyzing biblical writings; he occasionally foreshadowed approaches to the Bible taken by nineteenth-century critical scholars. He had a keen eye for discrepancies between different texts: "Any Corruption supposed therein, as there may well be, and Contradiction too, if the Books of *Samuel*, the *Kings*, and *Chronicles*, be critically, or but carefully considered, 1 *Sam.* 16.9, 10, 11. 1 *Sam.* 12.14. compared with 1 *Chron.* 2.13, 14, 15."[35] (In 1 Samuel 16, David is the eighth son of Jesse; in 1 Chronicles 2, David is the seventh son of Jesse.) He also pointed out a number of parallel passages that are so similar that it was clear to him that one of each pair must have been copied directly from the other:

> What thinkest thou of the History of *John, Mark,* which some have in that respect titled . . . a kind of holy Theft; is it not possible but that it might be some *Abreviation* of *Matthew*'s Story concerning Christ, there being little in it but what is well-nigh word for word in the other?[36]

> What thinkest thou of such parts and parcels of thy so called *Canon* as are each of them written in two several places or Books of thy Bible? one of which places and the respective parcels, whether Histories, or Prophecies, or Praises therein recited, are at most but Repetitions and meer Transcriptions out of the other, with some such Additions, or Ablations (or Alterations . . .) as is not unusually made among Transcribers, of which sort, for instance in a few, I refer thee, . . . to consider and compare *Psal.* 14 with *Psal.* 53. and 2 *Sam.* 22. with *Psal.* 18. also 2 *King.* 18.13. chap. 19. chap. 20. with *Isa.* 36, *Isa.* 37. *Isa.* 38. *Isa.* 39. also 2 *King.* 24. 18. chap. 25 throughout, with *Jer.* 39, *Jer.* 52. by which places perused, . . . it is yet plain and evident, that some of it was but Copied and Transcribed out of other some.[37]

The year of the restoration of the monarchy in England under Charles II (1660) brought an end to Puritan and Seeker hopes for the speedy arrival of the kingdom of God in England. This was also the year in which Samuel Fisher in *Rusticus ad Academicos*—daring as he was in his critical thinking— took the first step, among Friends, away from the empathetic reading and interpretation of the Bible, which I believe was the source of their world-shaking originality and dynamic power.

3

Later Seventeenth Century and Early Eighteenth Century

In 1666 William Penn, the young son of an English admiral, became a Quaker. Others who became converts to Quakerism in that year include a Scottish colonel, David Barclay, and his eighteen-year-old son, Robert Barclay. Robert Barclay studied theology at both the Roman Catholic Scots Theological College in Paris and the Calvinist University of Aberdeen. He was a prolific writer. His best-known and most influential work was his *Apology for the True Christian Divinity*. Barclay published his *Apology* first in Latin in 1676, then in English in 1678. His primary purpose in this book was to convince non-Quakers, especially Puritan students and theologians, of the truth of Quaker beliefs. But the *Apology* has been read mostly by later generations of Friends, many of whom have looked on it as the definitive systematic statement of Quaker beliefs and theology.

Although many Friends have assumed that Barclay simply spelled out more clearly and systematically the basic beliefs of George Fox and other first-generation Friends, some contemporary Friends have noticed significant differences in emphasis or tone between Barclay and earlier Quaker writers such as Fox and Isaac Penington. Maurice Creasey has observed: "When we turn from Penington to Barclay, we are conscious of moving, so to speak, from the Meeting to the Study."[1] And John Punshon wrote, comparing Fox and Barclay:

> There is a tantalising difference in atmosphere between the two men. Barclay is obviously a scholar, at home with the Fathers as well as the Bible, capable of taking nice points and making fine distinctions. Fox breathes the air of an Amos or Paul, and sees the whole sweep of God's covenant relationship with his Church in a far more dramatic and concrete way.[2]

Barclay's use of biblical references, in a few selections from his *Apology*, can serve as examples of this difference in atmosphere and tone between Barclay and the earliest Friends:

> This doctrine of universal redemption, or Christ's dying for all men, is of itself so evident from the scripture testimony, that there is scarce found any other article of the Christian faith so frequently, so plainly, and so positively asserted. It is that which maketh the preaching of Christ to be truly termed the gospel, or an annunciation of glad tidings to all. Thus the angel declared the birth and coming of Christ to the shepherds to be, Luke ii. 10, "Behold, I bring you good tidings of great joy, which shall be to all people:" he saith not, to a few. Now if this coming of Christ had not brought a possibility of salvation to all, it should rather have been accounted bad tidings of great sorrow to most people; neither should the angel have had reason to have sung, "Peace on earth, and good will towards men," if the greatest part of mankind had been necessarily shut out from receiving any benefit by it. How should Christ have sent out his servants to "preach the gospel to every creature," Mark xvi. 15, (a very comprehensive commission) that is, to every son and daughter of mankind, without all exception? He commands them to preach salvation to all, repentance and remission of sins to all; warning every one, and exhorting every one, as Paul did, Col. i. 28. Now how could they have preached the gospel to every man, as became the ministers of Jesus Christ, in much assurance, if salvation by that gospel had not been possible to all?[3]

But in a true church of Christ, gathered together by God, not only into the belief of the principles of truth, but also into the power, life and Spirit of Christ, the Spirit of God is the orderer, ruler and governor; as in each particular, so in the general. And when they assemble together to wait upon God, and to worship and adore him; then such as the Spirit sets apart for the ministry, by its divine power and influence opening their mouths, and giving them to exhort, re-prove, and instruct with virtue and power; these are thus ordained of God and admitted into the ministry, and their brethren cannot but hear them, receive them, and also honour them for their work's sake. And so this is not monopolized by a certain kind of men, as the clergy (who are to that purpose educated and brought up as other carnal artists) and the rest to be despised as laics; but it is left to the free gift of God to choose any whom he seeth meet thereunto, whether rich or poor, servant or master, young or old, yea, male or female. And such as have this call, verify the gospel, by preaching not in speech only, but also in power, and in the Holy Ghost, and in much fulness, 1 Thess. i. 5, and cannot but be received and heard by the sheep of Christ.[4]

I judge it fit to speak something in short concerning the preaching of women, and to declare what we hold in that matter.

Seeing male and female are one in Christ Jesus, and that he gives his Spirit no less to one than to the other, when God moveth by his Spirit in a woman, we judge it no ways unlawful for her to preach in the assemblies of God's people. Neither think we that of Paul, 1 Cor. xiv. 34, to reprove the inconsiderate and talkative women among the Corinthians, who troubled the church of Christ, with their unprofitable questions, or that, 1 Tim. ii. 11, 12, that "women ought to learn in silence, not usurping authority over the man," any way repugnant to this doctrine; because it is clear that women have prophesied and preached in the church, else had that saying of Joel been ill applied by Peter, Acts ii, 17. And seeing Paul himself, in the same epistle to the Corinthians, giveth rules how women should be-have themselves in their public preaching and praying, it would be a manifest contradiction, if that other place were taken in a larger sense. And the same Paul speaks of a woman that laboured with him in the work of the gospel: and it is written that Philip had four daughters who prophesied.[5]

I see nothing in these passages of the warm empathy with the biblical writers that jumped out at me in the writings of Fox, Burrough, and Fell.

Instead, Barclay used scriptural quotations as examples of the points he was making, or as stepping stones in his careful, logical arguments. I do find it interesting to compare Barclay's arguments for women's ministry with Margaret Fell's, in *Womens Speaking Justified*. It is remarkable that Fell made her case without ever appealing to Galatians 3:28—"There is neither Jew nor Greek, there is neither bond nor free, there is neither male nor female: for ye are all one in Christ Jesus" (KJV). In contrast, Barclay began his argument with that verse as the major premise: "Seeing male and female are one in Christ Jesus."[6] From there, he found it easy to insist that the passages that Fell also had to reckon with (1 Corinthians 14:34 and 1 Timothy 2:11-12) must be understood in ways that would not contradict the basic, fundamental principle of oneness in Christ. His reference to specific biblical examples of women who preached and prophesied—the heart and core of Fell's more personal approach—then became a way of demonstrating that the passages in 1 Corinthians 14 and 1 Timothy 2 must have been advices directed to special situations rather than comprehensive rules for the whole Christian church.

Nevertheless, Barclay was not completely unaware of the way in which the first Friends used the Bible. There is one very interesting passage in the *Apology,* which Michael Birkel has brought to our attention:

> Robert Barclay can offer helpful clues for understanding how Quakers read the Bible in this manner:
>
> > God hath seen meet that herein [in the scriptures] we should, as in a looking-glass, see the conditions and experiences of the saints of old; that finding our experience answer to theirs, we might thereby be the more confirmed and comforted, and our hope of attaining the same end strengthened.[7]
>
> To read the scriptures is to look in a mirror and find one's own inner life reflected in the lives of spiritual forebears.[8]

In this one sentence Barclay came closer than any other seventeenth-century Friend (as far as I have been able to discover) to recognizing that their primary approach to reading and interpreting scripture was the way of empathy—of entering without reserve into the strange new world of the Bible and identifying themselves with biblical writers, personalities, and communities.

Soon after William Penn was converted to Quakerism, he became a close associate and friend of George Fox. The two of them traveled together on several journeys in the ministry. In several controversies that broke out among Friends, Fox and Penn always stood together and supported each other's positions. In 1669, while Penn was in prison in the Tower of London, he wrote one of his best-known works, *No Cross, No Crown*. In 1682 he sailed to America to found the new colony, Pennsylvania. Also in 1682, he published a second, much longer edition of *No Cross, No Crown*. This work was addressed to those outside of Quakerism. The opening four paragraphs of the 1682 edition were part of the material that Penn added for that version:

I. THOUGH the knowledge and obedience of the doctrine of the cross of Christ, be of infinite moment to the souls of men; for that is the only door to true christianity, and that path the ancients ever trod to blessedness: yet, with extreme affliction, let me say, it is so little understood, so much neglected, and what is worse, so bitterly contradicted, by the vanity, superstition and intemperance of professed christians, that we must either renounce to believe what the Lord Jesus hath told us, Luke xiv. 27. "That whosoever doth not bear his cross, and come after him, cannot be his disciple:" or, admitting that for truth, conclude, that the generality of Christendom do miserably deceive and disappoint themselves in the great business of christianity, and their own salvation.

II. For, let us be never so tender and charitable in the survey of those nations, that intitle themselves to any interest in the holy name of Christ, if we will but be just too, we must needs acknowledge, that after all the gracious advantages of light, and obligations to fidelity, which these latter ages of the world have received, by the coming, life, doctrine, miracles, death, resurrection, and ascension of Christ, with the gifts of his Holy Spirit; to which add, the writings, labours and martyrdom of his dear followers in all times, there seems very little left of christianity but the name: which being now usurped by the old heathen nature and life, makes the professors of it but true heathens in disguise. For though they worship not the same idols, they worship Christ with the same heart: and they can never do otherwise, whilst they live in the same lusts. So that the unmortified christian and the heathen are of the same religion. For though they have different objects, to which they do direct their prayers, that adoration in both is but forced and ceremonious, and the deity they truly worship, is the god of the world, the great lord of lusts: to him they bow with the whole powers of soul and sense. What shall we eat? What shall we drink? What shall we wear? And how shall we pass away our time? Which way may we gather wealth, increase our power, enlarge our territories, and dignify and perpetuate our names and families in the earth? Which base sensuality is most pathetically expressed and comprized by the beloved apostle John, in these words: "the lust of the flesh, the lust of the eyes, and the pride of life, which (says he) are not of the Father, but of the world, that lieth in wickedness. [1 John ii. 16.]"

III. It is a mournful reflection, but a truth no confidence can be great enough to deny, that these worldly lusts fill up the study, care and conversation of wretched Christendom! and, which aggravates the misery, they have grown with time. For as the world is older, it is worse; and the examples of former lewd ages, and their miserable conclusions, have not deterred, but excited ours; so that the people of this, seem improvers of the old stock of impiety, and have carried it so much farther than example, that instead of advancing in virtue, upon better times, they are scandalously fallen below the life of heathens. Their highmindedness, lasciviousness, uncleanness, drunkenness, swearing, lying, envy, backbiting, cruelty, treachery, covetousness, injustice, and oppression, are so common, and committed with such invention and excess, that they have stumbled and embittered infidels to a degree of scorning that holy religion, to which their good example should have won their affections.

IV. This miserable defection from primitive times, when the glory of christianity was the purity of its professors, I cannot but call the second and worst part of the Jewish tragedy, upon the blessed Saviour of mankind. For the Jews, from the power of ignorance, and the extreme prejudice they were under to the unworldly way of his appearance, would not acknowledge him when he came, but for two or three years persecuted, and finally crucified him in one day. But the false christians' cruelty lasts longer: they have first, with Judas, professed him, and then, for these many ages, most basely betrayed, persecuted, and crucified him, by a perpetual apostacy in manners, from the self-denial and holiness of his doctrine; their lives giving the lye to their faith. These are they that the author of the epistle to the Hebrews tells us, "crucify to themselves the Son of God afresh, and put him to open shame [Heb. vi. 6.];" whose defiled hearts,

John, in his Revelation, stiles, the streets of Sodom and Egypt, spiritually so called, where he beheld the Lord Jesus crucified, [Rev. xi. 8.] long after he had been ascended. And as Christ said of old, a man's enemies are those of his own house; so Christ's enemies now, are chiefly those of his own profession: "they spit upon him, they nail and pierce him, they crown him with thorns, and give him gall and vinegar to drink [Mat. xxvii. 29-34]" Nor is it hard to apprehend; for they that live in the same evil nature and principle the Jews did, that crucified him outwardly, must needs crucify him inwardly; since they that reject the grace now in their own hearts, are one in stock and generation with the hard-hearted Jews, that resisted the grace that then appeared in and by Christ.[9]

William Penn specifically identified five biblical references in these four opening paragraphs of *No Cross, No Crown*. I was able to pinpoint three further biblical quotations:

the god of the world (2 Corinthians 4:4)

What shall we eat? What shall we drink? (Matthew 6:31)

a man's enemies are those of his own house (Matthew 10:36)

Only eight biblical references, in a selection longer than the pieces I quoted from George Fox and Edward Burrough in Chapter 2.

Beyond this obvious difference, my first reaction to this writing by William Penn is that its temperature is much lower than that of the writings by Fox, Fell, and Burrough. It is much less intense, much less immediately and intimately involved in the interior life-experience of the biblical writers. Empathy with the biblical worldview may not be completely absent, but for Penn the Bible seems to have become primarily a handbook, a collection of resources and guidelines for salvation and Christian living.

By the 1680s, many of the first leaders of Quakerism had died. Had Quakerism as a whole cooled off by that time, or did the survivors among the original leaders—such as George Fox and Margaret Fell—still display the old fire and intense involvement in the world of the Bible? To deal with this question, I looked closely at a brief 1683 epistle by Fox: number CCCLXXXV [385]—"To suffering Friends in prison at Bristol":

Dear friends,— With my love to all the prisoners and the faithful, as though I named them. It is the time now for all the faithful to keep in Christ their sanctuary, in whom you have all peace, rest, life, and salvation, and by the testimony of Jesus, and the blood of the Lamb, whose names are written in the Lamb's book of life, before the foundation of the world, they were they that did overcome, and did eat of the hidden manna, and had the new name. And therefore now is the time to keep the word of patience, and the testimony of Jesus; for they that keep the word of patience, the Lord will keep them in the hour of temptation, which will come upon the whole world, to try them which dwell upon the earth; for the word was before the world was, and the tempter; for all things were made by the word. And it is also the word of reconciliation, the word of power, the word of wisdom, and the word of life, and the word of salvation, by which people are reconciled to God, that are born again of the incorruptible seed by the word of God; and they feed and grow by the milk of the word, which lives, and abides, and endures for ever, which strengthens all the faithful, in all ages, in all their afflictions, imprisonments, and sufferings; and it is the same to God's people now in this day of trial, to preserve all his people every where, in his spirit and power, faithful to himself; for, he that endures faithful to the end shall be saved. And Christ saith, "He that is ashamed of me before men, him will I be ashamed of before my Father, and his angels which are in heaven." And therefore it is good to confess Christ before men, to be your priest, prophet, your shepherd, your bishop, your way, your mediator, that makes your peace betwixt God and you; and be valiant for his glorious name and truth upon the earth. And so with my love in the seed, in which you and all nations are blessed.[10]

As in Fox's earlier writings, the biblical quotations and citations are again densely packed—more than twenty-five of them in this short epistle. The issues with which Fox dealt here were more clearly defined than in his Epistle II, but the sense of empathy, of intimate involvement in the biblical world, shines through as intensely as in his earlier pieces. The sharp contrast between Fox and Penn in this regard is all the more striking, in that these two men were personal friends, frequent traveling companions, and regular supporters of each other when controversies arose within the Quaker movement. Somehow, in spite of his clear commitment and dedication to Quakerism, and his admiration for and close friendship with George Fox, William Penn was in the final analysis a second-generation Quaker, living at least in part off of the spiritual capital amassed by those who went before him.

There is one phrase in *No Cross, No Crown* that I find highly suggestive. In Chapter 2, I referred to early Friends and their fondness for biblical metaphors and symbolism. Of course, they were not sophisticated in linguistics and rhetoric; they could hardly have recognized that they were making rich use of metaphors. In this connection, I note William Penn's mention of "Sodom and Egypt, spiritually so called," with a reference to Revelation 11:8.[11] The Greek word translated "spiritually" in this verse in the King James Version is rendered in modern translations as "allegorically," "prophetically," "symbolic."

Fox and Burrough also did not have the sophistication to recognize consciously that they were reading the Bible empathetically—that they were shaping their own and their followers' moral character and identity by internalizing biblical themes, stories, figures of speech. Or, as Carole Spencer so well states it, for them "the Bible was not an external authority ('a paper Pope') but an internalized authority. Quakers lived, breathed and were infused by the words of Scripture."[12] The concept of "internalized authority," of course, was not part of even the most subtle seventeenth-century theological discourse. In that day, and for long since, the very concept of "authority" implied the imposition of *external* rules and ideas. We can see why George Fox, when writing to Friends, never mentioned the *authority* of scripture.

Most of the critics of early Friends were Puritans, for whom the authority of scripture was crucial. The earliest Friends struggled to find language that would enable them to challenge the Puritan, Calvinist view of the authority of scripture. Clearly, Fox, when addressing his opponents, had to reject the idea of scripture as an external, written authority:

Scripture is writing, and writing doth not endure for ever, but the word of the Lord endures for ever.[13]

Luke calls the scriptures a declaration, who was a minister of the word; and the scriptures are the words of God, and the words of Christ, and so not the word, but the words which the word Christ fulfills.[14]

Quite possibly it was the passage in Revelation 11 that suggested to Fox that his reading of scripture was "spiritual," that he lived in "the same spirit that the prophets and apostles were in"—even that scripture derived from "the spirit of God." "The spirit of God that led them to speak forth the scriptures, was the rule to the saints and holy men of God: . . . the spirit leads to see them again, and brings into unity with them and God."[15]

Samuel Fisher, in his defense of Quakerism against criticism from Puritan biblical scholars, took up George Fox's idea that the Spirit of God was the source and origin of scripture:

> The Apostles . . . wrote from the same Spirit of Faith with them of Old.[16]

> The Word *Light* and *Spirit of God* and *Christ within*, nigh in the heart, but not the *Letter without* is the *Gospel*, which *Paul* bare testimony to, and was sent to turn men to by his *Ministry*, and was not ashamed of, saying, its the *Power of God to Salvation, to everyone that believes in it.*[17]

Fisher also cautiously picked up on Fox's suggestion that the Spirit was "the rule to the saints," and carried through a further implication that scripture might be considered "a secondary rule":

> Let the thoughts hereof be far from us that the Scripture is the only Rule, for if we should grant it to be . . . a Rule at all, or a secondary Rule, which name of Rule is more then it any where calls itself by, yet the prime, most perfect Rule it is not, much less is it the only Rule to the Church or any men; and though we are as forward as any, on a due account, to own the profitableness of the very Letter, as it declares of the words of Truth and Uprightness, and the Doctrine that is according unto godliness, and to own its great usefulness, as to the purpose premised, and so affirm that the dead Letter . . . doth as truly answer and hold proportion with the Light, and Living Word, as the shadow doth with the Substance, the life-less Picture with the Living Person it represents.[18]

A decade and a half after Samuel Fisher published *Rusticus ad Academicos*, the Quaker theologian Robert Barclay, in his *Apology*, brought together these suggestions by Fox and Fisher into a definitive statement about the authority and place of the scriptures:

> Because they are only a declaration of the fountain, and not the fountain itself, therefore they are not to be esteemed the principal ground of all truth and knowledge, nor yet the adequate primary rule of faith and manners. Yet because they give a true and faithful

testimony of the first foundation, they are and may be esteemed a secondary rule, subordinate to the Spirit, from which they have all their excellency and certainty: for as by the inward testimony of the Spirit we do alone truly know them, so they testify, That the Spirit is that Guide by which the saints are led into all Truth; therefore, according to the scriptures, the Spirit is the first and principal leader.[19]

When George Fox wrote to Friends who shared his empathetic reading and understanding of the Bible, he had no need to spell out any doctrine or idea of biblical authority to them. Many Friends in later generations, finding a need to understand the place of the Bible in our faith, looked back to this statement by Robert Barclay as the official statement of what Quakers believe about the authority of the Bible. This statement has had widespread use as a teaching tool within Quakerism, as we have sought to understand and to teach one another and our children what Quakerism is all about. My argument is that we have, in so doing, not only completely missed the point of the meaning and significance of the Bible in original Quakerism; we have also left ourselves open to disastrous misunderstandings and divisions, as we have struggled to follow out the implications of Barclay's statement. I plan to spell this out in later chapters of this book.

The powerful impact of early Quaker spirituality came largely from their emphasis on personal example and on metaphors and symbolism in their reading of the Bible. One of the most original and striking of the biblical metaphors used by early Friends was "the Lamb's War." In my first chapter I noted how Hugh Barbour and Canby Jones brought the importance of the Lamb's War theme to the attention of contemporary Friends, and how Rob Tucker developed some of the implications of this theme. Doug Gwyn has also picked up on the Lamb's War as an important aspect of his interpretation of early Quakerism—not only in his book, *The Covenant Crucified*, but already in his first book, *Apocalypse of the Word.*[20]

Hugh Barbour has pointed out that the phrase, "the Lamb's War," "appears in the writings of almost every leading Quaker," and that "James Nayler used this phrase as the title for his most characteristic book."[21] I have noted that "similar terminology is found in the title of one of Burrough's controversial pamphlets: *A Discovery of some part of the War between the Kingdom of the Lamb, And the Kingdom of Anti-Christ.*"[22] Canby Jones, in his careful study, *George Fox's Attitude Toward War*, spelled out the category of the Lamb's War as the climax of Fox's thought about war and peace.[23]

The Lamb's War theme derives particularly from early Friends' reading of the biblical book of Revelation. From my study of the works of Edward Burrough, I have gained "a strong impression" that his thought and spirituality "originate primarily in the Book of Revelation."[24]

The book of Revelation is, indeed, one of the most difficult biblical books to interpret. John Calvin wrote commentaries on every book of the Bible—*except* Revelation. A major problem for the interpreter is the bold, lush use of metaphor, symbolism, even allegory in this book. As a result, many interpreters go off into one deep end or the other. One extreme is to rely entirely on an *allegorical* interpretation in which every physical detail is identified with a spiritual or figurative parallel meaning. The problem with the allegorical approach is that there are, and can be, no guidelines—anything goes. The other extreme is to insist on a strictly *literal* interpretation; but with the book of Revelation, full as it is of metaphorical and figurative language, this is literally impossible—with the result that, for those who attempt it, anything goes.

In the face of these difficulties with the book of Revelation, early Friends approached it with two important factors in their favor:

1. Empathy: they were ready to put *themselves* into the position of the original writer and readers.

2. Appreciation and appropriation of metaphor and symbolism: they *expected* to make what they called a "spiritual" interpretation—actually to make deep and full use of metaphor and symbolism.

Central to the early Quaker understanding of Revelation was the close connection between two metaphors for Christ in this book, Christ as lion and as lamb:

> Behold, the Lion of the tribe of Judah, the Root of David, hath prevailed to open the book, and to loose the seven seals thereof. And I beheld, and lo, in the midst of the throne and of the four beasts, and in the midst of the elders, stood a Lamb as it had been slain (Revelation 5:5-6 KJV).

Friends recognized this lamb/lion paradox throughout the book of Revelation. They zeroed in on the bloody images of a titanic war between Christ and his enemies:

> And I saw heaven opened, and behold a white horse; and he that

sat upon him was called Faithful and True, and in righteousness he doth judge and make war. . . . And the armies which were in heaven followed him upon white horses, clothed in fine linen, white and clean. And out of his mouth goeth a sharp sword, that with it he should smite the nations: and he shall rule them with a rod of iron (Revelation 19:11, 14-15 KJV).

A sword in his mouth? Taken literally, this would be strange and incongruous. But, as Edward Burrough recognized, the imagery in Revelation simply cannot be literal and physical: "We became Followers of the Lamb whithersoever he goes, and he hath called us to make war in righteousness; . . . and we war in Truth, and just Judgment; not with Weapons that are carnal, but by the Sword that goes out of his Mouth, which shall slay the Wicked, and cut them to pieces."[25]

This picture of "the sword that goes out of his mouth" makes sense if it is understood, as the early Quakers understood it, in light of the picture of the "whole armor of God":

Having your loins girt about with truth, and having on the breastplate of righteousness; And your feet shod with the preparation of the gospel of peace; Above all, taking the shield of faith, wherewith ye shall be able to quench all the fiery darts of the wicked. And take the helmet of salvation, and the sword of the Spirit, which is the word of God (Ephesians 6:14-17 KJV).

In this connection, Burrough insisted that the faithful are armed with "spiritual" weapons in this warfare:

Our Weapons are spiritual, and our victory and peace, is not of this World: And our War is against souls enemies, and against the powers of darkness, even by the Sword of the Spirit, which God hath given us . . . to convert people from sin and death, and from the very occasion of wars . . . about the things that are earthly.[26]

Just what are the weapons that the faithful wield in this war? The thought of early Friends was shaped by Revelation 12:7-11 (KJV):

And there was war in heaven: Michael and his angels fought against the dragon; and the dragon fought and his angels, And prevailed not; neither was their place found any more in heaven. And the great dragon was cast out, that old serpent, called the Devil, and Satan, which deceiveth the whole world: he was cast out into the earth, and his angels were cast out with him. And I heard a loud voice saying in heaven, Now is come salvation, and strength, and the kingdom of our God, and the power of his Christ: for the accuser of our brethren is cast down, which accused them before our God day and night. And they overcame him by the blood of the Lamb, and by the word of their testimony; and they loved not their lives unto the death.

Edward Burrough went a step further. Again and again he made "the point that one of the chief differences between the forces of Christ and the forces of Satan is the nature of the weapons which each side is using"[27]:

The Day of the Lord is come, . . . not by the multitude of an Host of men, nor yet by humane Policy and Wisdom, nor yet by carnal Weapons, nor by Goals [sic] nor Prisons, nor Persecutions, these are not the Lamb's Weapons, but these are Antichrist's and the Dragon's Armour and Weapons, which he makes War by, against the Lamb and his Followers: . . . But the Lamb's Weapons are Truth, Patience, Long-suffering, Meekness and down-right Sincerity of Heart and Tongue; and by these things shall Antichrist be slain, and these Weapons shall Conquer his kingdom.[28]

Here, then, in this mighty imagery of the Lamb's War from the book of Revelation, we find the basis for the peace testimony of the earliest Friends. Taking their stand here, they confronted the power of evil both in themselves and in the society of their time.

An interesting second-generation English Friend was John Bellers. He was born in 1654. Edward Burrough and other early ministers had set up men's and women's meetings in London to care for the needs of the poor among Friends.[29] In 1671 this responsibility was transferred to the newly-established "Six Weeks Meeting" in London. In 1677 this meeting instituted a scheme to buy flax and employ poor Friends in spinning it. In 1680 that body appointed the young John Bellers to act as treasurer of the funds provided for the flax-spinning plan. He served in this capacity until 1684, when the plan was apparently discontinued. This involvement apparently deeply impressed the young man with the sufferings of the unemployed, with their capacity for achievement when given an opportunity, and with the value of providing opportunities for them in the form of specific plans and programs. In 1696 Bellers formulated some proposals for giving employment opportunities to the poor in his "Proposals for Raising a lege of

Industry," which later became quite well known. A collection of his writings was published in 1935. These writings proposed a variety of social reforms, mostly directed toward improving the lot of the poor, but also calling for a council of European states, and for the maintenance of permanent lists of qualified voters.

Bellers often addressed identical proposals to Friends and to others, such as members of Parliament, and used similar arguments in both instances. The tenor of his writings was cool and rational. In his writings he appealed to a variety of authorities, from Solomon and Confucius to Isaac Newton.

His writings frequently included long lists of Bible passages, often quite brief, which Bellers apparently considered relevant to his arguments. When I studied his writings, I was able find a total of 317 biblical references. Certain books were clear favorites. Bellers quoted thirty-eight times from the gospel of Luke; other preferred books were the gospels of Matthew and John, the book of Proverbs, and the first epistle of John.

> There are four passages which Bellers quotes four or more times each: Luke 16:19-31 . . . (the parable of the rich man and Lazarus); Luke 16:9 ("And I say unto you, Make to yourselves friends of the mammon of unrighteousness; that, when ye fail, they may receive you into everlasting habitations." KJV); Matthew 25:31-46 (the parable of the sheep and the goats at the great judgment); and Acts 17:23-28 (from Paul's speech on Mars Hill in Athens: "God . . . dwelleth not in temples made with hands; . . . and hath made of one blood all nations of men; . . . they should seek the Lord . . . and find him; though he be not far from every one of us." KJV).[30]

The most remarkable aspect of Bellers's biblical references is the fact that a few themes recurred frequently in his quotations. His greatest emphasis was on the general theme of the last judgment or of judgment after death; fifty-eight of his references reflected this theme.

> Another significant theme . . . is an interest in the poor and the afflicted. Forty-three of his references comfort the poor, condemn the rich, or call for aid to the poor and afflicted. Nearly half of these passages (21) also reflect the theme of judgment, the ideas that the rich will suffer after the final judgment, that final rewards will go to the poor or to those who help the poor and suffering in their distress.[31]

In general, Bellers's use of the Bible was highly selective and represented strong, central religious and ethical concerns in his thinking—themes that were also emphasized in the text of his writings. These themes add up to an understanding of human beings as essentially rational; a rationalistic interpretation of religious truth; a pragmatic orientation toward human happiness, particularly eternal happiness after the last judgment; and a deep compassion for the sufferings of the poor. The Bible, for Bellers, had become largely a source book to back up these concerns, which in turn probably derived from his practical experiences in the work of the Society of Friends.

With the passing of the first generation of Friends, the sense of identification with the New Testament community appears to have been lost. The inability of George Fox and others to articulate the source of their understanding of the Bible was doubtless a major factor. The fact that the early leaders did not criticize Friends like William Penn, Robert Barclay, and John Bellers for using the Bible in a different way may also have contributed.

How, then, were Friends to interpret the Bible, particularly obscure or problematic passages? Other religious leaders, notably John Calvin, had produced significant commentaries on the Bible; Friends had not done this for themselves. And they had good reason for not trusting Calvin's commentary. We can see this clearly if we focus on several New Testament passages that relate to one issue on which Friends differed sharply from most Puritan groups—the legitimacy of women speaking or preaching in public worship:

> But this is that which was spoken by the prophet Joel; And it shall come to pass in the last days, saith God, I will pour out of my Spirit upon all flesh: and your sons and your daughters shall prophesy, and your young men shall see visions, and your old men shall dream dreams: And on my servants and on my handmaidens I will pour out in those days of my Spirit; and they shall prophesy (Acts 2:16-18 KJV).

> Now I praise you, brethren, that ye remember me in all things, and keep the ordinances, as I delivered them to you. But I would have you know, that the head of every man is Christ; and the head of the woman is the man; and the head of Christ is God. Every man praying or prophesying, having his head covered, dishonoreth his head. But every woman that prayeth or prophesieth with her head uncovered dishonoreth her head: for that is even all one as if she were shaven. For if the woman be not covered, let her also be shorn:

but if it be a shame for a woman to be shorn or shaven, let her be covered. For a man indeed ought not to cover his head, forasmuch as he is the image and glory of God: but the woman is the glory of the man. For the man is not of the woman; but the woman of the man. Neither was the man created for the woman; but the woman for the man. For this cause ought the woman to have power on her head because of the angels. Nevertheless neither is the man without the woman, neither the woman without the man, in the Lord. For as the woman is of the man, even so is the man also by the woman; but all things of God. Judge in yourselves: is it comely that a woman pray unto God uncovered? (1 Corinthians 11:2-13 KJV).

Let your women keep silence in the churches: for it is not permitted unto them to speak; but they are commanded to be under obedience, as also saith the law. And if they will learn any thing, let them ask their husbands at home: for it is a shame for women to speak in the church (1 Corinthians 14:34-35 KJV).

There is neither Jew nor Greek, there is neither bond nor free, there is neither male nor female: for ye are all one in Christ Jesus. And if ye be Christ's, then are ye Abraham's seed, and heirs according to the promise (Galatians 3:28-29 KJV).

I will therefore that men pray every where, lifting up holy hands, without wrath and doubting. In like manner also, that women adorn themselves in modest apparel, with shamefacedness and sobriety; not with braided hair, or gold, or pearls, or costly array; But (which becometh women professing godliness) with good works. Let the woman learn in silence with all subjection. But I suffer not a woman to teach, nor to usurp authority over the man, but to be in silence. For Adam was first formed, then Eve. And Adam was not deceived, but the woman being deceived was in the transgression (1 Timothy 2:8-14 KJV).

On direct reading, the implications of these passages seem to be in tension, perhaps even contradiction, with one another. The passage in Galatians 3 suggests that all social distinctions, including inequalities, are overcome within the Christian community. Acts 2 and 1 Corinthians 11 imply that women rightfully engage in at least one form of speaking—prophesying—in Christian worship, although the form of this practice is restricted in 1 Corinthians 11 in order to maintain women's subordination to men.

First Corinthians 14 and 1 Timothy 2 clearly deny women the right to speak or teach in Christian churches and insist that women should be obedient to male authority. The attempts of various sixteenth-, seventeenth-, and eighteenth-century Christian leaders and biblical interpreters to harmonize these and other relevant passages led to sharply varying conclusions about the rightness of spoken ministry by women and the proper status of women within the Christian community.

John Calvin was one of the best-known leaders of the Protestant Reformation in the sixteenth century. His leadership of the church in Geneva, Switzerland, from 1541 to 1564 made that city a strong center for the growth of the Reformed churches in Europe. Although he is famed as the author of the landmark work of systematic theology, the *Institutes of the Christian Religion*, he also wrote commentaries on all of the books of the Bible except Revelation, which were widely respected throughout the Reformed churches, including Scottish Presbyterianism and English Puritanism.

In his commentary on 1 Corinthians, John Calvin referred to the apparent tension between Galatians 3:28 and the passage in 1 Corinthians 11:

> The solution depends on the contexts of the two passages. When Paul says that there is no difference between man and woman, he is speaking about the spiritual Kingdom of Christ, where the outward characteristics . . . count for nothing, and are not taken into consideration, for it has nothing to do with the body, nothing to do with men's physical relationships with each other . . . , but it is concerned wholly with the spirit.[32]

For Calvin, the spiritual realm is here entirely separate from the physical, bodily world; it applies only "in the eyes of God, and inwardly in their conscience."[33] The spiritual has nothing to do with "the civil order"[34] or "the sphere of ecclesiastical polity."[35] Galatians 3:28 can therefore be disregarded when we consider questions such as the place of women in the church.

Concerning the tension between the apparent acceptance of women's prophesying, as long as it is not done bare-headed (in 1 Corinthians 11), and the forbidding of women to speak or teach in church (in 1 Corinthians 14 and 1 Timothy 2), Calvin answered,

> When the apostle disapproves of the one thing here, he is not giving his approval to the other. For when he takes them to task because they were prophesying bare-headed, he is not giving them

permission, however, to prophesy in any other way whatever, but rather is delaying the censure of that fault to another passage (chapter 14.34 ff).[36]

In light of later developments in the interpretation of these passages, we should take note of Calvin's definition of prophecy: "Prophets are (1) outstanding interpreters of Scripture; and (2) men endowed with extraordinary wisdom and aptitude for grasping what the immediate need of the Church is, and speaking the right word to meet it." The difference between prophesying and teaching is that "the task of teachers consists in preserving and propagating sound doctrines . . . so that purity of religion may remain in the Church."[37]

For Calvin, then, the controlling passages concerning women's place in the church are those in 1 Corinthians 14 and 1 Timothy 2. The emphasis is that women are to be obedient and in subjection; they have no right to exercise any authority in the church, even that of teaching or speaking. Indeed, Calvin went much further: "There is no doubt that wherever natural propriety itself has had its effect, women in all ages have been excluded from the control of public affairs. And common sense tells us that the rule of women is improper and defective."[38] How many of us today would agree that common sense says any such thing? Years ago, in a study of Calvin's ethics in his biblical commentaries, I noticed that he would sometimes appeal to " common sense" as a last resort in interpreting controversial passages in the Bible. The problem is that "common sense" often simply means the unexamined assumptions of the culture or society in a given time or place.

From the beginning, women were actively involved in Quaker preaching. Elbert Russell reported that "Elizabeth Hooten became the first woman preacher among Friends"[39] even before the great events of 1652. After those events, the band of traveling preachers who carried the Quaker message throughout the British Isles, and as far beyond as America and Turkey, included numerous women. George Fox went after critics of this practice in his 1656 tract, "The Woman Learning in Silence, or the Mystery of the Woman's Subjection to her Husband."[40]

In this pamphlet, Fox set out by citing one of Calvin's key passages regarding the ministry of women—in 1 Timothy 2: "Let your women learn in silence, with all subjection; here is a silent learning, a learning in silence; I suffer not a woman to teach, nor to usurp authority over the man, but to be silent."[41] He moved on from this passage to the one in Acts 2: "Here all may see the spirit of the Lord not limited, but upon the handmaids and the servants is the Lord's spirit poured, . . . and they shall prophesy, . . . *Joel* 2.28; and in *Acts* 2."[42]

George Fox then devoted the bulk of his tract to trumping the 1 Timothy 2 passage by pointing out as counter-examples the numerous women who preached the gospel, taught, and exercised leadership in the early church:

> Philip had four daughters that did prophesy, which the apostle did not forbid; and saith the apostle, despise not prophesying.[43]

> Anna the prophetess, . . . spake of Christ, to all them that looked for redemption in Jerusalem. Here was a large testimony borne of Jesus by Anna the prophetess.[44]

> Priscilla; . . . Phebe the sister, the servant of the church.[45]

> It was Mary Magdalen that was sent to declare his resurrection, and she was to tell the brethren (the disciples) whither Christ was to go. . . . It was Mary that first declared Christ after he was risen.[46]

Then came the climax of Fox's argument:

> Who is it that dare stop Christ's mouth? that now is come to reign in his sons and daughters, Christ in the male, and Christ in the female? and you that will not have him to reign in the female as well as in the male, you are against scripture, and will not have him to reign over you.[47]

Puritans and others who would deny women the right to proclaim the gospel or prophesy were not simply misinterpreting the Bible, they were outright negating the authority of scripture and rejecting the kingship of Christ.

As I review my summary of Margaret Fell's *Womens Speaking Justified*, first published in 1666, I note that her argument took the same track that George Fox had followed ten years earlier. She added several points that filled out and clarified the structure of this argument. She began by noting that the ground of the objection "against Womens speaking in the Church" was "taken from the Apostles words"[48] not only in 1 Timothy 2:11-12 but also in 1 Corinthians 14:34-35. She concluded from the context in 1 Corinthians 14 that the injunction against women's speaking was directed only to the situation specifically prevailing in Corinth. (In an addition at the end of *Womens Speaking Justified*, Margaret Fell similarly argued, regarding the prohibition in 1 Timothy 2:11-12: "If it were to all Women, that no Woman might speak, then *Paul* would have contradicted himself; but they were such Women that the Apostle mentions in *Timothy*, That *grew wanton, and were busiebodies, and tatlers, and kicked against Christ.*"[49] Fell also expanded Fox's list of specific examples by adding several women prophets from the Old Testament.

I noted earlier in this chapter that Margaret Fell made no reference to Galatians 3:28 as a general principle calling for equal roles for men and women in the church; the same was the case with George Fox in "The Woman Learning in Silence." It remained for Robert Barclay, with his preference for finding general logical principles rather than lively personal examples in scripture, to take that step.

In the early eighteenth century, a biblical commentary was published that interpreted the passages in 1 Corinthians, regarding the ministry of women, in a new way. The English philosopher John Locke is best known today for his writings on philosophy of knowledge and political philosophy. In the late seventeenth century he had argued eloquently for religious toleration. Locke died in 1704. After his death, between 1705 and 1707, his *Paraphrase and Notes on the Epistles of St. Paul* was published in two volumes.

Locke found a new way to reconcile the passages in chapters 11 and 14 of 1 Corinthians—by re-defining prophecy: "Prophesying as St Paul tels us Ch: XIV.3 was speaking unto others to edification exhortation, and comfort: But . . . only then when such speaking was a spiritual gift performed by the immediate and extraordinary motion of the holy ghost."[50] Noting "that the spirit of god and the gift of prophesie should be powerd out upon women as well as men in the time of the gospel is plain from Acts. II.17,"[51] he was ready to comment on 1 Corinthians 14:34-35: "I apply this prohibition of speakeing only to reasoning and purely voluntary discourse, but suppose a liberty left women to speak where they had an immediate impulse and revelation from the spirit of god."[52]

But, according to Locke, there was reason for Paul's insistence that women should keep their heads covered when prophesying:

When they thus either prayd or prophesied by the motion and impulse of the holy-ghost care was taken that whilst they were obeying god who was pleasd by his spirit to set them a speaking, the subjection of their sex should not be forgotten, but owned and preserved by their being covered. The Christian religion was not to give offence by any appearance of suspition that it took away the subordination of the sexes and set the women at liberty from their natural subjection to the men. And therefore we see that, in both these cases, the aim was to maintain and secure the confessed superiority and dominion of the man and not permit it to be invaded soe much as in appearance. Hence the arguments in the one case for covering and in the other for silence are all drawn from the natural superiority of the man and the subjection of the woman.[53]

Even though Locke did paraphrase Galatians 3:28-29 in his commentary, he wrote no notes on that passage; he apparently did not look on it as offering any challenge to women's "natural subjection to the men."

We owe thanks to scholar Peter A. Huff for bringing to light a controversy between two British Friends, who were attempting to understand Locke's views on the ministry of women and to apply his insights to Quaker practice.[54] In the early eighteenth century, Friends were apparently divided as to the exact role of women in Quaker ministry and church government. They did not find clear guidance in the writings of the earliest Friends on this issue. They found cause to pay attention to Locke's interpretation. Locke was not only an advocate of religious toleration, he had been a personal friend of William Penn. Unlike Calvin and his Puritan followers, Locke had insisted that Paul's writings did allow for at least some forms of vocal ministry by women.

Locke's writings on this subject did have some ambiguity. Two Friends, in attempting to resolve these ambiguities, came to differing conclusions and expressed their disagreements in print. "In 1715, Benjamin Coole, a Quaker preacher from Bristol, published *Some Brief Observations on the Paraphrase and Notes of the Judicious John Locke: Relating to the Women's Exercising Their Spiritual Gifts in the Church*."[55] Josiah Martin, a London Quaker scholar, replied in 1716 in *A Letter to the Author of "Some Brief Observations."* In 1717 Coole came back with *Reflections on "A Letter to the Author of 'Some Brief Observations,'"* and Martin responded with *A Vindication of Women's Preaching*. Coole's death in the same year brought the debate to an end.

Taking Locke as his justification, Coole confined women and their ministry to the realm of charismatic, "extraordinary" utterances under direct divine inspiration. He thought it was perfectly appropriate for men to engage in the less charismatic ministries of proclamation and instruction. "Women could prophesy, he argued, but only men could preach."[56] Coole did note Locke's failure to discuss Galatians 3:28-29. He stated that Paul here was speaking of Christians solely as "Abraham's seed" and "heirs according to the promise"—"The purpose of Galatians 3:28 is not to underline a radical unity overcoming race, class, and sex, but to indicate simply that all Christians are children of the covenant through faith."[57] Coole insisted: "This Text do not prove a Woman to be all one with a Man. . . . The Order of Nature, as well as Nations, is no ways inverted by this Text."[58] If women are allowed to "Talk Magisterially, Positively and with . . . a Masculine Air and Assurance,"[59] then the foundations of society will be shaken.

According to Martin, on the other hand, Locke's understanding of Paul allowed women to engage in a ministry involving the full range of apostolic responsibilities: preaching, teaching, and evangelizing. Martin appealed to Robert Barclay in rejecting the Puritan idea of an ordinary, educated, ordained ministry. He therefore rejected the Puritan distinction between an ordinary ministry and an extraordinary ministry. *All* ministry must be under direct inspiration from God. Not only women but also men are forbidden to speak in Christian ministry on any basis other than immediate, charismatic inspiration. Martin went back to the traditionally Puritan definition of prophecy as "whatsoever is included in the Term Preaching."[60] "To speak of preaching apart from the supernatural promptings of the Spirit, he declared, betrays an unbiblical deference to human wisdom. Neither women nor men, he asserted, possess the right to speak without the inspiration of God."[61] Finally, Galatians 3:28 is really the controlling passage. This passage and Paul's letter to Philemon (on the brotherhood, in Christ, of master and slave) proclaim "the Effects of Christianity in its true Colours."[62]

But even Martin did not come to a full sense of biblical equality. Following Margaret Fell, he suggested that the command to "ask their husbands at home" (1 Corinthians 14:35 KJV) applied to married women—but not to single women. He could still speak of the "natural Subjection of the Married Woman."[63]

Friends in the middle of the seventeenth century may have claimed the title "the despised people called Quakers" as a badge of honor. Friends in the early eighteenth century longed to be recognized as a respectable part of English society. The idea of women as preachers was still a wildly radical innovation; some Friends had a deep need for a "judicious" justification or even watering down of this Quaker practice. But the reckless radicalism of the Lamb's war was still waiting to break out—and it did so, in 1737, in the writings of a little, hunchbacked Friend, born in England but eventually transplanted to Pennsylvania—Benjamin Lay:

Christ was not ashamed to call such spiritual Souls his Brethren, which worship God in Spirit, and in his Church which is his Kingdom, saying *I will declare thy Name unto my Brethren*; and after his blessed Resurrection sent forth a Woman Preacher the very first, to declare of it, and I believe to preach freely as she had freely receiv'd of him; *Go tell my Brethren I am risen, and that I ascend to my Father and your Father, to my God & your God.* O glorious Message! one of the best that ever was, and yet sent by a Woman! the glad Tidings of great Joy, that their Lord was alive that they thought was dead. They did not reject the Testimony because it came by a Woman; no more than the *Samaritans*, the Woman that *Jesus* sent from *Jacob's* Well, as I can find; but they went or ran to see for themselves.

Although I have writ thus much for Womens Preaching, yet I would have none go before they are sent of the Lord, no more than Men; for it is alike hateful for me, and many worthy Friends, to my certain Knowledge. I could willingly pray to the Lord with all my Soul and Spirit, that he would be pleased to stop the Mouths of all those Lyars, who say *Thus saith the Lord*, when he never spake by them. Male and Female are all one in Christ the Truth, the true Church or Congregation which is in God, and God in his Church which is his Kingdom, where he rules and reigns, and is blessed for evermore. *So be it.*[64]

I hear in these words echoes of Francis Howgill's ecstatic identification of the true church with the kingdom of God and of George Fox's deeply prophetic notes. There is Robert Barclay's recognition of the centrality of Galatians 3:28, stripped of his pedantic scholarly tone. Above all, there is Margaret Fell's ultimate appeal to the living personal witness of biblical women, boiled down to perhaps the two most dramatic examples of all: Mary Magdalene, from whom Jesus had cast out seven devils (Mark 16:9; Luke 8:2 KJV), who was the first witness to the resurrection of Jesus; and the one whom even Margaret Fell had failed to mention—the woman of Samaria who had had five husbands and was living with another man without benefit of clergy, and who was the first person to proclaim publicly that Jesus was the Messiah (John 4:5-39).

4

Eighteenth Century Antislavery and Quietist Friends

One of the earliest Quaker antislavery writings was a book, *The American Defence of the Christian Golden Rule, Or An Essay to prove the Unlawfulness of making Slaves of Men*, written by John Hepburn and published in 1715. "Little is known about Hepburn, except that he came to Pennsylvania as an indentured servant and considered himself a Quaker."[1] Hepburn's argument that slavery was wrong boiled down to a single saying, from Jesus' Sermon on the Mount (Matthew 7:12; Luke 6:31):

> This Practice contradicts Christs command, who commanded us, *To do so to all men as we would they should do to us*, or as we would be done by. Now the buying and selling of the *Bodies* and *Souls* of Men, was and is the Merchandize of the Babylonish Merchants spoken of in the *Revelations*. Now the Tyranizing over and making Slaves of our Fellow Creatures, the Negroes, every one knows, or may know, this is not the way they would be done unto.[2]

Another antislavery Friend was Ralph Sandiford, a shopkeeper in Philadelphia who had migrated from England.

He poured out his feelings in a little book which Benjamin Franklin printed for him in 1729—although the discreet Franklin took care to see that the printer's name did not appear on the title page. Sandiford called the book *A Brief Examination of the Practice of the Times*. He addressed it in particular to the Philadelphia Friends.[3]

Even the title page of this book teems with biblical quotations and allusions:

Whereby is manifested, how the Devil works in the Mystery, which none can understand and get the Victory over but those that are armed with the Light, that discovers the Temptation and the Author thereof, and gives Victory over him and his Instruments, who are now gone forth, as in the Beginning, from the true Friends of *Jesus*, having the Form of Godliness in Words, but in Deeds deny the Power thereof; from such we are commanded to turn away.[4]

Here is a longer selection that shows the same flowing, impassioned biblical style:

The earthly Tabernacle, which is centred to its Original as a Seed, which will be cloathed with its own Body, whether of Light or of Darkness; therefore while we have the Light, let us walk in it, that we may be raised to a glorious Immortality with the Saints in Light, forever to adore and admire that Power by which we were redeemed; that dwelt in that Body, that suffered the Wrath due to us; in which he perfected the Will of God, who went about doing Good: giving Sight to the Blind, and causing the Lepers to be cleansed, and unto the Poor is the Gospel preached freely; by him who dispossess'd the Devils, whereby the Creature that was in Bondage and Captivity was set free; by the great *Jubilee* and Prince of the Law of Liberty— not only to the *Jews*, but to all Nations: who when he was reviled, reviled not again, but suffered all things from his enemies for whom he waded through that bitter Conflict In the Garden, which he finished on the Cross, when the Sins of the whole World was upon him, under which he cried, *My God, my God why hast thou forsaken me!* and he that had known Hunger in the Wilderness now suffered Thirst, and they gave him Vinegar to drink; in which the Scripture was fulfilled, and when he had received it, he said, *It is finished*, and he bowed his Head and gave up the Ghost. Oh! The unparallel'd Love of Christ, the immaculate Lamb, to Enemies! for whom he prayed on the Cross; tho' he had Power over all Creatures, in Heaven and Earth, that he might have commanded Legions of Angels for his Deliverance: But such was the Love of our Redeemer, in whom there was no Offence, to suffer for Offenders! in which is manifested his great Mercy, and wonderful Love and Charity, which the Angels themselves cannot fathom! the infinite Extension of the Love of God in Christ, which is incomprehensible! yet unto us is this Grace given, that we might partake of the unsearchable Riches of Christ; which neither Principalities nor Powers, whether of Angels, or Men, or Devils, should be able to separate us from him, who is both Precept and Precedent to his Church; and if the Green Tree thus humbled himself, much more shall the Dry. Shall we Lord it in the Creation, in Opposition to his Command which saith, *It shall not be so amongst us*; Or can we behold him in his Sufferings he went thro' for Sin, and yet commit these Things whereby we should crucify him afresh, and put him to open Shame, and deny his Gospel, which brings Life and Immortality to those that obey the Light thereof; a Measure of which is given to every Man, to make known the Mystery, which from the Beginning of the World hath been hid in God, who created all things by Jesus Christ, who in the Beginning moved by his Spirit on the Face of the Deep, for the carrying on and perfecting of the outward Creation; so he moveth in our Hearts by his Spirit for our new Creation in Christ, whose first Appearance may be as a Grain of Mustard-Seed against Sin, yet as the first Work of Faith we are to believe in it, as a Measure of the Revelation of Christ, which was promised should first reprove for Sin, which was in order to bring those that obey it out of Sin whereby, like the Leaven in the Meal we may be changed into its Nature, by which we encrease in the Faith, and the Comforts thereof are known; which can not proceed from Nature, because it contradicts the Natural Man, which wars against it to keep the Creature in Bondage to Lust; Neither will the Devil reprove for Sin for then Satan would war against himself.[5]

As I read passages like these, I can easily imagine that I am in the midst of something written by George Fox or Edward Burrough. That is, until I come up against passages like these:

Love to God, and Hospitality to Strangers, was recommended

under all Dispensations. *Whereby*, saith the Apostle, *some have enter-tained Angels unawares*, whose Mission was to the righteous Souls that sought the Good of all Men, as was testified of just *Lot*, that his righteous Soul was grieved with *Sodom's* filthiness.[6]

Also *Abraham*, in whose righteous Seed all the Families of the Earth are blessed, is eminent for his Regard to the Lord's Covenant, in that he caused all his Household, both Children and Servants, whether born in his House, or bought with Money, to be circumcised with him, that they might keep the Way of the Lord, *Gen.* xviii.9. So that herein *Abraham* sought them to the Lord, in the Faith, which was accounted to him for Righteousness, and his End was answered, for *Abraham* believed God with all his House, which, had he come by them as we do by the *Negroes*, or *Indian* Slaves, they would hardly have regarded *Abraham*, or believed in the Lord, or his Ordinance. But does this appear in this Trade that we seek them to the Lord and his Gospel or their Liberty and Property to us and our Children, let the Impartial judge since we go for them for that very End. Therefore you are short of the Law which must be fulfilled before a higher Dispensation is known, which *Moses* testifyed of, that those Souls that would not obey should be cut off; yet *Moses* was faithful in that Dispensation, in ministering to *Pharaoh* and *Egypt* for their Oppression.[7]

But to return to the Law, that was given to a hard-hearted People, unto whom many Things were suffered on that Account, that they made Captives of those they were at War with, and drove out the Inhabitants that possessed the promised Land, which they had forfeited by their Wickedness; but what is that to us, who are not at War with these Negroes, neither can we say their Country is given unto us, or that we have a Command or a Dispensation for the Trade; . . . yet ready are you to fasten on the hardest Thing that was suffered to them, while you pretend to the Dispensation of that Grace and Truth that comes by Jesus Christ. Yet even amongst the *Jews*, if One became poor to be sold unto a Brother or to a Stranger, any of his Kin may redeem him, or, if able, he may redeem himself; and the Price of his Redemption shall be according to the Number of Years to the Year of *Jubilee*; and if he fails of these Opportunities of Redemption, the *Jubilee* shall release him, not only from Servitude, but shall restore him to his Family and Possession.[8]

Righteousness may be put to the Plumb-line, which will discover the Uprightness thereof; that we may be polished and made fit for our eternal Habitations with God, who will recompence to every Man according to his Deeds; therefore let not Dust and Ashes contend with its Maker, but submit the Work to Trial; and if it contradicts the foregoing Dispensations of Angels, and of *Moses* and the Prophets, and even *John* the Baptist, who testifies that he was to decrease, how shall it agree with the Dispensation of Christ who in his Bodily Appearance, wherein he laid down to us many Duties, yet he sums up all in this new Commandment that we love one another, as the Badge unto the World of our Discipleship for he that loveth him that begat loveth him so that is begotten of him and not only so, but we are to love our Enemies for if we forgive not Men their Trespasses against us, how shall we expect Forgiveness of Christ, who died for us, when Enemies; which is the highest Expression of Love, in which his Gospel consists, and those that have receiv'd it in the Power of it, beat their Swords into Ploughshares, and their Spears into Pruning-hooks, having no Use therewith; whose Weapons are not for the Destruction of the Body, yet mighty through God, to cut down Sin in the Creature; that the Spirit may be saved in the Day of the Lord Jesus, who first loved us, therefore do we love him; and in this do we manifest it, by keeping his Commandments; and he that dwelleth in Love, dwelleth in God who is Love, and God in him by his Spirit, which gives Boldness in the Day of Judgment, when none will be able to stand before him, but those that are clothed therewith; who when he commissioned his Disciples to preach unto the World, before whom the very Devils were subject, because of the Power that dwelt in them yet when some resisted the Power, it raised the Zeal of the Apostles, to desire that Fire might have fell from Heaven to have destroyed them; and tho' they produced a Precedent of one of the Prophets in a former Dispensation, yet they were rebuked by our Lord, that they knew not what Manner of Spirit they were of.[9]

In contrast, George Fox rarely used the word "dispensation," and when he did so, it was mostly in quotations from Paul's letters. Fox did not look on God's revelation or action in history as falling into a specific series of stages, with each of these "dispensations" replacing or setting aside the previous stage. Sandiford's main point is that the ethical principle of hospitality to strangers persists through all of the successive dispensations. Wouldn't it have been simpler for him just to omit or bypass the whole idea of "dispensations"? My own suspicion is that Sandiford dwelt on this term only because it was a prominent concept in William Penn's preface to Fox's *Journal*:

> Divers have been the dispensations of God since the creation of the world unto the sons of men; but the great end of all them has been the renown of his own excellent name in the creation and restoration of man.[10]

The outward dispensation that followed the benighted state of man after his fall, especially among the patriarchs, was generally that of angels, as the Scriptures of the Old Testament do in many places express, as to Abraham, Jacob, &c. The next was that of the law by Moses, which was also delivered by angels, as the apostle tells us. This dispensation was much outward, and suited to a low and servile state; called therefore that of a schoolmaster, to point out and prepare that people to look and long for the Messiah, who would deliver them from the servitude of a ceremonious and imperfect dispensation, by knowing the realities of those mysterious representations in themselves. In this time the law was written on stone, the temple built with hands, attended with an outward priesthood and external rites and ceremonies, that were shadows of the good things that were to come, and were only to serve till the Seed came, or the more excellent and general manifestation of Christ, to whom was the promise, and to all men only in Him, in whom it was Yea and Amen, even life from death, immortality and eternal life.

This the prophets foresaw, and comforted the believing Jews in the certainty of it; which was the top of the Mosaical dispensation, which ended in John's ministry, the forerunner of the Messiah, as John's was finished in Him, the fulness of all. And God, who at sundry times, and in divers manners, had spoken to the fathers by his servants the prophets, spoke then by his Son Christ Jesus, who is heir of all things; being the gospel-day, which is the dispensation of sonship; bringing in thereby a nearer testament and a better hope, even the beginning of the glory of the latter days, and of the restitution of all things; yea, of the restoration of the kingdom unto Israel.

Now the Spirit, that was more sparingly communicated in former dispensations, began to be poured forth upon all flesh, according to the prophet Joel; and the light that shined in darkness, or but dimly before, the most gracious God caused to shine out of darkness, and the day-star began to arise in the hearts of believers, giving unto them the knowledge of God in the face (or appearance) of his Son Christ Jesus.[11]

And to this great and blessed end of the dispensation of the Son of God, did the apostles testify, whom he had chosen and anointed by his Spirit, to turn the Jews from their prejudice and superstition, and the Gentiles from their vanity and idolatry, to Christ's Light and Spirit that shined in them. . . . So that the Light, Spirit and Grace, that comes by Christ, and appears in man, was what the apostles ministered from, and turned people's minds unto, and in which they gathered and built up the churches of Christ in their day.[12]

Sandiford did more than use Fox and Burrough's biblical style and Penn's dispensational approach to biblical revelation. He referred specifically to several significant aspects of George Fox's thinking. He noted that Fox advised some slaveholders to modify some of the severity of their mastership:

Our Friend George Fox, in a Sermon taken in Shorthand as it was preached at a Monthly Meeting in Barbados, tho in the Beginning of Time, when many were convinced that had Slaves, he advised them to use them well, and to bring them up in the Fear and Knowledge of God, and after a reasonable Service to set them free; as we may also see in his Journal, pag. 354. which was far from encouraging them to buy more after their Convincement. For if they had gone back again into that Trade, what had their Convincement done for them, but bring them into greater Judgment for their Disobedience to the Manifestation?[13]

In his specifically biblical arguments, Sandiford quoted several verses from Isaiah, including one, which he noted Fox had already cited:

We may see Chap. lviii. 6. where the Lord ordains the Fast that he will accept of, which is to loose the Bands of Wickedness, to undo the heavy Burdens, and to let the Oppressed go free, and that ye break every Yoke, or in vain were all their Oblations and Sabbaths to him, who delights in Mercy rather than Sacrifices; which Passage our Friend George Fox made use of against the Oppressors and Persecutors of those Times.[14]

Sandiford also appealed to Fox's example in using biblical language to denounce Christians who fell away from the purity of their faith:

Our worthy Elder and Father in Christ, George Fox observed that such as had heard the Lord's Voice and come out of *Egypt* and through the Red Sea and praised God on the Banks of the Seashore, where they have beheld the Goodliness of *Israel's* Dwelling; also such who in the Gospel Times can preach Christ in Words, but forsake him in Life, to follow the Wages of Unrighteousness, like *Balaam*; these he saw in the Vision of Life, were and would be the greatest of Deceivers, who lead the World after them by their evil Example.[15]

Sandiford not only looked back to such early Friends as George Fox and William Penn for leadership and guidance; I am convinced that he was reading their writings with empathy. As he went to the Bible to establish his case against slavery, he read the Bible through the eyes of Fox and Penn. Just as Fox and Penn themselves were unaware that they were reading the Bible in very different ways, so Sandiford was no more aware of the inconsistencies between their approaches to the Bible. I believe this accounts for the apparent fact that his own interpretation of the Bible was uneven and problematic at times. In spite of these problems, I am impressed that Sandiford was able to produce a strong and far-reaching biblical argument against slavery. He showed clear insight in drawing on such biblical themes as hospitality toward strangers, proclaiming liberty to the captives, freeing the oppressed, even release from servitude in the Jubilee year, as crucial to the question of the morality of slaveholding and the slave trade.

Sandiford did not live to see the modest results of his crusade. Cast out of the Society of Friends, and broken in health, he retired in 1731 to a small farm near Philadelphia where two years later he died. His tombstone recorded the great passion of his life as well as the date of his premature death: "In Memory of RALPH SANDIFORD, son of John Sandiford of Liverpool, he Bore A Testimony against Negro Trade & Dyed the 28th. of the 3d. Month 1733. Aged 40 years."

During his last illness Ralph Sandiford received visits from his friend, the strange little hunchbacked Quaker and abolitionist, Benjamin Lay. Lay hated slavery more violently even than Sandiford did. Convinced that his friend's delirium and death had resulted from ill treatment by slaveholding Friends, Benjamin Lay took up the crusade where Ralph Sandiford had laid it down.[16]

Benjamin Lay was born in England. In 1710 he migrated to the island of Barbados in the West Indies. Barbados was a British colony. The economy and social structure of Barbados were heavily dependent on the institution of slavery. "During the second half of the seventeenth century and early part of the eighteenth there was a sizable Quaker community in Barbados."[17] Friends built six meeting houses in Barbados. Many Friends owned slaves, who worked on their plantations.

Benjamin Lay and his wife, Sarah, ran a store; many of their customers were slaves from the plantations. Benjamin "became deeply interested in the condition of the slaves. His violent denunciations of the practice of slaveholding excited the anger of the planters, and he was compelled to leave the island."[18] Benjamin and Sarah Lay moved to Philadelphia in 1731. Benjamin soon learned that many of the leading elders in Philadelphia Yearly Meeting were slaveholders. Their slaveholding practices may have avoided the excesses that went along with the plantation system, but they had no intention to give up their ownership of slaves or to abandon the practice of buying and selling slaves or to permit the yearly meeting to take any firm stand against slaveholding or the slave trade.

Not long after the death of his new friend Ralph Sandiford, Benjamin Lay began a campaign against the slaveholding Quaker elders. Not only did he verbally denounce their slaveholding and slave trading, he also engaged in dramatic actions that were clearly inspired by the prophetic symbolism that had been carried out by such persons as Elijah, Isaiah, John the Baptist, and Jesus. Seventeenth-century Friends had also practiced prophetic symbolism: James Nayler rode into Bristol on a donkey, just as Jesus had ridden into Jerusalem; Robert Barclay walked the streets of his city naked, as a sign, just as Isaiah had done. Benjamin Lay showed more originality in his actions, but his inspiration came from the biblical prophetic tradition. He and Sarah moved to a small farm in Abingdon, on the outskirts of Philadelphia, and lived there in a cave; his vegetarian diet and clothing made of flax came from crops that he grew on his farm. (Think of Elijah and John the Baptist living in the wilderness, wearing a hairy garment and leather belt, and eating locusts and wild honey.) His most notorious act—pulling out a sword in the hallowed gathering of Philadelphia Yearly Meeting and thrusting it into a book filled with red juice, which splattered over the gathered Friends—had all of the prophetic energy and emotion of Jesus in the courts of the temple in Jerusalem overturning the tables of the money changers. In some ways, these actions portray an empathy with the people of the Bible even more profound than that of the first Friends; in another way, however, I believe Benjamin Lay's empathy and identification with the prophetic tradition fell short. I know of no evidence that he wept for his people or interceded with God on their behalf, as Moses, Amos, and Jeremiah had done, or that he asked God to forgive the Friends who disowned him, as Jesus and Stephen had done for those who killed them.

Sarah Lay died in 1735. For quite a few years, Benjamin Lay kept up a friendship with Benjamin Franklin. In 1737 Benjamin Lay took a number of papers he had recently written to Benjamin Franklin, who printed them as a book, titled *All Slave-Keepers that Keep the Innocent in Bondage*. Franklin (as he had done with Ralph Sandiford's work) prudently left his own name out of the book.

In this book, Benjamin Lay proved himself to be a masterful user of biblical language as a weapon for denouncing slaveholders:

No greater Sin Hell can invent, than to prophane and blaspheme the pure and Holy Truth, which is God all in all, and remove God's Creatures made after his own Image, from all the Comforts of Life, and their Country and procure for them, and bring them into all the miseries that Dragons, Serpents, Devils, and Hypocrites, can procure and think of; these things are carried on by Christians, so called, and Ministers too.[19]

Matth. vii.17. *Every good Tree bringeth forth good Fruit, but a corrupt Tree bringeth forth evil Fruit.* Is there any eviler Fruit in the World than Slave-keeping? Any thing more devilish? It is of the very Nature of Hell itself, and is the Belly of Hell.

Verse 18. *A good Tree cannot bring forth* such cursed *evil Fruit* as Slave-trading, if this Practice be the worst, the greatest Sin in the World (with what goes and grows with it) as it is, to be sure.[20]

As *God gave his only begotten Son, that whosoever believed in him might have everlasting Life*; so the Devil gives his only begotten Child, *the Merchandize of Slaves and Souls of Men*, Rev. xviii. 13. that whosoever believes and trades in it might have everlasting Damnation.[21]

We may safely say, without Breach of Charity, by these Prophets or Ministers before-mentioned, as *Micajah* said by *Ahab's* four hundred false Prophets, 1 *Kings* xxii. 23. that there is a *Lying Spirit* in the Mouths of all them that keep or trade in Slaves, and say it is lawful in this blessed Gospel Day.[22]

Now Friends, you that are Slave-Keepers, . . . you are got beyond
Gospel, Law, *Abraham*, Prophets, Patriarchs, to *Cain* the Murtherer,
and beyond him too, to the Devil himself, beyond *Cain*, for he
Murthered but one, that we know of, but you have many Thousands,
or caused 'em to be so, and for ought I know many Hundreds of
Thousands, within 50 Years.[23]

For all of his eloquence in using the Bible to castigate slaveholders, when
I searched to find how Benjamin Lay used the Bible to show why slaveholding
was wrong, he seemed to be remarkably tongue-tied. He barely went beyond
referring to a couple of basic principles: "No greater nor no better Law, say
I, than to love God above all, and all our Fellow-Creatures as ourselves; these
two contain Law, Prophets and Gospel, do to all as we would be done by."[24]

I find evidence in Lay's book that his opposition to slaveholding came
not from the Bible but from his personal awareness of what slavery actually
meant. The passion and pathos in these passages are overwhelming:

I say my own Experience when I lived in *Barbadoes* about 18 Years
ago, where we had much Business in Trading, and the poor Blacks
would come to our Shop and Store, hunger-starv'd, almost ready
to perish with Hunger and Sickness, great Numbers of them would
come to trade with us, for they seemed to love and admire us, we
being pretty much alike in Stature and otherways; and my dear Wife
would often be giving them something for the Mouth, which was
very engaging you that read this may be sure, in their deplorable
Condition. Oh! my Soul mourns in contemplating their miserable,
forlorn, wretched State and Condition that mine Eyes beheld them
in then.[25]

These Wretches being in Town in this miserable Condition, with
not a Crum of good or bad to put into their Mouths, ready to drop
as they walked or crawled along the Streets, they many of them
hearing of us, for we were very much known amongst them, they
would come to our Door; if they came before we were gone to
Meeting, and there they would stand as thick as Bees, but much
more like *Pharaoh's* lean Kine, and I may say their Appearance was
dismal enough to move a very hard Heart; so we used to give them
a little of something at Times, as we found some Freedom, considering our Circumstances; But if we gave to some, and did not to all,
as to be sure we could not, oh how the poor Creatures would look. I

say many Hundreds would come and flock about us; and them that receiv'd, O how thankful, with bended Knees; but them that did not what Words can set forth the dejected sinking Looks that appeared in their Countenances. Shall I ever forget them?[26]

An especially heart-wrenching incident involved a slave owned by a Barbados Friend:

My dear Wife has often spoke of a Passage in or near *Spikes's* in *Barbadoes*; going hastily into a very plain-coat outside Friend's House, there hung up a Negro stark naked, trembling and shivering, with such a Flood of Blood under him, that so surprised the little Woman she could scarce contain; but at last a little recovering, she says to some in Family, *What's here to do?* They began exclaiming against the poor miserable Creature, for absconding a day, or two, may be by reason of his cruel Usage, as by this Barbarity we may imagine.[27]

The contrast between Benjamin and Sarah Lay's empathy for the slaves, whom they had come to know as customers in their store, and the callous indignation of the Quaker slave-owning family, speaks for itself. Inspired as Benjamin was by the great example set by the original Quakers, how could he help being chagrined and angry at what he was seeing in the beloved community to which he belonged:

But my dear and tender Friends, how does this cruelty and partiality agree with our principles as a People, which have been preaching up Perfection in holiness of Life, for near a Hundred Years and the universal Love of God to all People, of all colours and Countries, without respect of Persons: Have we forgotten this blessed Testimony for which our dear Friends suffered in *Old* and *New-England?*[28]

Benjamin Lay clearly felt deep empathy for the slaves whom he knew. He was unable to feel similar empathy for the Quaker slave owners and slave traders whom he confronted. Who, indeed, could have identified himself deeply with both groups of people in such circumstances?

Faced with what may be a human impossibility, we are reminded of "the immeasurable greatness of [God's] power" (Ephesians 1:19). What God accomplished was to empower a Friend to grow into this depth and breadth of empathy. With this spiritual power, John Woolman (1720-1772) became a major mover in bringing Friends as a body to the point where they first gave up the practice of slaveholding themselves and then went on to become significant leaders in the struggle to abolish slavery in America and in the British empire.

An important source of Woolman's influence consisted in the ways in which he used and appropriated the Bible. Phillips Moulton, editor of the 1971 edition of John Woolman's major writings, noted that for Woolman, "The saturation of his thought with the Bible is attested by some seven hundred quotations or allusions ranging widely over both Old and New Testaments. This is particularly evident in the essays."[29]

In his essays, "Some Considerations on the Keeping of Negroes" and "Considerations on Keeping Negroes: Part Second," Woolman began with some expressions of basic biblical principles (following the practice of Quaker antislavery pioneers such as John Hepburn): "Seek ye first the kingdom of God, and his righteousness; and all these things shall be added unto you" (Matthew 6:33); "Forasmuch as ye did it to the least of these my brethren, ye did it unto me" (Matthew 25:40); "Oppression maketh a wise man mad" (Ecclesiastes 7:7); "The stranger that dwelleth with you shall be as one born amongst you, and thou shalt love him as thyself" (Leviticus 19:34); "Thou shalt not oppress a stranger, for ye know the heart of a stranger, seeing ye were strangers in the land of Egypt" (Exodus 23:9); "I am the Lord, which exercise lovingkindness, judgment, and righteousness in the earth; for in these things I delight" (Jeremiah 9:24); "Ye shall not respect persons in judgment, but you shall hear the small as well as the great" (Deuteronomy 1:17).[30]

In the second part of this essay, Woolman quoted numerous Old Testament passages that the supporters of slavery were citing in approval of the practice. Many of these were specific instances where God directed the Hebrews to make slaves of particular groups of people such as the descendants of Ham and the Gibeonites. But Woolman had prefaced these references by quoting from Ezekiel: "The son shall not bear the iniquity of the father" (Ezekiel 18:20); and so he provided for a fitting conclusion to his argument:

> To suppose it right that an innocent man shall at this day be excluded from the common rules of justice, be deprived of that liberty which is the natural right of human creatures, and be a slave to others during life on account of a sin committed by his immediate parents or a sin committed by Ham, the son of Noah, is a supposition too gross to be admitted into the mind of any person who sincerely desires to be governed by solid principles.[31]

Woolman showed himself to be a master of sophisticated argumentation: he always made biblical principles central, such as love, justice, and universality, along with philosophical principles such as the natural right of all humans to enjoy liberty; and he subordinated all other specific biblical precepts or practices to these underlying principles.

Between 1999 and 2002, I presented courses at Reedwood in which I traced the ways in which Friends used the Bible over the whole course of Quaker history, from the seventeenth century to the present day. What I have written up to this point about John Woolman and the Bible directly reflects what I said about Woolman in those classes. Since that time, two books about Woolman, both published in 2003, have helped me to substantially expand and develop my understanding and appreciation of how he perceived and used the Bible in his writings. In one of these books, *The Tendering Presence: Essays on John Woolman*, edited by Mike Heller, the essays by J. William Frost and Michael Birkel deal most directly with Woolman's interpretation of the Bible. Michael Birkel's essay, "Preparing the Heart for Sympathy: John Woolman Reading Scripture," presents in brief form some interesting and important themes that he spells out more fully in his 2003 book, *A Near Sympathy: The Timeless Quaker Wisdom of John Woolman.*

Frost points out that there seem to be sharp inconsistencies between Woolman's essays and his *Journal*. In the essays, Woolman appealed to natural reason as well as to scripture, and he argued rationally from scriptural principles. In the *Journal*, his appeals to scripture seem to be more in line with traditional Christianity and Quakerism. In conclusion, Frost suggests that Woolman "tailored his vocabulary to fit his audience, his genre, and his purpose in writing."[32] Frost has convinced me that I have to consider both groups of writings in order to fully appreciate Woolman's use of the Bible. But it was Michael Birkel who provided me with a key to discover how Woolman was reading the Bible in his *Journal*.

In my 1999 class, I had stated flatly that Fox's, Fell's, and Burrough's empathetic way of reading and understanding the Bible had disappeared after the first generation of Quakerism. Michael Birkel showed me that there was at least one major exception: John Woolman had read the Bible with deep empathy, and this reading had remarkable consequences for his own spirituality and for his sensitivity to the conditions of people in all walks of life in his own day.

Birkel demonstrated that, like George Fox, Margaret Fell, and Edward

Burrough, John Woolman had also entered sympathetically and imaginatively into the life and thought of the Hebrew and early Christian communities and was looking at the world through the window of biblical faith:

> His entry in his *Journal* for May 28, 1772, demonstrates an appreciation of the multi-layered meanings of reality that underscore the profound connectedness of all of life. So here we come to a complex relationship: John Woolman read the Bible in terms of his own particular inward experiences, yet he perceived his world in profoundly Biblical terms. His spiritual experiences shaped his reading of the Bible, and the Bible shaped his understanding of his experiences. He did not simply read the Scriptures. He lived them.[33]

Birkel showed that Woolman even went beyond the earliest Friends in his empathetic reading of scripture. The key to this insight was his capture of the ways in which Woolman used the phrase, "a near sympathy." Woolman expressed a near sympathy to Moses: "I had a near sympathy with the prophet in the time of his weakness, when he said, 'If thou deal thus with me, kill me I pray thee out of hand, if I have found favour in thy sight' (Numbers 11:15)."[34] Unlike Fox and Burrough, Woolman here demonstrated conscious awareness that he was reading the Bible with empathy. And then Woolman went a step further: he also showed his "near sympathy" in his remarkable ability "to identify with the oppressed of his day."[35] Woolman wrote, during his visit to the Delaware Indians at Wyalusing,

> I was led to meditate on the manifold difficulties of these Indians, . . . and a near sympathy with them was raised in me; and my heart being enlarged in the love of Christ, I thought that the affectionate care of a good man for his only brother in affliction does not exceed what I then felt for that people.[36]

Birkel argued convincingly that it was Woolman's "near sympathy" with the biblical prophets that opened the way to his "near sympathy" with Native Americans and black slaves:

> He used the same expression, "near sympathy," to describe his relationship with both prophets and martyrs, on the one hand, and with the victims of injustice, on the other. He was aware of the connection between a sympathetic reading of scripture and the sympathetic love for others that is the fruit of inward transformation.[37]

Sympathy for others is the fruit of inward transformation, and the sympathetic reading of Scripture which he has been demonstrating in the *Journal* passage for May 28, 1772, prepares one's heart for this sympathy.[38]

James Proud's 2010 collection of writings by John Woolman includes a previously unpublished fragment; nearly half of this fragment consists of a long paragraph in which Woolman focused his attention on the account of Jesus calming a storm at sea (Mark 6:45-52; parallels in Matthew 14:22-33 and John 6:16-21). In his narration, John Woolman added touches in which he portrayed the emotions of Jesus' disciples: "Notwithstanding their reluctance to enter without him into a ship. . . . They imagined that their toil was unknown to their master though it was perfectly present to him. . . . Which they so little expected that they were all frightened." These touches were fine examples of the "near sympathy" (with the disciples), which he referred to in his *Journal*. But then came a jarring note—Woolman called "this history . . . only a type" of "the inward and spiritual miracle" in our own lives—showing clear unconcern (much less empathy) for the historically-centered focus of the gospel writer. And then he drew it all together: "We think ourselves alone and without Jesus Christ, nay we imagine he has abandoned us, and we scarce know him again when he offers himself at break of day."[39] In this very disconnect between history and contemporary spirituality, we find ourselves drawn into deep empathy with the disciples.

The contrasts within this brief paragraph suggest to me a key issue in learning to appreciate Woolman's approaches to the Bible. When I reread John Woolman's *Journal* in light of Michael Birkel's insights, I came up against a remarkable problem. We have seen how the writings of Fox, Burrough, and Fell were crowded with biblical quotations and allusions, put together in a flowing, breathless style or expressed with personal warmth. In John Woolman's *Journal* we read page after page interrupted by only occasional biblical quotations. His writing, like his way of life, was careful and disciplined. Only in two daily entries, during the final week and a half of his voyage to England,[40] do we find biblical citations packed closely together in a way that reminds us of those earliest Friends. These are the passages that Michael Birkel depended on most heavily in demonstrating Woolman's near sympathy with biblical writers and with the poor and oppressed people in his own time.

By using Earlham School of Religion's online Digital Quaker Collection, I discovered that the phrase "near sympathy" or "nearer sympathy" occurred only four times in Woolman's *Journal*. Indeed, the word "sympathy" was present only eight times in all. In contrast, the word "truth" appeared ninety-five times in the *Journal*. Other words and their appearances in the *Journal* were:

"pure" and "purity"—seventy-five times

"wisdom"—fifty times

"duty"—twenty times

"righteous" and "righteousness"—twenty-five times

A number of Woolman's phrases converge to suggest a pattern in his thought or spirituality: pure truth, pure life of truth, pure wisdom, pure Spirit, pure love, pure righteousness, pure obedience. These phrases and very close parallels can be found in about forty instances in the *Journal*.

I have indicated how George Fox's empathetic reading of the Bible was closely tied in with what Alan Kolp called his affective spirituality. Kolp made use of a typology, which contrasted "affective" spirituality (more emotional, spontaneous, and love-empathic) with "speculative" spirituality (more intellectual, formal, and duty-oriented).[41] I see John Woolman's spirituality, as it emerged in his *Journal*, as being very much of the speculative type, except where his "near sympathy" or empathy came to the fore and to that extent leavened his careful formality and duty-orientation.

An empathetic understanding of the Bible was an important aspect of John Woolman's spirituality, but I believe that it was clearly not the center or linchpin of his understanding of Quakerism or of the Christian faith. It was, rather, a grace note that enriched his theology and spirituality, sweetened the austerity of his lifestyle, and deepened his remarkable sensitivity to persons of all conditions and walks of life.

Anthony Benezet was a close friend and ally of John Woolman in the struggle against slavery. Benezet was born in 1713 in France. His parents were devout Huguenots; in the face of the terrible persecutions that the Huguenots were then facing in France, they fled with their family in 1715 to the Netherlands and then to England. Anthony Benezet's father joined Friends in England. In 1731 the family migrated to Philadelphia. Anthony's father, John Stephen Benezet, and a couple of Anthony's sisters soon left the Quakers and became active Moravians. (The Moravians were descendants of the Bohemian Brethren, followers of the fifteenth-century religious pioneer, John Huss, who broke with the Roman Catholic church a century before Martin Luther; this movement was being revitalized in the early eighteenth century under the leadership of Count Nikolaus von Zinzendorf, and had spread through active missionary work to Great Britain and the colonies in America.)

Soon after arriving in America, young Anthony Benezet joined Friends. In 1736 he married Joyce Marriot, a Friends minister. Three of his brothers, "born with an instinct for big business, were soon engaged in exporting peltry and other merchandise, and importing dry goods and sundries from London."[42] Anthony also

> started out to use the mercantile training he had received in England in buying and selling commodities, trading with a group of Friends, including the Barneys of Nantucket and Newport; . . . but he found such an occupation uncongenial. Unlike most young men, starting out in a new world, he steadily rejected every opportunity of a lucrative position in an effort to find himself.[43]

> When the opportunity to teach the youth of Germantown in the year 1739 presented itself, it was like reaching port after stormy seas. This school at Germantown was opened on December 30, 1701, and Anthony Benezet succeeded the learned Francis Daniel Pastorius, the school's first master.[44]

(Pastorius had been one of the earliest opponents of slavery in America; in 1688 he and three other Friends signed a formal protest against slavery on behalf of a small group of Dutch and German Friends in Germantown, Pennsylvania. "These Dutch and German Friends deserve full credit as pioneers of the Spirit. They were the first Americans to see slavery as it really was."[45] Pastorius died in 1719 or 1720.) Anthony Benezet spent the rest of his life as a schoolteacher, mostly in Philadelphia—except for short periods when poor health forced him to take breaks from his work.

From his correspondence we get brief insights into why Anthony did not follow the paths his brothers and sisters took in business and religion. Some time between 1740 and 1743, "he expressed his dislike for a business career, in a letter to Sarah Barney: 'I find being much amongst the buyer and seller rather a snare to me, as I am of a free, open disposition. I had rather be otherwise employed, and more retired and quiet.'"[46] In 1751, he learned that his sister Susanna Pyrleus and her husband were planning to become Moravian missionaries. He wrote to them:

Our brother Pyrleus intends for Europe, knowing that he has formerly thought this his duty. Whether it be, or be not, his duty at this time to go abroad on this errand we will leave to the great Judge and tryer of hearts; though we would caution him not to take it upon trust, because other men think proper; but by humiliation and prayer, try as Gideon did the fleece, again and again, lest he should be as one beating the air, and it be said in conclusion, Who has required this at thy hand? However, we wish him good speed in the Lord.

But as to our Sister Susanna, we must declare our dislike and our *disunion* with her intended voyage. It is certainly her duty to take care and watch over the children that God has given her. . . . We think it would be much more edifying to the church of God in general, if she was to stay where she is, and, as the Apostle advises the young women in his day, *mind her own business*, and learn in silence, and by watching and prayer seek after true acquaintance with her own heart.[47]

The spirituality of most Friends throughout the eighteenth century, and of many Friends well into the nineteenth century, is commonly called Quietism. Quietism was based on the conviction "that God is known only through the prayer of inward silence when all human thought and feeling is quieted."[48] More explicitly,

Only in the "silence of all flesh" can God make himself heard; . . . only when all "creaturely activities" of reason, forethought, planning and organization are suspended can God work in and direct the soul through some invasion, a "breaking in" . . . of the Divine.[49]

The term "Quietism" was originally used to describe a movement among Roman Catholic mystics in France and Italy in the late seventeenth century. The best known Quietists were Madame Jeanne Marie Bouvier de la Motte Guyon, Archbishop François Fénelon, and the priest Miguel de Molinos. Beginning in 1772, the writings of these three Quietists were translated into English, "most of them by James Gough, a noted Quaker schoolmaster of Bristol. They interested Friends chiefly because of their kinship with views that they already held in some measure and which these works powerfully reinforced."[50] I find it easy to believe that Anthony Benezet became a Friend because he was strongly attracted to its Quietist spirituality.

Anthony Benezet became a prolific letter-writer. Many of his letters have been preserved—written not only to Quakers in Philadelphia, New England, and England, but to a wide variety of other persons including Benjamin Franklin, Patrick Henry, John Wesley, the English antislavery attorney Granville Sharp, and the Queen of England. He also published tracts on a variety of subjects including war, prayer, alcoholic beverages, the rights of Native Americans, the plight of the French Acadians who had been forcibly exiled from their homes in Nova Scotia and—most notably— in opposition to slavery. His antislavery tracts were widely read in England and the American colonies.

In his later years, Benezet opened an evening school in his home for African American children. He became a Quaker elder. During the eighteenth century, elders were becoming increasingly influential as upholders and enforcers of moral and spiritual discipline among Friends. In 1752 Philadelphia Yearly Meeting appointed him an overseer of the press. This was a position of great authority, as the overseers of the press had the final say on what writings on religious matters could be published by any Friends. Since Philadelphia Quakers did not agree to disown members for slaveholding until 1776, the extraordinary trust that Friends placed in him must have come about because they recognized his deep commitment to their Quietist spirituality.

Finally, "Anthony Benezet, worn out by his many labors on behalf of the Negroes, died in May, 1784, mourned by the greatest assembly which had ever been seen at a Philadelphia funeral. Whites and Negroes alike walked in the procession to his grave."[51] In the year after his death, a student at Cambridge University in England, Thomas Clarkson, entered an essay contest on the assigned topic of the rightness of slavery. Searching for information on the topic, Clarkson came across Benezet's book, *Some Historical Account of Guinea.* Clarkson later wrote:

"In this precious book I found almost all I wanted" for the essay. He not only came to terms with the reality of slavery, he also won the contest and in the process of having his essay published decided to devote his life to working against slavery.

From that time he continued gathering data. His findings contributed heavily to the 1807 victory when England abolished the Slave Trade, after which he worked toward the next goal to end slavery in British possessions, legislated in 1833, and fulfilled in 1838.[52]

In recent decades, many of Anthony Benezet's writings have become generally available. Since 1937 many of his letters and a substantial number of his tracts have been reprinted in books by George Brookes and Irv Brendlinger on Benezet's life, thought, and influence. Two of Benezet's tracts and two letters have been reprinted in J. William Frost's collection of Quaker antislavery documents. *Some Historical Account of Guinea* has been reprinted as a separate volume by several publishers. I have used this reprinted material as my source for studying Benezet's use of the Bible.

Like John Bellers, Anthony Benezet quoted widely from a variety of authors, modern and ancient. Quotations from the Bible are liberally, if irregularly, scattered throughout his writings. He apparently looked to all of these sources as resources undergirding his positions on moral issues. In a tract on the evils of the slave trade, he concluded:

> I have considered the Trade as inconsistent with the Gospel of Christ, contrary to natural Justice, and the common feelings of Humanity, and productive of infinite Calamities to many Thousand Families, nay to many Nations, and consequently offensive to God the Father of all Mankind.[53]

This suggests that we can learn the will of God both through scripture and through the exercise of natural reason and feelings.

A major reason for the far-reaching influence of Anthony Benezet's writings is the cumulative effect of the evidence that he gathered and presented about the condition and situation of Africans, contrasting their former lives in freedom in their native lands with the misery of their existence as slaves. This evidence consisted largely of long quotations from travelers, merchants, and others who had observed all of this.

Most of Benezet's scriptural references were fairly brief. In one letter to a Friend, he went into more detail than usual in an interesting attempt to apply Jesus' parable of the good Samaritan to contemporary life:

> Should thou, or I, meet with an accident, such as breaking a limb, &c., in some part where we were not known, and lay in the road unable to help ourselves; and should the proper officers either through prejudice or neglect of duty not take care to relieve us; how should we feel, and what should we think of such of the neighbours who saw, or even only heard that we were in that situation, and unrelieved, if they should suffer us to perish there for fear of the trouble, or the charge which might fall upon them, and make themselves easy

under so palpable a neglect of duty, by concluding that a charge of this kind ought to fall on the public, and was no business of theirs? Did the good Samaritan hold himself excused from relieving the wounded traveller, because there were laws in Judea, and persons to whom the duty of taking care of the distressed stranger belonged? But probably this was the argument the Priest and the Levite made use of to themselves to excuse their hardness of heart. It is much to be wished, that a greater concern prevailed in the Society for the promotion of practical Christianity, as it would be the most likely way to remove that selfishness which is the parent of obduracy of heart and of most other vital evils. I do not mean barely the act of giving to the poor, but I mean true charity, i.e., the love which was in Christ, which is the root of everything that is good. If this love prevailed, it would certainly manifest itself by fruits as well as words.[54]

This is a valiant attempt to apply reason and imagination in the interpretation of a biblical passage.

Once, in a letter to another Friend, Benezet did go on at some length in biblical language, gathering together a wide variety of biblical references:

As a people we are called to dwell alone, not to be numbered with the Nations content with the comfortable necessaries of life; as Pilgrims & Strangers; to avoid all incumbrances, as was proposed to Israel of old, to be as a Kingdom of Priests, an Holy Nation, a peculiar people to show forth the praise of Him that hath called us, in our plain innocent, self-denying lives, in which we may depend upon experiencing the fulfilling of the Promise to Jacob "I will never leave nor forsake thee." Great is the energy and Power of Truth to support those whose dependence is on God alone, in opposition to the power & wisdom of the world. Our Saviour thro' the whole of the Scriptures, but more especially in his sermon on the Mount, calls his immediate followers to this happy state of separation from the world, its corrupt & vain selfish spirit.

"Ye are not of the world, saith this blessed Redeemer, as I am not of the world, therefore the world hateth you." Whenever we propose to advance ourselves in the world by any other means but those proposed by the Gospel, in meekness & humility, we depart from the safety & nobility of our calling; and unmindful of these great advantages thus proposed to us, be as a Society like the Israelites of old, too generally lusting after the flesh Pots in Egypt: the delights, the honours & profits of this world, notwithstanding our own better experience, and the falling away of so many others, if we look about us, & retain a feeling knowledge of the truth it must convince us, that our ability to do good, must arise from another power, than that which the spirit & wisdom of this world which is so much at enmity with God gives. Moses, tho' so greatly learned in all the wisdom of the Egyptians, before he was qualified to lead the people from their state of captivity, was obliged to undergo a forty years sequestration in the humble life of a shepherd; a situation which, doubtless on account of its simplicity and abasedness, as we read, abhorred by the wise Egyptians; thus it still is, at this time, the simple & innocent track to which the Gospel leads, that exposes those, who are willing to walk therein, to the abhorrence of that spirit which so strongly prevails in the world, even amongst too, too many, who profess themselves members of our Society.

The Recabites, of whom so honourable mention is made by the Prophet Jeremiah, attained to that preference by their strict adherence to their Fathers injunction, which was, to stand in a state of contemplation & special separation from the world & its spirit. Indeed, from the beginning to this day, the choice has been of those who were low & of little esteem in their own eyes, as well as the eyes of the world. "The Lord (says the holy Virgin Mary) has regarded the lowliness of his handmaid." These have chiefly been made use of in the promulgation of the Gospel, & tho' by means of these lower ones, many of a higher class, even Philosophers & Kings were called in, yet predominantly the choice has been of these little ones, agreeable to that of the Apostle, "Not many wise, not many noble; but God hath chosen the foolish & weak things, such as are esteemed base things of the world, & even things which are not, to bring to pass things that are" for this plain reason "that no flesh should glory." But adds the Apostle, speaking to the Christians of that day, "Ye have despised the poor" yielding themselves up to that wretched disposition, so natural to the corrupt state of human heart, to exalt & support that which is esteemed by the world, tho' hateful in the divine acceptance. Many of the great ones in our Saviour's days were ready to judge & conclude with respect to the Multitude, who being more free from worldly prejudices &

attachments, followed our Lord in disinterestedness & simplicity are said "to have heared him gladly." "Many of the Rulers of the Pharisees, said they, believed on him, but this people who know not the Law are accursed." From these considerations, it is plain, that it is only in a self-denying state of mind, a state of separation from the world, as Pilgrims & Strangers, making our wants & the wants of our Children as few & small as may be, that we & they may the better submit to what Truth requires, that we shall attain to any good degree of establishment in the Truth; it is thus that, laying aside every weight & burden, we may rightly follow him that has called us to be soldiers in his warfare.[55]

These biblical references do not flow out in the free, unselfconscious style of George Fox and Edward Burrough. Anthony Benezet, instead, was choosing his passages and stringing them together carefully in order to construct a rationally persuasive argument. Yet he was hardly showing himself to be a man of the eighteenth-century Enlightenment, exalting reason above all other sources of understanding and wisdom. His reasoning showed less careful precision than John Woolman demonstrated in his essays. Even in his efforts to be rationally persuasive, Anthony Benezet was distrustful of "the spirit & wisdom of this world." As he wrote to Moses Brown, an influential Rhode Island Friend:

Our blessed Savior enjoins his disciples not to resist evil but to overcome evil by good—Himself overcame & gave a deadly blow to sin by suffering and letting evil spend his strength on him. "Thinkest thou said this meek redeemer to Peter that I cannot pray my father for more than twelve legions of angels, but it became him to suffer he was led as a lamb to the slaughter and as a sheep dumb before the shearer. This is the mystery which is hid from the wise the rich and the great of this world, its too deep for natures reason to fathom.[56]

I have gone fairly rapidly through Benezet's available writings in order to gain a sense of the breadth of his choice of biblical passages. I found that, like John Bellers, he was highly selective in his use of the Bible. Certain types of books were clear favorites. Nearly a third of his biblical references were teachings of Jesus from the Synoptic Gospels (Matthew, Mark, and Luke). Another full third were from New Testament epistles and Old Testament books of the prophets. Among the epistles, the First Epistle of Peter was his clear favorite. His quotations from the prophets were mainly from the books of Isaiah, Jeremiah, and Ezekiel.

There were a few passages that he quoted frequently, which were clearly his favorites:

"Thou shalt love the Lord thy God with all thy heart . . . and . . . Thou shalt love thy neighbor as thyself" (Mark 12:30-31 KJV).

"As ye would that men should do to you, do ye also to them" (Luke 6:31 KJV).

And three passages from the second chapter of the First Epistle of Peter:

"But ye are a chosen generation, a royal priesthood, a holy nation, a peculiar people" (1 Peter 2:9 KJV).

"Dearly beloved, I beseech you as strangers and pilgrims, abstain from fleshly lusts, which war against the soul" (1 Peter 2:11 KJV).

"For even hereunto were ye called: because Christ also suffered for us, leaving us an example, that ye should follow his steps" (1 Peter 2:21 KJV).

He quoted a number of passages from the prophets and from the Epistle of James, which emphasized God's concern for the poor. Benezet clearly found strong support in the Bible for his sensitivity to the needs of the poor and weak, in particular of slaves and exiles.

Anthony Benezet's commitment to Quaker Quietism and his interest in the similar spirituality of the European Quietist mystics is noticeable in two letters that he wrote to George Dillwyn, a Friends minister. In each letter he referred favorably to a recently published volume that included a biography or an English translation of the works of a Quietist mystic. In 1774, he wrote:

The case of many high professors amongst us is I think well expressed in the words of ye translator of ye Book I now send, in his acc't of the life of Lady Guion well worthy our most serious notice.

"Many people (he says) who pass for persons of extraordinary piety. . . . To become of no reputation; to forsake all, & to be forsaken of all, for his names sake; to watch, diligently lest spiritual pride, in one shape or other arise, in order to get it subdued & slain; to live wholly and singly *to him who died for us*."[57]

In 1779, Benezet wrote to Dillwyn: "Has thou read Michl. Molinos's spiritual Guide? Would it be agreeable. Its more especially tends to establish that nothingness of self in which true greatness & peace consists."[58]

In the phrase "nothingness of self" Anthony Benezet surely touched the heart of Quietism—of the deep spirituality shared by those Roman Catholic mystics and those eighteenth- and nineteenth-century Friends. I wonder whether this spirituality had any impact in itself on the ways in which Quietist Friends approached and interpreted the Bible.

At least through the end of the eighteenth century, Friends recognized two primary groups of religious leaders: ministers and elders. Ministers were recorded as having the gift of speaking helpfully in meetings for worship. Elders took responsibility for convening, guiding, and ending these meetings; for the spiritual and moral health of the Quaker community; and for encouraging and guiding the ministers. John Woolman was a minister; Anthony Benezet was an elder. Hugh Barbour and Jerry Frost have pointed out some of the ways in which

> Quietism dominated the practice of the ministry. A minister was a spokesperson for God and was forbidden to speak out of his or her own will. The divine origins of messages became apparent in the practices of prophecying, telling visions, and speaking to individual states.[59]

> Quietists constantly worried about their motives and questioned the purity of their messages.[60]

John Churchman (1705-1775) was a Quaker farmer and surveyor. He lived his entire life in Nottingham, Pennsylvania. He was recorded as a minister when he was about thirty years old, and from then on he spent a great deal of time—much of it during the winter months—traveling to visit Friends in many parts of the American colonies. He made an extended visit to Great Britain, Ireland, and Holland from 1750 to 1754. His wife, Margaret Churchman, was also a recorded minister. Like many traveling Friends ministers, he wrote a journal of his life and ministry, which was published in 1779.

Entries in John Churchman's journal show that he was clearly Quietist in his spirituality:

> I then loved retirement and inwardly to feel after the incomes of life, and was often fearful lest I should again fall away. In this time it was manifested to me, that if in patience I stood faithful, I should be called to the work of the ministry; I loved to attend religious meetings, especially those for discipline, and it was clearly shewn

me, that all who attend those meetings should inwardly wait in great awfulness, to know the immediate presence of Christ the head of the Church.[61]

I leave this remark, to excite all to dwell in meekness and fear, and to beware of the will of the creature, and the reasonings of flesh and blood, which lead into doubting and disobedience.[62]

I . . . found it my place to exhort friends to retire deeply inward in all their meetings, humbly waiting to be admitted into the heavenly presence.[63]

John Churchman sometimes struggled at length over his motives in speaking and over the question of how purely he was expressing what God intended him to say:

I had a very bright opening as I thought, and expected to stand up with it very soon, but being willing to weigh it carefully was not very forward, viewing its decreasing brightness, until something said as it were within me, "is the woe in it," is necessity laid upon thee, 1 *Cor.* ix. 16. And therefore woe if thou preach not the gospel. This put me to a stand, and made me feel after the living presence of him, in whose name and power I desired to speak, if I appeared in testimony; and not feeling the pure life and power of Truth, so as to stand up, the brightness of the Vision faded, and left me quiet, humble, and thankful for this preservation; the drawing strength and lusting desire of the unstable, who centre not to the pure gift in themselves, are as the many waters, or sea of Mystery Babylon, for her merchants to sail their ships and trade upon. This was a time of inward growing to me.[64]

On first day I thought I had an engagement to stand up, and considerable matter before me, and after speaking three or four sentences which came with weight, all closed up, and I stood still and silent for several minutes, and saw nothing more, not one word to speak; I perceived the eyes of most of the people were upon me, they, as well as myself expecting more; but nothing further appearing, I sat down, I think I may say in reverent fear and humble resignation, when that remarkable sentence of *Job*, chap. i, 21. was presented to my mind, *Naked came I out of my mothers womb, and naked shall I return; the Lord gave, and the Lord hath taken away; blessed be the name of the Lord,* and for, I suppose, near a quarter of an hour I remained in a silent quiet; but afterwards let in great reasonings and fear lest I had not waited the right time to stand up, and so was suffered to fall into reproach; for the adversary who is ever busy, and unwearied in his attempts to devour, persuaded me to believe that the people would laugh me to scorn, and I might as well return home immediately and privately, as attempt any further visit on the Island; after meeting I hid my inward exercise and distress as much as I could, when night came I lodged with a sympathizing friend and experienced elder; . . . when I awoke, I remembred that the sentences I had delivered in the meeting, were self evident truths, which could not be wrested to the disadvantage of friends, or dishonour of the cause of Truth, tho' they might look like roots or something to paraphrase upon, and altho' my standing some time silent before I sat down might occasion the people to think me a silly fellow, yet they had not cause to blame me for delivering words without sense or life; thus I became very quiet, and not much depressed, and was favoured with an humble resignation of mind, and a desire that the Lord would be pleased to magnify his own name and truth, and preserve me from bringing any reproach thereon.[65]

These passages appear to me to be exercises in discernment; Churchman was learning to recognize and distinguish more clearly what was coming from God, and what was simply from his own mind or emotions.

William Taber, in his remarkable study of the ministry of Quietist Friends, observed that

many of those who stayed steadily in the Light, and who were faithful to the tasks of reordering and to the increasing flow of love, found that the dimensions of reality continued to widen until they could "feel" beyond the usual senses. Gifts of spiritual discernment and a sensing of "states," occasional telepathy, and foreknowledge might develop.[66]

John Churchman recorded a striking example of this apparently "supernatural" sensitivity to the spiritual conditions of others:

As the meeting broke up I stept to a young woman, a friend, who lived near the meeting house, and desired her to step forward and turn the few friends in there, as she knew them, and let the others go by, which she readily performed; when we were all set down round the room, it soon felt to me that if I delivered my concern in general terms, the intended end would not be answered, being in pain for their good, and close matters spoken might be taken by such to whom they least belonged, and being greatly humbled, I was desirous to be rightly instructed, (not knowing their names) to speak to them separately; the Lord who never fails those who humbly trust in him, shewed me where and with whom to begin, and so to the next, and mine eye being fixed on the person to whom I directed my speech, each knew what was delivered to them in particular, and I hope the opportunity was beneficial; for I had great peace: When the friends were gone I asked the young woman, who seemed in some surprize, what ailed her, she said that several were very exactly told their condition, and feared they would judge her for an informer; I told her she need not matter that, as she knew herself to be innocent. I mention this occurrence as a remarkable kindness from the merciful Lord to the children of men, for their help and instruction, and that his servants may be encouraged to wait upon him for instruction to discharge their duty as faithful stewards in his sight, who knows the secrets of all hearts, and taught his servant in old time to know the wife of Jeroboam, tho' she feigned herself to be another woman. Blessed, and magnified be his holy name who is over all worthy for ever and ever![67]

That event occurred during John Churchman's visit to Friends in Ireland. He recorded another occasion, after he returned to England, in which a dream played a key role in his speaking to the "condition" of his hearers:

I . . . reached Rawcliff in Yorkshire on first day; on the night before I had a dream which much affected me; "I thought I heard a kind of melody and singing at my left hand, whereupon I said, What do ye rejoice at; which continuing I said, your singing is somewhat like David's rejoicing before the ark, but I see it not, and heard a voice on my right saying, the ark is in the land of the Philistines, where it was taken through the wickedness of the priests and sins of the people, who removed the ark from Shiloh to strengthen them in battle;" whereupon I awoke and was under some exercise for a time, concluding it was ominous, but saw no further, until we went to meeting in the forenoon, where I soon heard a kind of tuneful sighing, which kept increasing, and turning my head to discover from whence it came, found it to be at my left hand; after a while a person stood up and spoke a few sentences of extraordinary enjoyments which were to be felt; my mind was pained, and after he sat down I stood up and said, What are ye doing? and what do you feel to occasion this rejoicing? and should have proceeded to have told them my thoughts, but instantly my dream came into my mind, and so with little addition sat down very sorrowful; after the meeting I went to dinner, but could not eat much or be chearful; at the afternoon meeting we had the same tune until my spirit was afflicted; but labouring to know that quiet which is not easily disturbed, I received strength in a loving frame of mind to inform them, that I feared they were mistaken in their states and conditions, for that death reigned, and it was rather a time of mourning: . . . In the evening having the company of the chief singer among them, I had a singular freedom simply to relate my dream to him, with a desire that he might examine whether the ark enclosing the pure testimony was preserved safe amongst them; which shut up further conversation. In a few days after, an intimate friend asked me how I fared there, I repeated to him my dream, and he told me it was very significant, for that a withering had taken place in that meeting, and that person had several children who were married to such that did not profess with us, and being treated with as a parent, he said it might be a means of increasing the meeting, if those they had married came to meeting with them, and discouraged friends from dealing with them, lest it should prevent them.[68]

The disciplines of Friends yearly meetings in the early eighteenth century forbade marriages between Friends and non-Friends, but many meetings did not enforce this rule. The main responsibility for teaching children the Quaker way of life lay with their parents. In practice, where the parents came from differing religious backgrounds, they were less likely to train their children in those Quaker principles and practices that differed from those of other Christians. The long-run effect was that looseness in enforcing the marriage regulations was tending to make Quakers more like other Christians. John Churchman, like John Woolman and Anthony Benezet and numerous other Quaker ministers and elders, was convinced that the distinctiveness of the Quaker way of life was essential to full Christian discipleship. These Friends were reformers, who were committed to persuading Quaker local and yearly meetings to enforce the whole spectrum of Quaker practices, including the marriage rules.

Late in 1761, John Churchman suffered a severe illness. A friend who visited him wrote down a number of things that he spoke during that illness and the beginning of his recovery. These written reports were added to his journal when it was published. In one of these discourses he related a dream or vision:

I thought I saw Noah's Ark floating on the deluge, or flood, with Noah and his Family in it, and looking earnestly at it, I beheld the window of the Ark, and saw Noah put out the dove; and I beheld her flying to and fro, for some time; but finding no rest for the soal of her foot, I thought she returned, and I saw Noah's hand put forth to take her in again. After some time I thought I beheld her put forth a second time, and a raven with her, the dove fled as before for some time, and then I saw her return with a green olive leaf in her mouth, as a welcome token of the flood's being abated; I thought I saw also the raven fly, cawking, to and fro, but he did not return; and it came into my mind, this is a ravenous bird, and seeks only for prey to satisfy his own stomach, otherwise he might have returned to the Ark with good tidings, or some pleasant token, as well as the dove: Again, after a short space, I thought I beheld the mountain tops, and some of the tree tops, beginning to appear above the waters, and that I could perceive the flood abate very fast; and as the waters fell away I saw the trees began to bud and a gradual greenness of new leaves came upon them, and I heard the voice of the turtle, and saw many symptoms of a pleasant and happy season approaching, more than I can now relate; and the prospect thereof ravished my soul; I beheld the trees blossoming, the fragrant valleys adorned with grass, herbs, and pretty flowers, and the pleasant streams gushing down towards the ocean; indeed, all nature appeared to have a new dress; the birds were hopping on the boughs of the trees, and chirping; each in their own notes, warbled forth the praise of their creator. And whilst I beheld these things, a saying of the Prophet was brought fresh in my memory, and applicable as I thought to the view before me, viz. *The mountains and the hills shall break forth before you into singing, and all the trees of the field shall clap their hands; instead of the thorn shall come up the fir tree, and instead of the brier shall come up the myrtle tree, and it shall be to the Lord for a name, for an everlasting sign that shall not be cut off*," see Isaiah, lv. 12-13.

When I awoke, the prospect remained clear in my mind, and

had a sweet relish, which now continues with me; and the application of the Vision seems to me in this manner: The flood which
appeared to cover the face of the earth, is the corruption and darkness which is so prevalent over the hearts of mankind; the Ark represents a place of safe (tho' solitary) refuge, wherein the Almighty
preserves his humble attentive people, who, like Noah, are aiming
at perfection in their generation. The dove sets forth the innocent,
harmless, and loving disposition, which attends the followers of the
lamb who are always willing to bring good tidings, when such are to
be had: The raven represents a contrary disposition which reigns in
the hearts of the children of disobedience, who chiefly aim at grati-
fying their own sensual appetites; the waters gradually abating, the
trees appearing, and afterwards budding, the voice of the turtle, and
the pleasant notes of the birds, all seem clear to me, to presage the
approach of that glorious morning, wherein corruption and iniquity shall begin to abate, and be swept away; and then every thing
shall appear to have a new dress: I am fully confirmed in the belief,
that that season will approach, which was foretold by the prophet,
wherein the glory of the Lord shall cover the earth, as the waters
cover the sea; and in a sense of these things my soul is overcome.[69]

The "application of the Vision" is clearly an allegorical interpretation of
the biblical story of Noah's ark. An allegory is "the treatment of an ancient
tradition (generally narrative in form) whereby one ignores its literal meaning and discovers new, hidden meanings in each term of the tradition."[70]
This type of interpretation was used by a number of the early Church
Fathers—notably by Origen in the third century. It gradually fell out of
use, as thinkers came to recognize not only that it lost any connection to
the historical concreteness of the biblical writings, but also that it was an
approach that had no boundaries or guidelines, except for the limits of the
interpreter's imagination.

This was not the only time that Churchman resorted to allegory in his
interpretation of scripture. He was convinced that God called women as well
as men to minister by speaking in meetings for worship. What was he to do
with a verse such as 1 Corinthians 14:34: "Let your women keep silence in
the churches: for it is not permitted unto them to speak" (KJV)? His solution:

The creaturely will, would choose and would be busy with questioning, is it not, or may it not be so and so; this is that womanish
part, which is not permitted to speak in the church, it runs first into

transgression, for want of learning of the husband at home, or being in subjection to him.[71]

He also sought to derive a spiritual lesson from the sordid story of Jacob's fearful attempt to bribe his brother Esau with gifts of sheep, cows, and other animals, in order to escape Esau's wrath over the ways in which Jacob had tricked him:

> Choosing rather, that the Lord in his infinite wisdom and mercy, should deal out to me my daily bread according to his own pleasure, *I passed over this Jordan with my staff and now I am become two bands,* was the saying of Jacob *Gen.* xxxii. 10. As this saying of the good Patriarch came fresh in my mind, I thought, that altho' I could not see myself much increased in heavenly treasure, I came poor, and had only the staff of Faith to lean upon, yet I had to bless the Lord that he was now pleased to favour me with the same staff in my return.[72]

When John Churchman encouraged Friends to "let their language in words be the real language of Truth," by avoiding the use of the word *you* in speaking to single individuals and refusing to use heathen names for months or days of the week, he even felt the need to improve on the homely examples that Jesus was wont to use in his teachings:

> *Neither do men,* said our blessed instructor, *light a candle and put it under a bushel; but on a candlestick, and it giveth light to all that are in the house,* Mat. v. 21. Nor doth the Lord enlighten his candle, that is the spirit of man, with the pure knowledge of Truth, that we should cover it, either with an easeful disposition to save ourselves trouble, or hide the work thereof under the covering bushel of worldly saving care, after the gain and treasure of this world.[73]

(The quotation about a candle and a bushel is actually Matthew 5:15; I presume that Churchman may have confused the reference with Mark 4:21: "Is a candle brought to be put under a bushel, or under a bed? and not to be set on a candlestick?" [KJV].)

> Perhaps such who baulk their testimony to the pure Talent of Truth given them to profit withal, may one day have their portion appointed with the wicked and slothful servant, see *Mat.* xxv. 24-25 *&c.*[74]

On one occasion John Churchman spelled out his basic principle for interpreting scripture: during his travels in England, he was attending a large "general meeting" of Friends, where

> it became my concern to recite the words of our blessed Lord, John 5 v. 39-40. *Search the Scriptures for in them, ye think ye have eternal life, and they are they which testify of me, and ye will not come to me that ye might have life,* from whence I had to shew them the danger of trusting to information and knowledge, whether by reading the Scriptures, or hearing them preached, and neglecting to attend unto the inspeaking voice of Christ immediately in the heart, which is the only sure interpreter of the scriptures, leading those who attend to his instruction in the sure way to life eternal.[75]

In practice, this approach seems to have led him to minimize the historical context of the original passage and instead to "spiritualize" it in applying it to the inward situation of himself or of the person or people he was addressing. He described his situation in his late teens as one of disobedience and temptation to despair, intensified by the death of his father, and then

> in the fall of the year after I had arrived to the age of 20 years; it pleased the Lord to remember me, who had been an Exile, in captivity under the old taskmaster in Egypt spiritually, and by his righteous judgments mixed with unspeakable mercies, to make way for my deliverance.[76]

On a visit to a meeting in New Jersey, Churchman believed that another Friend who spoke had gone on longer than the Lord had actually led him to speak:

> Afterwards being in company with the friend above hinted, and he being down in his mind and perhaps not fully knowing the cause, asked me what I thought of the meeting, to which I was not forward to answer; he said, tell me what I have done this day? whereupon I asked him privately and in a pleasant manner, what Gideon did to the men of Succoth? *Jud.* viii. 16. at which he was greatly humbled, fully understanding what I meant, and did not in the least resent the hint; which I thought was truly great in him, and very becoming a minister.[77]

Referring to Gideon, Judges 8:16 (KJV) reads: "And he took the elders of the city, and thorns of the wilderness and briers, and with them he taught the men of Succoth."

One of his most unusual interpretations of scripture involved Hebrews 12:26: "Now he hath promised, saying, Yet once more I shake not the earth only, but also heaven" (KJV), which in turn was a paraphrase of Haggai 2:6: "For thus saith the LORD of hosts; Yet once, it is a little while, and I will shake the heavens, and the earth, and the sea, and the dry land" (KJV). In both contexts, the passage is clearly eschatological, describing cosmic catastrophes to come at the end of the age. In a sermon in his home meeting at East Nottingham in 1756, Churchman spoke:

A piercing cry and lamentation ran through me, thus, *Alas for the day! Alas for the day! Woe is me!* (several times repeated) and a voice which seemed to be connected with the foregoing, said further, yet once more saith the Lord, I shake not the earth only but also heaven: Not only the situation of those that know not any place of safety or refuge, that which is outward and earthly; but also those who assume a higher place and in their specious appearances and false pretences amongst men, do value themselves on their assumed goodness, and would fain be accounted of the highest rank, and even place themselves among the saints, and are by some accounted as stars in the firmament; yet in the day of my power wherein I will shake the heavens, and the earth, those stars shall fall to the ground.[78]

John Churchman's "spiritualizing" interpretations of biblical texts did not lead him simply to a concern for deeper religious experience and inner piety. Quakerism had from the beginning had a firm emphasis on holiness in living, both individually and as a community. If any Friends failed to live up to the high ethical standards professed by the church, they would be "disowned"—Friends would publicly declare in their business meetings that such persons did not speak for or represent true Quakerism. Churchman on numerous occasions expressed his concern about the decline in this discipline; about the failure of Friends corporately to enforce the highest Quaker standards in their lives. During his visit to Friends in England:

Not being easy in my mind to leave this county without being at the quarterly-meeting for business to be held at Glastonbury, I returned thither, and was concerned to lay before friends the declining state of the society in that county, and to exhort them to put the discipline in practice, that the church might be cleared from disorders, which caused reproach; it was thought by friends to be the most solid quarterly-meeting which had been held in that county for many years.[79]

Much further on in his English visit, he reported:

> Several friends coming to take leave of me, I had an opportunity
> to remark to them the reason that their meetings were so dull and
> cloudy; for I thought I clearly saw there was a neglect among them
> of putting the discipline in practice, where disorders were evident;
> and that this neglect had caused them to suffer, which would still
> continue and increase, until they set the testimony of Truth over the
> heads of such who by disorderly walking had brought a reproach
> thereon: The friends were affected, and acknowledged they believed
> it to be the case amongst them. We parted in tenderness and I pro-
> ceeded on my journey with an income of solid peace.[80]

In regard to Quaker ethics, John Churchman was not a mere tradition-
alist, reaffirming the standards that Friends had held for nearly a century.
In several areas of life, he was a reformer and innovator. Along with John
Woolman and Anthony Benezet, he was active in extending Quaker principles and ethics in new directions. In 1756:

> As it were in a moment mine eyes turned to the case of the poor
> enslaved Negroes: And however light a matter they who have been
> concerned with them may look upon the purchasing, selling, or
> keeping those oppressed people in slavery, it then appeared plain
> to me, that such were partakers in iniquity, encouragers of war and
> the shedding of innocent blood, which is often the case, where those
> unhappy people are or have been captivated and brought away for
> slaves.[81]

This was the time of the French and Indian War; Churchman had
already been actively working with Benezet and Woolman on issues of war
and peace. These two Friends had written on the evils of slavery; it is tempt-
ing to speculate that their influence had been at work in Churchman's mind,
and that his "as it were in a moment" was simply the point at which these
influences emerged into clarity for him. Indeed, Churchman and Woolman
were before long laboring together on the slavery issue. Churchman reported that in 1759

> I was also engaged with my friend John Woolman in visiting some
> active members of our society, who held slaves, first in the city of
> Philadelphia, and in other places; also in New-Jersey, in which ser-
> vice we were enabled to go through some heavy labours, and were
> favoured with peace.[82]

But not only on the slavery issue. John Churchman also worked with Woolman and Benezet and other reform-minded Friends in forging new directions for the Quaker peace testimony. He may, in fact, have been the pioneer thinker in this area. From the founding of Pennsylvania until 1756, Friends had played a major role in the government of the colony. In particular, they held strong, often dominating, majorities in the colonial legislature (the Assembly) all through that period. Jack Marietta has well summarized Friends' views on war-and-peace issues during those years:

Friends believed that a Christian could ethically supply money to his sovereign even when the sovereign—a non-Quaker—used it to prosecute wars. That was the construction that seventeenth-century Friends put upon Jesus' response to the Pharisees in Matthew, chapter 22: "Render therefore unto Caesar the things that are Caesar's and unto God the things that are God's." The precept required all Quaker private citizens to pay their taxes to their sovereign without protest. By extrapolating from the individual taxpayer to the Pennsylvania Assembly, where Friends predominated, the Society required that Quaker legislators supply the king or queen's demands for money. Historically the monarch rarely demanded money from the colonial legislature and then only in wartime. Sometimes the monarch asked explicitly for supplies or the payment of troops. All the Friends ever gave was money "for the King's [or Queen's] use." The king or queen was well satisfied with the money.[83]

In 1748, Pennsylvania's governor pressed the Assembly to appropriate funds "to station a ship of force at Delaware capes, also to encourage the building of a battery below the city."[84] In this situation, Churchman reported:

One night as I lay in my bed, it came very weightily upon me to go to the house of assembly, and lay before the members thereof the danger of departing from trusting in that divine arm of power which had hitherto protected the Inhabitants of our land in peace and safety; the concern rested on me several days, which occasioned me with earnest breathings to seek the Lord, that if this was a motion from him, he would be pleased to direct my steps therein, so that I might be preserved from giving just cause of offence to any, for it seemed to be a very difficult time; many, even of our society, declaring their willingness that a sum of money should be given to the King, to shew our loyalty to him, and that they were willing to part with their substance for his use, tho' as a people, we had a testimony to bear against all outward wars and fightings.[85]

He was here at least uneasy with the traditional Quaker practice of granting funds for military purposes under the formula, "for the king's use." Before long, believing the Lord was calling him to do so, he went to the State House and addressed the members of the Assembly:

> Under an apprehension of the difficulties before you, I feel a strong sympathy with you, and have to remind you of a just and true saying of a great minister of Jesus Christ in his day, *The powers that be, are ordained of God.* Now if men in power and authority, in whatsoever station, would seek unto God (who will be a spirit of judgment to them that sit in judgment) for wisdom and counsel to act singly for him that ordained the power, and permitted them to be stationed therein, that they should be his ministers; such will be a blessing under God to themselves and their country; but if those in authority do suffer their own fears and the persuasions of others, to prevail with them to neglect such attention, and so make, or enact laws in order to their own protection and defence by carnal weapons and fortifications, styled human prudence, he who is superintendant, by withdrawing the arm of his power, may permit those evils they feared to come suddenly upon them, and that in his heavy displeasure. . . . May you be rightly directed at this time, many of whom do fully believe in the immediate influence of Christ, the wisdom of God, which is truly profitable to direct![86]

Six years later, when John Churchman returned from his extended visit to England, the French and Indian War had broken out. At the same time, the Pennsylvania Assembly was embroiled in a continuing political power struggle with the colony's proprietor, Thomas Penn, and with a succession of governors appointed by the proprietor. When the military situation on the Pennsylvania frontier grew increasingly dire in 1755, the governor requested urgent appropriations for military defense. The Assembly passed a series of military appropriations bills that were vetoed by the governor, because they included a tax on Penn's properties in Pennsylvania. Because the Assembly distrusted giving too much power to the governor and the proprietor, these bills also would have put responsibility for spending these funds into the hands of a special commission, whose membership included some Friends.

This situation was the context for a significant entry in John Woolman's *Journal*:

> A few years past, money being made current in our province for

carrying on wars, and to be sunk by taxes laid on the inhabitants, my mind was often affected with the thoughts of paying such taxes, and I believe it right for me to preserve a memorandum concerning it. I was told that Friends in England frequently paid taxes when the money was applied to such purposes. I had conference with several noted Friends on the subject, who all favoured the payment of such taxes, some of whom I preferred before myself; and this made me easier for a time. Yet there was in the deeps of my mind a scruple which I never could get over, and at certain times I was greatly distressed on that account.[87]

Jack Marietta has reported what happened next:

Some Friends became increasingly restive over the Assembly's behavior even before the tax became law. At the annual convention of Philadelphia Yearly Meeting in late September they opened a discussion about the ethics of paying taxes that financed war. John Woolman, one of their number, reported that they were uneasy about paying such taxes. Since he did not qualify that expression of uneasiness, he apparently meant *any* taxes, and not just those that Friends expended. Their grievance was so general it could shake the basic presumptions of Quaker statesmen, Quaker ethics, and provincial politics. At the 1755 Yearly Meeting a committee was appointed to consider the difficult question these Friends had raised; no answer was even remotely in sight.[88]

In October John Churchman attended a couple of Quaker business meetings in New Jersey:

As the sound of war and public commotions, had now entered the borders of these heretofore peaceful provinces, some solid thoughts attended my mind at Shrewsbury, respecting the nature of giving money for the King's use, knowing the same to be intended for the carrying on of war.[89]

On his way home

I felt an engagement of mind to go to Philadelphia; . . . when we came to the city the Assembly of Pennsylvania being sitting, we understood that a Committee of the House was appointed to prepare a bill, for granting a sum of money for the King's use to be issued in paper bills of credit, to be called in and sunk at a stated time by a tax on the inhabitants, on which account several friends were under a close exercise of mind.[90]

Churchman met with a number of Friends in Philadelphia; early in November "upwards of twenty" of them drew up and signed an Address to the Assembly. They "went together to the House, and presenting it to the Speaker, it was read while we were present."[91] The heart of the address asserted:

> As the raising sums of money, and putting them into the hands of committees, who may apply them to purposes inconsistent with the peaceable Testimony we profess, and have born to the world, appears to us in its consequences, to be destructive of our religious liberties; we apprehend many among us, will be under the necessity of suffering, rather than consenting thereto, by the payment of a tax for such purposes.[92]

Even though five Quaker legislators voted against the tax, the bill was quickly passed by the Assembly. Since the bill embodied a momentary compromise with Thomas Penn, the governor did not veto it, and it was enacted into law. The law put expenditure of the funds into the hands of a commission appointed by the Assembly; two or three Friends were members of that commission. For the first time, Friends had direct responsibility for spending taxpayer funds for military use.

In December the two committees appointed by the yearly meeting to consider the war-tax question met in Philadelphia:

> Friends thus met were not all of one mind in relation to the tax. . . . It was a conference the most weighty that ever I was at, and the hearts of many were bowed in reverence before the Most High. Some Friends of the said committees who appeared easy to pay the tax, after several adjournments withdrew; others of them continued to the last.[93]

> After several solid opportunities of waiting on the Lord to be rightly instructed, in which being favoured with a renewed sense of the ownings of truth, many friends thought they could not be clear as faithful watchmen, without communicating to their brethren, their mind and judgment concerning the payment of such a tax; for which purpose an Epistle was prepared, considered, agreed to, and signed by twenty one friends.[94]

This *Epistle of Tender Love and Caution to Friends in Pennsylvania* was signed December 16, 1755. The twenty-one signers included Woolman, Churchman, and Anthony Benezet. A key paragraph of the epistle read:

> And being painfully apprehensive that the large sum granted by the late Act of Assembly for the king's use is principally intended for purposes inconsistent with our peaceable testimony, we therefore think that as we cannot be concerned in wars and fightings, so neither ought we to contribute thereto by paying the tax directed by the said Act, though suffering be the consequence of our refusal, which we hope to be enabled to bear with patience.[95]

This was the first time that any Friends refused to pay taxes for war.

Nearly all of the signers of this Epistle were members of Philadelphia Yearly Meeting. One of them, however, was Samuel Fothergill, a Quaker minister from London Yearly Meeting, who was on a religious visit to Friends in America.

John Churchman had forged a friendship with Samuel Fothergill during his traveling ministry in England. Churchman reported that he and his American traveling companion, John Pemberton, "went to our friend Samuel Fothergill's at Warrington, where we continued from the second to the fourteenth of the first month (New-stile) 1752, he and Susanna his wife being tender and kindly affectionate, we were refreshed in their company."[96] When Churchman left England in August 1754 to return to America,

> Samuel Fothergill before mentioned, came over with me on a religious visit to friends in America; and during our passage, great nearness was between us; we held meetings constantly on the first and fifth days of the week, and landed near Wilmington in New-Castle County on Delaware on the twenty-fourth of the ninth month (1754) in the forenoon.[97]

As Samuel Fothergill visited Friends in Pennsylvania and other colonies in America, he became increasingly concerned about the involvement of many Friends in the French and Indian War. Early in November 1755 he wrote to his wife:

> The deviation of many from our testimony, and their desertion of an arm which has been their sure defence above seventy years, and guarded them from hostile invasions and bloodshed, and now, leaning on their own strength, and actually putting the people in arms

in some places, seems to be a presage of distress they will find hard to bear.[98]

On the day after he signed *An Epistle of Tender Love and Caution to Friends in Pennsylvania*, Samuel Fothergill wrote from Philadelphia to his sister:

> The sure mercies of our Heavenly Father are new every morning, conveying along with them renewed obligations to awful worship, and some degree of holy ability to offer it to him. . . .
>
> A number of substantial Friends from divers parts of this province having appointed a meeting for conference together, in this city, and requesting my meeting them, I found some engagement of mind for the service. Our conference continued, by several adjournments, until last evening.[99]

He was keenly aware of the possibly divisive outcome of the action he and the other tax-refusers had taken. In January he wrote to his wife:

> The assembly here have passed a law imposing a tax upon the inhabitants of this province; and as a great part of the money is to be laid out for military purposes, many solid Friends cannot pay it, which is likely to bring such a breach and division as never happened amongst us since we were a people; may it be finally conducive to the glory of the ever worthy Name, if it issue in the winnowing of the people.[100]

What did happen among Pennsylvania Friends was dramatic, though not as dire as Fothergill anticipated. "In April 1756, five of the eight . . . who had been commissioned to expend the £60,000 asked the governor to declare war upon the Delawares and offer bounties for their scalps." Two of the commissioners who signed this request were Friends: "they were disowned by the end of the month."[101] Some Friends sent an address to the Assembly; they

> begged the Quaker legislators "by the Profession you make of being the Disciples and Followers of our Lord Jesus Christ, the Prince of Peace," and for "the Honour of God," stop the proclamations of war and bounties. But the Assembly did nothing more than discuss the request. . . . On 14 April, the governor proclaimed war and offered on behalf of the commissioners $130 for every scalp of a male Delaware and $50 for a female.[102]

This was too much for some Quaker legislators. On June 4, six Friends, including James Pemberton (brother of John Churchman's traveling companion, John Pemberton), resigned from the Assembly.

In 1756 Samuel Fothergill returned home from America. He faced severe criticism from some Friends for signing the *Epistle of Tender Love and Caution*:

As he recounted to John Churchman, when he went to a meeting in London:

I had a continued chain of hard labor. . . . I found in almost every mind a secret displeasure against the friends who signed the Epistle of caution and advice; and fully expected to be tried by the Meeting for Sufferings for being concerned in it.[103]

But he also had strong supporters; the Meeting for Sufferings (the executive body of London Yearly Meeting) took no action against him. What the Meeting for Sufferings did do at its meeting on July 9, 1756, was to choose two Friends, John Hunt and Christopher Wilson, to travel to America and to command Friends in Pennsylvania "to withdraw from the House, and also to pay their taxes."[104] While the two Friends were on a slow voyage to Pennsylvania, many Pennsylvania Friends boycotted the special election to replace the six legislators who had resigned and the regular annual election in October. Only twelve Friends were re-elected to the Assembly. Hunt and Wilson arrived five days after the October election; they quickly persuaded four Quaker legislators to resign. Friends never again controlled the Pennsylvania Assembly.

Hunt and Wilson had little success in changing the minds of the Friends who were refusing to pay the war tax; instead, they came to understand the position of the tax protesters.

Hunt and Wilson . . . were free to devote their energies to a problem that English Friends were hardly aware of. The Society in Pennsylvania was badly divided over the behavior of the Assembly and the Friends still remaining in it. Some Friends talked as though schism lay ahead. During their year in Pennsylvania Hunt and Wilson tried with a large measure of success to mediate the differences between the two camps.[105]

John Woolman's comments summarize the situation from the viewpoint of the tax protesters:

When the tax was gathered, many paid it actively and others scrupled the payment, and in many places (the collectors and constables being Friends) distress was made on their goods by their fellow members. This difficulty was considerable, and at the Yearly Meeting at Philadelphia, 1757, the matter was opened,[106]

despite the hope of some influential Friends

that no one in the protestors' camp would rashly raise the issue. . . .

The issue did arise and the Yearly Meeting appointed a large committee of forty-three members to consider the tax question and report back. On the committee were the most prominent ministers and reformers—Churchman, Woolman, William Brown, Joseph White, Anthony Benezet; only one assemblyman or former assemblyman; and five English Friends including Hunt and Wilson.[107]

Woolman described what then took place:

We met and, sitting some hours, adjourned until the next morning. It was a time of deep exercise to many minds, and after some hours spent at our second meeting, the following report was drawn and signed by a Friend in behalf of the committee:

. . . As we find there are diversity of sentiments, we are for that and several other reasons unanimously of the judgment that it is not proper to enter into a public discussion of the matter, and we are one in judgment that it is highly necessary for the Yearly Meeting to recommend that Friends everywhere endeavour earnestly to have their minds covered with fervent charity towards one another.[108]

The Yearly Meeting adopted the committee's report. Considering the unorthodoxy of the radical pacifists' protest, that was a victory for them.[109]

This accommodation was to hold firm for at least a quarter century; during the Revolutionary War, many Friends refused to pay war taxes levied by the Pennsylvania Assembly, while others paid the tax. Both positions were accepted by the yearly meeting.

At the end of the war, the Meeting for Sufferings expressed gratification at the number of Friends who had learned spiritual discipline from the trials and sacrifices of the war: "They have measurably seen and felt the sufficiency of his protecting power, and in the day of their humiliation have been permitted to sit under the sensible covering of his paternal care."[110]

Samuel Fothergill (1715-72) was a Quaker minister as was his father. Samuel's older brother, John Fothergill, was a physician and served three times as clerk of London Yearly Meeting. Unlike John Woolman and John Churchman, Samuel Fothergill did not write a journal. More than seventy years after his death, a Friend, George Crosfield, published an extensive collection of his correspondence, together with some of his father's correspondence and some brief narratives to provide context for the letters, as *Memoirs of the Life and Gospel Labours of Samuel Fothergill*.[111]

Samuel Fothergill traveled extensively among Friends in the British isles, and made one trip to Friends in America (1754-56). His visits among Friends in the American colonies sharpened his views not only on war and peace but also on slavery. A few months after his return to England, he wrote to a Friend:

Maryland is poor; the gain of oppression, the price of blood, is upon that province—I mean their purchasing, and keeping in slavery, negroes—the ruin of true religion the world over, wherever it prevails. . . .

North Carolina is the next. . . . The largest body of Friends here seems to me the weakest; they have been a lively people, but negro purchasing comes more and more in use amongst them, and the pure life of Truth will ever proportionably decay.[112]

Like John Churchman, Samuel Fothergill readily quoted from a wide variety of biblical writings. I noticed that he preferred to use quotations that included vivid or unusual phrases:

Oh that I may keep to the Rock of the righteous generation, who is able to preserve.[113]

In all cases where contrary sentiments occur, and where we are required earnestly to contend for the faith, the more the meekness of the Lamb is adopted and abode in, the more indisputably He is known to be the Lion of Judah's tribe, going forth conquering and to conquer. I sympathise nearly with such amongst you who dare not turn aside from the directions of Heaven, but follow the ark into Jordan.[114]

He especially seems to have delighted in putting together quotations or references from a variety of biblical contexts, so that they combined into striking, even dramatic, word pictures. I give several examples next; after each quotation from one of Fothergill's letters, I list the biblical passages (all from the King James Version) that I was able to identify. This may give some sense of the literary skill and technique that he used in his correspondence with family members and friends:

I am thankful to the great Master that we have fathers, as well as instructors, in mercy continued amongst us; such as by a long course of experience have explored the great mystery of godliness and ungodliness; watchmen that are placed upon Zion's walls, whose trumpets give a certain sound.[115]

Isaiah 62:6: I have set watchmen upon thy walls, O Jerusalem.

1 Corinthians 14:8: If the trumpet give an uncertain sound, who shall prepare himself to the battle?

A faithful following and service of him who is ever worthy of fear and obedience. In this and this only we shall rejoice in our lots, every one under his own fig-tree, that has been planted, pruned, and made fruitful by the cultivation of the right hand of the great Husbandman.[116]

Micah 4:4: They shall sit every man under his vine and under his fig tree; and none shall make them afraid.

Luke 13:6: He spake also this parable; A certain man had a fig tree planted in his vineyard; and he came and sought fruit thereon, and found none.

Luke 13:8-9: Lord, let it alone this year also, till I shall dig about it, and dung it: And if it bear fruit, well.

Abundantly good and gracious hath he vouchsafed to be to my soul, in this painful labour in which I am engaged, and hath often filled with his own holy rain, his heritage; and made, at times, as a sharp threshing instrument in his hand, to thresh the lofty mountains to pieces, and to bow the sturdy oaks of Bashan. It hath been his own work and gracious condescension, and to him over all be the praise ascribed, who is God of the mountains, and lifter up of the low valleys.[117]

Isaiah 41:15: I will make thee a new sharp threshing instrument having teeth: thou shalt thresh the mountains, and beat them small.

Isaiah 2:12-14: For the day of the LORD of hosts shall be . . . upon all the oaks of Bashan, And upon all the high mountains.

Zechariah 11:2: Howl, O ye oaks of Bashan; for the forest of the vintage is come down.

Isaiah 40:4: Every valley shall be exalted, and every mountain and hill shall be made low.

Being made to know I go not in this warfare at my own expense, but though spiritually without bag, scrip, staff, or shoes on my feet, of my own providing, yet the inexhaustible storehouse, armoury, and wardrobe, where all the living generations have sought and received supplies, is often opened to my humbling admiration, and though I have travelled at great expense, the bag continues to be filled with fresh riches, the scrip with suitable bread, and the staff strong to support in arduous, painful pilgrimage; and though I have travelled amongst sharp, cutting rocks, rending thorns, and even amongst scorpions and serpents, my feet are not bruised, but shod with the preparation of the Gospel of peace and light.[118]

Matthew 10:9-10: Provide neither gold, nor silver, nor brass in your purses, Nor scrip for your journey, neither two coats, neither shoes, nor yet staves.

2 Corinthians 10:4: The weapons of our warfare are not carnal, but mighty through God to the pulling down of strong holds.

Jeremiah 50:25: The LORD hath opened his armoury, and hath brought forth the weapons of his indignation.

Luke 10:19: Behold, I give unto you power to tread on serpents and scorpions, and over all the power of the enemy.

Ephesians 6:13-15: Take unto you the whole armor of God. . . . Stand therefore, having . . . your feet shod with the preparation of the gospel of peace.

He that loved us and gave himself for us remains the Ancient of Days, yet new every morning.[119]

Daniel 7:13: One like the Son of man came with the clouds of heaven, and came to the Ancient of days.

Lamentations 3:22-23: His compassions fail not. They are new every morning: great is thy faithfulness.

We sorrowfully know that we have amongst us traditional formalists, having a name only, by outward inheritance; yet there remains a worm Jacob, the feeble, yet faithful wrestlers with God amongst us, whose life is hid with Christ in God, and who, through the virtue of sacred unction, have not an absolute need of man's teaching, but are gathered in spirit into the Lord's mountain, where the Lord of Hosts makes unto all his people a feast of fat things, and where he destroys the face of the covering, and the veil that is spread over all nations.[120]

Isaiah 41:14: Fear not, thou worm Jacob, and ye men of Israel; I will help thee, saith the LORD.

Genesis 32:24-25: Jacob was left alone; and there wrestled a man with him until the breaking of the day. And when he saw that he prevailed not against him, he touched the hollow of his thigh; and the hollow of Jacob's thigh was out of joint, as he wrestled with him.

Genesis 32:28: And he said, Thy name shall be called no more Jacob, but Israel: for as a prince hast thou power with God and with men, and hast prevailed.

Colossians 3:3: Your life is hid with Christ in God.

1 John 2:20: Ye have an unction from the Holy One, and ye know all things.

Isaiah 25:6: In this mountain shall the LORD of hosts make unto all people a feast of fat things.

Isaiah 25:7: He will destroy in this mountain the face of the covering cast over all people, and the veil that is spread over all nations.

Another distinctive aspect of Samuel Fothergill's use of the Bible showed up in the way he sometimes used the Bible as a resource in addressing life's issues. Here are a few examples:

Oh! that in this day of thy visitation thou might be wise in heart, and give up to the sword that which is for the sword. If there was a willingness to be divested of every beloved, inconsistent with the will of Him that hath called thee, thou would experience more help, and a gradual removing of those things that interfere between thee and the joys of God's people.[121]

He was taking two quotations from the book of Jeremiah. In Jeremiah 15:2: "Thus saith the LORD: Such as are for death, to death; and such as are for the sword, to the sword; and such as are for the famine, to the famine; and such as are for the captivity, to the captivity," the prophet was listing punishments that God would visit on his people because of the evil they had done during the reign of King Manasseh. In Jeremiah 43:11: "When he cometh, he shall smite the land of Egypt, and deliver such as are for death to death; and such as are for captivity to captivity; and such as are for the sword to the sword," the prophet was declaring how the Lord, through the hand of the Babylonian king, would punish Egypt for that land's sins and idolatry. Fothergill was using the phrase, "give up to the sword that which is for the sword," to mean what Isaac Watts expressed in his famous hymn: "All the vain things that charm me most, I sacrifice them to His blood. . . . Love so amazing, so divine, Demands my soul, my life, my all."

The concluding meeting for ministers and elders was held on Seventh-day, which was solemn and bowing; the enlivening, encouraging Presence was richly manifested to a small handful, that seemed like the mournful prophet under the juniper-tree.[122]

When Queen Jezebel threatened to kill the prophet Elijah, he fled for his life; Elijah "went a day's journey into the wilderness, and came and sat down under a juniper tree: and he requested for himself that he might die" (1 Kings 19:4). The mournfulness to which Fothergill referred was not fear of death or persecution, but simply distress that such a small number had showed up for a meeting.

It is a most solemn and awful thing to assume the name of the Lord's ambassador; I believe thou considers it so. Thence ought we also to consider the high obligations we are under to receive from him, not only his instructions, but our credentials. . . . These will not be withheld, if we wait our Master's time; his sound will be certain, and his discoveries clear. We shall not say, like Ahimaaz,—"When I ran, there was a tumult;" but distinctly receive and deliver our Master's message, in his own wisdom and spirit.[123]

King David's son, Absalom, had led a revolt. David had ordered his generals, including Joab, to put down the revolt, but to spare Absalom's life. When Absalom was captured, Joab disobeyed this order and had Absalom killed. When Ahimaaz volunteered to take the news to David, "Joab said unto him, Thou shalt not bear tidings this day" (2 Samuel 18:20). When Ahimaaz ran and arrived in Jerusalem, David asked him, "Is the young man Absalom safe? And Ahimaaz answered, When Joab sent the king's servant, and me thy servant, I saw a great tumult, but I knew not what it was" (2 Samuel 18:29). Ahimaaz was clearly lying at Joab's orders. Fothergill was suggesting that if a Friends minister spoke before he or she had waited until God's message became clear and distinct, then the "tumult" in the minister's mind would result in God's word for the day not being properly delivered to the congregation. This view was characteristic of Quaker Quietism. In these quotations applying the Bible to contemporary life, I observe that Fothergill paid little attention to the context of the biblical passages he cited, or to the biblical history that they reflected.

Like John Churchman, John Woolman, Anthony Benezet, and other Quaker reformers, Samuel Fothergill's commitment to extending the peace testimony and his opposition to slavery were in essence part of a broader concern to maintain and strengthen the complete Quaker lifestyle. They saw Quaker discipline, with disownment being the sanction of last resort, as the way to maintain high ethical standards and to preserve Quakerism as a community separate and distinct from the "world." Fothergill may well have believed that his crowning achievement was reflected in the minute of the 1753 London Yearly Meeting—"The proposal made by our Friend Samuel Fothergill respecting the establishment of a Yearly Meeting of Ministers and Elders, being re-considered, was referred to the consideration of the Committee for drawing up the Epistle,"[124]—and in the actual establishment of that body by the yearly meeting in the following year. 1754 was also the year in which Fothergill sailed to America. After nine or ten months of visiting Friends in America, he wrote to the clerk of Philadelphia Yearly Meeting:

> I know not what advantage may redound to the church, but it brought me great peace, in the sense of a discharge of my duty, in this labour for the revival of that discipline which divine wisdom placed as a hedge about his vineyard, when he planted it in the morning of our day.[125]

In his song of the vineyard, Isaiah wrote:

My well beloved hath a vineyard in a very fruitful hill: And he fenced it, and gathered out the stones thereof, and planted it with the choicest vine: . . . he looked that it should bring forth grapes, and it brought forth wild grapes. . . . I will tell you what I will do to my vineyard: I will take away the hedge thereof, and it shall be eaten up; and break down the wall thereof, and it shall be trodden down (Isaiah 5:1-5).

The vineyard of the LORD of hosts is the house of Israel (Isaiah 5:7).

In his parable of the wicked husbandmen, Jesus said, "A certain man planted a vineyard, and set an hedge about it, and digged a place for the winevat, and built a tower, and let it out to husbandmen" (Mark 12:1). When the husbandmen refused repeatedly to pay rent in kind to the absentee landlord, "What shall therefore the lord of the vineyard do? he will come and destroy the husbandmen, and will give the vineyard unto others" (Mark 12:9). In both Jesus' parable and Isaiah's song, the hedge and the wall were incidental details, not essential to the main point of the story. Fothergill took this detail and made it a central scriptural justification for the Quaker discipline.

Many Quaker ministers, including John Woolman and John Churchman, told of going through a period of adolescent rebellion against their Quaker upbringing. Samuel Fothergill also reported that in his late teens,

I wandered far from the garden enclosed, and laid myself open to the enemy of my soul: I kept the worst company, and subjected myself to almost every temptation, broke through the fence of the sacred enclosure, and trampled it under my feet. . . . At length, alas! I beheld the strong wall broken down, the garden wall destroyed, the mound left defenceless, and no hope left of returning peace to my afflicted soul![126]

In the Song of Solomon, the king was describing his beloved: "A garden inclosed is my sister, my spouse; a spring shut up, a fountain sealed" (Song of Solomon 4:12). In the book of Proverbs, "I went by the field of the slothful, and by the vineyard of the man void of understanding; And, lo, it was all grown over with thorns, and nettles had covered the face thereof, and the stone wall thereof was broken down" (Proverbs 24:30-31), is the sort of common-sense prudence that Benjamin Franklin would have delighted in. It appears to me that Fothergill was using these figures of speech to refer to his early rebellion against the "fence" or "wall" of strict Quaker discipline.

In a letter to his wife, describing his travels in the southern American colonies, Samuel Fothergill misquoted a biblical passage, subtly, but with the effect that he turned its meaning upside down:

> Accommodations were scarce enough, though we made shift to get into some cabin or other at nights, but had not my clothes off for several nights successively, or anything at times to lie down upon but a bear skin or boards; but sufficient was the day for the evil thereof. I was favoured with a state of perfect good health.[127]

Jesus' saying was actually, "Sufficient unto the day is the evil thereof" (Matthew 6:34). The context makes it clear that he was advising against "borrowing trouble": we have enough problems to deal with right now, without adding to them by worrying about the future. Fothergill interchanged the subject of the sentence and the object of the preposition, and made it into an expression of gratitude that he had been spared consequences more serious than the discomforts of the moment.

I find it noteworthy that Samuel Fothergill saw no significance in the rootage of the biblical writings in the concrete events of history. He used the Bible as a storehouse of sayings, to be appropriated for their rhetorical impact or for their usefulness in justifying or reinforcing the Quaker way of life, to which he was committed.

Job Scott, a Quietist Friends minister in New England Yearly Meeting, was born in Providence, Rhode Island, in 1751. He noted that "my parents . . . were accounted honest people, though my father made but little profession of religion. My mother was more zealous, and attended Friends meetings when she conveniently could."[128] His mother died when he was ten years old.

> As I grew to fifteen and upwards, in violation to clear inward convictions, in opposition to the dictates of the Holy Spirit, I began to run into company, learned to dance and play at cards, and took great delight therein. . . .
>
> My Father sometimes reproved me in those days for my conduct; but sinning against divine light and visitation, hardened me against his advice. I grew more and more vain, proud, airy and wanton. . . .
>
> Thus I went on frolicking and gaming, and spending my precious time in vanity.[129]

For a time Job Scott was attracted to the Baptists and attended Baptist church services. In 1770, when he was nineteen, he finally began attending Friends meetings regularly. He first spoke in Meeting in 1774; by 1776 he had begun traveling in the ministry.

In 1774 Job Scott began teaching children in Friends schools. In 1780 he married Eunice Anthony. He made trips in the ministry to Friends—at first within New England, next to New York, and then to New Jersey and Pennsylvania. In 1789 and early 1790 he made an extended trip to Friends going as far south as Georgia. His wife died in 1791. When he next made a trip to Friends in Connecticut, "I took a solemn leave of the family (that is, my father-in-law Daniel Anthonys) living in my house, and in whose family I left my own father, and my two youngest children."[130] In December 1792 he sailed to Europe and began visiting Friends in the British Isles. While in Ireland he came down with smallpox; he died of that disease in Ballitore, Ireland, November 1793. His *Journal* was published in Rhode Island in 1798.

A significant passage in his *Journal* was this:

For the want of close attention to the word of divine life in my own soul, I made a blunder in my publick testimony, which greatly humbled me, and made me very careful and watchful afterwards. O! it is good to trust in the Lord with all our hearts, not leaning to our own understandings. It was relying too much on my own understanding and memory which brought this great anxiety upon me. And I record it for future caution, mean-while beseeching God Almighty to preserve me, and all his true gospel ministers in the right line of safety and divine qualification, which is in and with the opening of the Spirit, and with the understanding also.[131]

This distrust of natural reasoning when speaking in meeting is a typical Quietist emphasis; it came out time and again in Scott's *Journal*. Many times during his travels he felt "closed up" and unable to speak, because he felt no opening from God—even though he believed Friends were longing to hear what a visiting minister would have to say.

Just as Anthony Benezet and John Churchman, with the support of John Woolman and Samuel Fothergill, had refused to pay war taxes during the French and Indian War, Job Scott was one of the Friends who refused to pay war taxes during the American Revolutionary War—and who even carried the peace testimony a step or two further. In 1775, it being a time of war, and preparations for war between Great-Britain and America, and the rulers of America having made a paper currency professedly for the special purpose of promoting or maintaining said war; and it being expected that Friends would be tried by requisitions for taxes, principally for the support of war; I was greatly exercised in spirit, both on the account of taking and passing said money, and in regard to the paying of such taxes, neither of which felt easy to my mind. I believed a time would come when christians would not so far contribute to the encouragement and support of war and fightings, as voluntarily to pay taxes that were mainly, or even in considerable proportion, for defraying the expenses thereof; and it was also impressed upon my mind, that if I took and passed the money that I knew was made on purpose to uphold war, I should not bear a testimony against war, that for me, as an individual, would be a faithful one.[132]

It did not take long for him to come to a decision on the matter:

After some strugglings, and a length of close exercise attended with much inward looking to the Lord for direction and support, I was enabled to cast my care upon him, and to risk myself and my all for his service, come whatever might come, or suffer whatever I might suffer, in consequence thereof. I was well aware of many arguments and objections against attending to such scruples; and some seemingly very plausible ones, from several passages of scripture, especially respecting taxes; but I believed I saw them all to arise from a want of clear understanding respecting the true meaning of said passages; and I knew I had no worldly interest, ease, or honour, to promote, by an honest attention to what I believed were the reproofs and convictions of divine instruction.[133]

In 1778 he was put to the test:

An old acquaintance of mine, being now collector of rates, came and demanded one of me. I asked him what it was for? He said, to sink the paper money. I told him, as that money was made expressly for the purpose of carrying on war, I had refused to take it; and for the same reason could not pay a tax to sink it, believing it my duty to bear testimony against war and fighting. . . . He appeared moderate, thoughtful, and rather tender; and after a time of free and pretty full conversation upon the subject, went away in a pleasant disposition of mind, I being truly glad to see him so. Divers such demands were made of me in those troublesome times for divers years.[134]

Job Scott's reflections on these events were remarkably full of biblical language:

> The Lord, who is ever attentive to the good of souls and the exaltation of his kingdom, is on his way, and truth will more fully break forth; righteousness will come into dominion; the mountain of the Lord's house will surely be established above all the other mountains; but many of the called, through want of faithful attention to the call, may never become the chosen, and so never come forth valiantly in the testimony, nor stand immovable, nor triumph victoriously, in the Lamb's warfare.[135]

Such a passage, culminating in an appeal to the Lamb's War theme, suggests the extent to which Job Scott was intending to read the Bible through a seventeenth-century Quaker lens. He was also seeking to confirm the peace testimony in the context of the corporate life of the Quaker community:

> At our yearly meeting this year, 1779, the subject of Friends paying taxes for war came under solid consideration. Friends were unanimous, that the testimony of truth, and of our society, was clearly against our paying such taxes as were wholly for war; and many solid Friends manifested a lively testimony against the payment of those in the mixture; which testimony appeared evidently to me to be on substantial grounds, arising and spreading in the authority of truth. It was a time of refreshment to an exercised number, whose spirits I trust were feelingly relieved, in a joyful sense of the light which then sprung up among us. On the whole, I am renewedly confirmed, that . . . the Lord will raise up a band of faithful followers, who, preferring Jerusalem's welfare to their chiefest joy, will press through the crowd of reasonings, and follow the Lamb whithersoever he leadeth them.[136]

At several points in his *Journal*, Job Scott looked to people in the Bible, from Abraham to Jesus, as examples for Christian living. As a young boy sitting with his mother in Meeting, "I even had longing desires to become truly religious, and to serve and fear God, as Abraham Isaac and Jacob did, and others that I read or heard of."[137] When he moved with his family in 1782 from Providence to Gloucester, eighteen miles away, "I fully expected to return again some time or other, but did not know when it might be.

I remembered the movements of Abraham, Isaac, and Jacob, and in the recollection thereof, a degree of solid satisfaction was afforded me."[138] On his journey to the southern states, in Virginia,

> I was at Caroline meeting, silent here also, and more painful and distressing than any I had been at in this journey before. I remembered the account of Christ's agony, his sweating as it were drops of blood, and crying out to his heavenly Father, "My God, my God, why hast thou forsaken me!" [Matt. xxvii. 46] I saw the propriety of his passing through this trying scene: and I believed it necessary for me to go through that proportion of sufferings assigned me: and though he passed through this for our sakes, he . . . set us an example of faith, patience, and perseverance through all; and that he might both feel and manifest this resignation in the most conspicuous manner possible, he was so far stripped as to feel as if he was forsaken; yet even in this extremity, though as man, he was ready to wish the cup to pass from him, yet he centered in—"not my will, but thine be done." [Luke xxii. 42.] I saw that there was no way for me to get rightly along, but through the like submission.[139]

He similarly looked to the experiences of biblical people as evidence of God's love and care for us:

> My mind was livingly opened to a fresh and humbling sense of the unspeakable love and goodness of God to poor, frail, finite man, in ancient days—particularly I was bowed in consideration of his wonderful dealings with Noah; and how he was with him in the ark; and how he taught him to prepare it for his own and family's preservation: how he was with Abraham when he left his father's house at his command, and went forth not knowing whither he was to go: also how he was with Israel in Egypt, through the Red sea, the wilderness, and Jordan; with David, when he fled from Saul, being hunted as a partridge upon the mountains; with Jonah, in the whale's belly; with Daniel, in the lion's den; and the three children, in the fiery furnace; with his own well beloved son, in the great trials and temptations which he was led through in the wilderness and among men: also how he was with the apostles, and supported them when men rose up against them; and through all their perils by sea and land, and by and among false brethren. What shall I say? he hath ever been a sanctuary and safe hiding place for the righteous in all ages, and remains to be so still; and as truly and powerfully so

now as ever.—And as my mind was thus led and opened, earnest breathings were begotten in me, that we of the present generation, who have known his loving kindness, may walk worthy of the continuance thereof, and never distrust his care and providence.[140]

A book by Job Scott on baptism in the New Testament was published during the final year of his life. His argument was long-winded, with close attention to every minute detail of the evidence in the New Testament. A key point in his argument was the idea that God's revelation came through in a series of states or dispensations, each of which replaced the preceding one:

It was necessary, that in the course of God's divine Providence, and divers dispensations, he who was to go *before* our Lord in the *power and spirit of Elias*, thus to prepare his way, should be sent seasonably to begin and *"fulfil his course,"* in that ministration and *baptism* which was in order to the manifestation of the great gospel baptizer, *before* the publication of that word which *began* from Galilee, *after* his baptism.[141]

And even though John should sit higher, shine brighter, and be far greater in the kingdom of eternal glory, than many of these, yet *as* the Baptist, *or baptizer in water,* he was under a dispensation that was vastly *low* in comparison of that pure gospel state which these *little* ones all witness in the *new covenant dispensation;* which water baptism could no more be a part of, or belong to, than circumcision, burnt offerings, or any other rituals of the Mosaic dispensation. And if *Moses*, however faithful in all his house, as a servant, must as to his law of ceremonials, his dispensation of signs and shadows, *decrease* and give place to the Son, surely so must *John*.[142]

I presume that Job Scott, like Ralph Sandiford, picked up the concept from William Penn that God's revelation came about in a series of dispensations in the course of history.

Job Scott was clearly concerned about the right understanding of scripture. He wrote:

The Scriptures, other good books, religious conversation, contemplation upon the works of creation and providence; all these are very good means of information; but none of them, nor even all of them, without the Holy Spirit's sealing operation and evidence upon the mind, can ever make a man sure of his duty to God in any one thing. . . . It may be said the scriptures are certain. Very well, but what certifies thee that they are certain, or that thou knowest their meaning? Do not the professed masters in reasoning widely differ upon many passages in the sacred writings? they all say they have reason on their side. But believe them not: nor believe that any thing is or can be certainly known to man, of the divine authority of the scriptures, without the light and evidence of the Holy Spirit.[143]

And again, during his final visit to Ireland: "The scriptures are good, very good; discipline, good rules, and good order, all very necessary; but still it is the spirit that quickens and giveth life."[144] We are again hearing him echo themes from seventeenth-century Friends, such as James Nayler: "None can rightly understand the Scriptures, but they who read them with the same spirit that gave them forth; for 'the natural man understands not the things of God, for they are spiritually discerned' (I Corinthians 2:14)."[145] In a book published thirty years after his death, Scott gave some suggestions for reading scriptures with the aid of the Holy Spirit:

The safe state is that of a careful, inward waiting for direction, looking to the Lord for help, in times of awful silence and profound stillness before him, and in reading the Scriptures, and other books, or in viewing the works of creation and Providence. God alone can give the right turn and direction to our minds, and profitably influence our thoughts, meditations, inferences, conclusions, and devotions in any of these times and occasions. Haste is almost always dangerous, but waiting on the Lord for clearness, direction and qualification is always safe, and never, if rightly exercised, fruitless.[146]

Job Scott apparently carried this idea of spiritually discerning the things of God a step further, in his reference to "the spiritual import, meaning, and mystery of many passages"[147] in the scriptures:

It has been gradually from time to time opened and sealed on my mind, that a part of the scriptures, which many generally understand to speak only of outward things, may be understood by the truly enlightened to convey inward and spiritual instruction.[148]

It is obvious to the enlightened mind, that many passages in scripture have both an outward or literal, and an inward and mystical meaning.[149]

Job Scott also picked up on some thoughts of Samuel Fisher:

> There are Prophets, and Men Moved, Led and Guided, by Gods infallible Spirit, that by it are fitted . . . to open Scripture; nor was it ever since it was a Scripture more opened by this Infallible Spirit, then now it is, and soon to be; yet for all this, men that have no more then the outward *Moses*, and the Prophets, do not Believe, nor Repent, because they listen not to the Light within, that calls for doing to all as they would be done by, which is the *Law* and the *Prophets*, saith Christ, *Mat. 7.*[150]

And so—on listening to the Light within—Scott insisted:

> As soon as they *know any thing* as they *ought*, they see and know that they knew nothing by or of themselves; but are altogether beholden to a spiritual discerning from the divine light shining in their hearts, to give them this knowledge. Hence says the apostle, 'God, who commanded the light to shine out of darkness, hath shined (take notice where this shining is) in our hearts, to give the light of the knowledge of the glory of God in the face of Jesus Christ.' (2 Cor. iv. 6.)[151]

Job Scott concluded: "The scriptures will ever remain in a great degree a sealed book to the mere natural understandings of the wisest of men."[152] He went on to ponder on the opening of the seals, in the book of Revelation:

> There is the *one thing needful* wanting, which, while it is *wanting, cannot be numbered*; for indeed we can never number or perceive it clearly, truly and fully, so long as the *seventh seal* remains unopened to us. For until they are all opened, we shall ever be liable to be guessing, contriving, inventing. . . . Those to whom they are opening and opened, know they have their opening here in time progressively: but this is only as God is *waited upon*. . . . In this attentive, single, waiting state, deep mysteries are opened. . . . In this work of redemption, renovation, and removal of the seals, (for it goes on gradually together) the Lord who is light in himself, and ever dwells in the light, that is, in his own essence, appears to our minds as breaking through the clouds.[153]

Great part of the Revelations, as well as other mysterious scriptures, is livingly known in the work and progress of regeneration. . . . The scripture is a sealed book; it is abundantly wrapped up in parable, metaphor, and mystery—yea many, very many things in it, which men whose minds are outward will read and understand of outward things, are mainly meant of internal operations, discoveries, and overturnings, which God in his dealings with the soul, leads it along through. He that hath an ear, let him hear.[154]

But just as for the first Friends the outcome and test of spiritual enlightenment was a high standard of ethical, righteous living, "doing to all as they would be done by," so for Job Scott the heart of the unfolding mystery was not some sort of esoteric consciousness, but perseverance in ethical living, even in the face of suffering and persecution:

> After these sore trials are in a good degree endured, the fifth seal opens, and brings to view the persevering follower of the Lamb, the *holy altar*, and under it the "souls of those that were slain for the word of God, and the testimony which they held," ver. 9. Here the state of sufferings and persecutions, endured by the righteous, is seen, and also the state of rejoicing and triumph which follows after: for here they are heard, availingly calling on the Almighty God, holy and true, for judgment.[155]

Even though Job Scott, as a good Quietist, sought to avoid "relying too much on my own understanding" in religious matters (particularly on speaking in meeting), and though he insisted that "the Holy Spirit's sealing operation and evidence upon the mind, . . . the light and evidence of the Holy Spirit" is essential to properly understanding the meaning of scripture (in contrast to the "professed masters in reasoning," who "say they have reason on their side"), I found him on at least a couple of occasions making use of rational arguments or using critical reasoning, when he dealt with scripture. One occasion was his review of his teenage wavering between Baptists and Friends. He wrote there, referring to the "Great Commission" (Matthew 28:19-20):

> Thus the apostles fulfilled the commission. They taught baptizingly. The commission is not "teach, and then baptize," as two separate acts. It is "teach, baptizing"—and those who livingly witness the *gospel*, the power of God to salvation, preached unto them, they feel it, and receive it in, and only in "the Holy Ghost, sent down from heaven," they are "taught baptizingly, in the demonstration of the spirit and of power." [I Cor. ii. 4.] And no preaching has a whit more of the gospel in it, than it has of the Holy Ghost, the alone

166

true baptizing power. I don't marvel that the letter-learned teachers of our day, who run unsent, who are *always ready*, are ignorant that a true gospel minister is clothed with baptizing authority from on high. . . . Of the subject of baptism, . . . there is and can be but *one* in the gospel, and that this is and must be spiritual.[156]

On a later occasion, he wrote:

I cannot believe or conceive it probable, or even consistent with the truth of God, or of the very mystery of divine things, that Christ, after his crucifixion, descended into hell; yet I have no doubt that, in the course of his sufferings and agony, he really did feel, endure, and also conquer the force, and power, and pains of hell.[157]

(Many commentators had found—and still do find—biblical evidence for Christ's descent into hell in Ephesians 4:9: "Now that he ascended, what is it but that he also descended first into the lower parts of the earth?" [KJV] and 1 Peter 3:18-20: "Christ also hath once suffered for sins, . . . being put to death in the flesh, but quickened by the Spirit: By which also he went and preached unto the spirits in prison; Which sometime were disobedient, when once the long-suffering of God waited in the days of Noah" [KJV].) Here, even though he lacked Samuel Fisher's formal theological and biblical education, Job Scott was attempting the sort of critical reasoning that Fisher had used in his interpretation of the Bible.

One paragraph shows just how far Job Scott had gone beyond his Quietist heritage:

By asserting the absolute inadequacy of reason, unassisted by Divine influence, to discover Divine truths or the meaning of parables and deep mysteries, ever designed by Eternal Wisdom to be hid from mere creaturely wisdom, it is not at all intended, nor indeed implied, either that these are in the least inconsistent with reason, or that reason is not to be an assistant in propagating truth. On the contrary it is our rational faculties, that receive the illuminations of Divine light, and being thereby rectified, are brought to comprehend, in a greater or less degree, what this light is, and the certainty and reality of its teachings: that it is truly Divine, an emanation from God, the very life of the Eternal Holy Word, and that its teachings are all perfectly agreeable to the mind and will of God.[158]

Here we no longer have pure Quietism's absolute distrust of the use of reason in the spiritual life.

The eighteenth-century leaders among Friends—ministers and elders— were united in their commitment to a Quietist spirituality. The reformers, including John Woolman, Anthony Benezet, John Churchman, Samuel Fothergill, and Job Scott, were also united in their ethical stance; they insisted on enforcing the traditional Quaker moral standards and also on pushing beyond these in the direction of abolishing slavery within the Society of Friends and of refusing to pay taxes for war. These same Friends varied widely in their approaches to interpreting the Bible. How to read and understand the Bible was not a crucial issue for them; they enjoyed deep friendships and spiritual unity in spite of their differences in this area. Friends in the next generation became convinced that these differences did matter: greatly, vitally—disastrously.

5

The Hicksite-Orthodox Separation

Throughout the eighteenth century, Friends appealed to Robert Barclay's *Apology* as the decisive authority on Quaker theology. Quietist Friends found support from Barclay in their distrust of reason in the religious life: Barclay referred to "the carnal mind, which is at enmity with God;"[1] and he asked, "Why need we set up our own carnal and corrupt reason for a guide to us in matters spiritual?"[2] He also complained: "As to reason, I shall not need to say much; for whence come all the controversies, contentions and debates in the world, but because every man thinks he follows right reason?"[3]

But Barclay could also be referenced in support of the use of reason as a way to test claims that Friends are actually being guided by the Holy Spirit:

> We then trust to and confide in this Spirit, because we know, and certainly believe, that it can only lead us aright, and never mislead us; and from this certain confidence it is that we affirm, that no revelation coming from it can ever contradict the scripture's testimony nor right reason, not as making this a more certain rule to ourselves,

but as condescending to such, who not discerning the revelations of the Spirit, as they proceed purely from God, will try them by these mediums.[4]

In addition, William Penn claimed that philosophers, even before Christ, had come to true knowledge of God through the use of reason:

Socrates, That *Good Heathen,* if, without Offence to the Professors of Christianity, I may say so, not only confesseth to *One God,* but, I am of Opinion, they will think he gives good Reason why he doth so.[5]

Plato, the famous Doctor of *Gentile-Divinity,* Scholar to *Socrates,* whom the *Greeks* for his Heavenly Contemplation, and Pious Life, sirnam'd, *Divine,* gives us his Faith of God in these Words, . . . *He is said to be* GOOD, *because he bestows his Benefits upon all.* . . . By all which it is as evident, how True, how Reasonable, and how Firm a Belief *Plato* had, of *One Eternal Being and Father of all.*[6]

The eighteenth century has been called the "Age of Reason"; a major movement in that century was the Enlightenment, led by thinkers such as Voltaire, Benjamin Franklin, Thomas Jefferson, and Thomas Paine. Many practiced a religion with a foundation of reason rather than one of revelation.

When Job Scott claimed that reason could be of use in coming to know truth about God, was he influenced solely by words from Barclay and Penn and by Samuel Fisher's use of critical reason in studying the Bible? Or had he also caught some of the spirit of the Enlightenment from the thought-world around him? I cannot at this point answer the question; but it is clear that, by the end of the eighteenth century, an increasing number of Friends—especially younger and rural Friends—were being moved by Enlightenment thinking. A few were even identifying the Light Within with the light of reason.

Many other Friends were being swept up in a contrary trend: the Evangelical Movement, founded in large part by the preaching of John Wesley. In the religious fervor of the Methodists they saw a resurgence of the enthusiasm of the first Friends. The Evangelicals' insistence on correct doctrine reminded them of the intensely Christ-centered character of early Quakerism. Friends, especially in England, found such Evangelical leaders as John Wesley, Granville Sharp, William Wilberforce, and Thomas Clarkson to be valuable allies in their struggle to abolish slavery.

Job Scott spent the final two weeks of his life, ill with smallpox, in the home of a Quaker widow, Elizabeth Shackleton, in Ballitore, Ireland. Elizabeth's stepson, Abraham Shackleton (1752-1818), was headmaster of Ballitore School, which had been founded by his grandfather. A sensitive Quietist elder, "Abraham Shackleton may have been influenced, and was certainly strengthened, by the visit of a saintly . . . Friend, Job Scott."[7] War clouds were gathering, in reaction to the French Revolution; in 1796, "the always smoldering resentment of the Irish against the English flared up in a protest against conscription."[8] Armed rebellion soon broke out in Ireland.

In the midst of this turmoil, Abraham Shackleton became convinced that God could not have commanded certain immoral acts as reported in the Old Testament. In particular, he insisted that God could not really have commanded the utter destruction of the Canaanites in war; belief that God had done so was "highly derogatory of the character of the unchangeable God."[9] He could not believe that the loving God revealed in the New Testament, the God who commanded Friends to abstain from all war, could ever have commanded anything so horrible as war, cruelty, or vengeance. Therefore, Shackleton insisted, some passages in the Old Testament could in no way claim to be "holy" or the authoritative word of God. In 1797 he became involved in a discussion with another elder, Samuel Woodcock, who insisted that it was "an essential article of Christian faith" to believe that the Hebrew wars "were undertaken by the express command of God."[10]

In spite of the reforms achieved by Friends like Woolman, Benezet, and Fothergill, toward the end of the eighteenth century many ministers and elders were still feeling discouraged about the spiritual health of the Quaker community. Quite a few came to contrast the lukewarmness within Quakerism with the fervor and vitality that they saw in the Evangelical Movement. They were impressed by the similarities between the spiritual power of seventeenth-century Quakerism and of eighteenth-century evangelicalism. Believing that evangelicalism *was* true Christianity, they became evangelicals themselves and strove to restore Quakerism to its original evangelical purity.

One of these evangelical Friends was David Sands, a minister from New York Yearly Meeting. He made an extensive visit to Ireland in the 1790s where he found much support among Irish Friends. But he also met strong opposition. Abraham Shackleton did agree with the evangelicals in diagnosing the situation: "Shackleton deeply felt that the religious Society to which he belonged was in a low and declined spiritual state, that the inner life and power had waned, that external forms of discipline and custom had come into sway in an unbearable degree."[11] He believed, however, that the evangelicals were part of the problem, not part of the solution: "He felt that Friends had declined spiritually and were trying to restore the Society's spiritual life by going back to old doctrines and creeds, rather than returning to true Quaker principles."[12] A considerable number of Irish Friends shared Shackleton's reaction to evangelicalism. They were intuitively aware of important differences between evangelicalism and early Quakerism.

I am able to clarify a couple of these differences by using the word-study tools provided in Earlham School of Religion's Digital Quaker Collection. I begin with words that David Sands used in his preaching: "Christ Jesus your Saviour and Redeemer; he who suffered his precious blood to flow to wash away your sins."[13] Searching through Robert Barclay's *Apology*, the eight-volume *Works of George Fox*, and the *Collection of the Works of William Penn*, I found *no* examples of the phrase "precious blood." (Even though Fox and Penn fairly frequently used the adjective "precious.") I could find only two passages with even slight resemblance to Sands' wording: "The blood of Christ . . . doth redeem, and wash, and cleanse, and purify from all sin," by George Fox;[14] and "Entertain Him in thy Soul, that He may wash thee, and cleanse thee by *His Own Spirit*, and by *His Own Water*, and by *His Own Blood*," by William Penn.[15] At the very least, it appears that Sands was living quite a different spirituality from Fox, Penn, and Barclay. (Curiously enough, my concordance turned up nothing like "suffered his precious blood to flow" in the King James Version of the Bible; the closest to "suffered his precious blood . . . to wash away your sins" was in Revelation 1:5—"Jesus Christ . . . loved us, and washed us from our sins in his own blood"—which was echoed by Penn and Fox at least as closely as by Sands.)

An even more telling sign of innovation in Quaker doctrine can be seen in an account of David Sands's travels among Irish Friends, supplied by his editor: that he believed himself "called upon to unite with the sound Friends in earnestly contending for the faith of the gospel, against those who denied the Godhead of Christ, and the efficacy of his propitiatory sacrifice."[16] The editor observed that a while later, in England,

> the Society generally was too well persuaded and convinced of the importance of faithfully maintaining our testimony to the doctrine of the Godhead of Christ, and his propitiatory sacrifice; and of the Divine authority and inspiration of the Scriptures of truth, to be greatly shaken.[17]

The phrase, "propitiatory sacrifice," central for the Irish and English evangelical Friends, appeared in the published *Works of George Fox* only twice—both times in quotations from non-Quaker opponents whom he was refuting. The phrase did not appear at all in William Penn's *Collection of the Works*, and only twice in Robert Barclay's *Apology*—once as a summary of Roman Catholic teaching about the Eucharist, and once, in passing, as part of his arguments against the predestination of many souls to eternal damnation.

Shackleton and his Irish allies rejected the outside influence of evangelicalism. They were, however, immersed in Enlightenment thinking and convinced of the importance of reason in dealing with religious questions. These were underlying issues as the dispute between Abraham Shackleton and Samuel Woodcock came before their Yearly Meeting:

> The national Yearly Meeting of Ireland for 1798 emphasized the necessity of keeping "unity in faith and principle," and was "sorrowfully convinced that a disposition hath appeared tending to weaken the general testimony, which we as a people have maintained, as to the origin, use and advantage of these records [Scriptures]." The body of Friends at this time expressed the judgment that "a standard should be lifted up against the spirit of speculation and unbelief," and that Friends who "persist in maintaining such sentiments and doctrines and do not condemn their conduct" should be disowned.[18]

By 1801, Abraham Shackleton and his supporters had all been disowned or had voluntarily withdrawn from their meetings.

In 1799 Hannah Barnard, an outspoken Friend from New York Yearly Meeting, was traveling in the ministry and came to Ireland, where she met Abraham Shackleton and recognized that his views corresponded with some questions she was beginning to ask. Controversy followed her from Ireland to England:

> She challenged the Old Testament's assertions that God had commanded the Israelites to carry on bloody warfare against their enemies. At no time, she affirmed, had "the great and merciful Creator ever commissioned any nation or person to destroy another"; war occurred because of human passions, not divine authorization.[19]

She was asked what she believed about the virgin birth of Jesus, and replied that "it had not been revealed to her."[20] Disciplinary proceedings began with a refusal in England to grant her request to continue into

Germany on her travels in the ministry, and concluded in 1802 when her home monthly meeting disowned her.

Henry Tuke (1755-1814) of York, England, worked with his father, William Tuke, in founding The Retreat, a pioneering mental hospital, and in operating a grocery business. "As an adjunct to the grocery, a chocolate factory was set up,"[21] which many decades later became famous, after it passed into the hands of the Quaker Rowntree family. In 1801 Henry Tuke published a small volume "of carefully chosen excerpts from the writings of early Friends, the selections being chosen with the obvious purpose of proving that the founders and early leaders of Quakerism were evangelical and orthodox Christians."[22]

In 1805 he published a book that he himself wrote: *The Principles of Religion, as Professed by The Society of Christians, Usually Called Quakers*. In his "Introduction," he suggested that the book was needed because "the ample and excellent *Apology* of Robert Barclay, is too diffuse for the generality of young readers; and it requires a more close and patient attention than many are willing to bestow."[23] He continued:

> With respect to those principles which are peculiar to our Religious Society, I hope that, however singular they may appear to some, they will, on close examination, be found consistent with the nature and spirit, of the gospel. . . . I trust, we are able to give such reasons for our dissent from other Christians, as may, at least, excuse it to those from whom we differ.[24]

Actually, his purpose was much more ambitious. He was one of many leaders in London Yearly Meeting who felt that the preaching of Friends such as Abraham Shackleton and Hannah Barnard was a dangerous threat to the Christian faith of the Quaker community. Twentieth-century evangelical Quaker missionary, educator, and historian, Walter Williams, noted that Henry Tuke "labored at the very opening of the nineteenth century to turn back the tide of unsound doctrine," and that in his *Principles of Religion*,

> written at a critical moment in Friends history, the author was seeking to aid his contemporaries in avoiding the errors of unbelief which were threatening his beloved Society. He brought to the reader's attention the cardinal evangelical doctrines of the New Testament. This work proved helpful to multitudes. It became at once a "best seller" among Friends. By the middle of the nineteenth century it had passed through twelve English editions, and had been printed

by several of the American Yearly Meetings as well. . . . It was used of God to steady the faith of many while the storm of threatened unbelief raged on.[25]

Henry Tuke was clearly arguing that the principles of Quakerism were solidly based on the scriptures. I can readily see the ways in which he carried out this argument:

> The Scriptures inculcate those principles of piety and morality, which contribute to the happiness of mankind, both here and hereafter; and there is not any general duty, religious or moral, in which they do not afford instruction and direction. [26]

He wrote of "considering the Scriptures, and endeavouring to build systems upon them."[27] After quoting John 1:1-4 and John 1:14, he went on: "Here we have a clear and full testimony both to the Divinity and the humanity of Christ; and we have, ever since we were a people, borne testimony to this Scripture doctrine."[28] He referred to "those arguments, which the miracles performed by Christ and his apostles, afford for the truth of the Christian religion."[29]

Tuke wrote that "the gift of the Holy Spirit . . . is a doctrine on which we insist."[30] He went on:

> In considering this subject, it may be proper to advance and support the following positions:
>
> 1. The necessity of the assistance of the Holy Spirit, for understanding the things, and for working the works, of God. . . .
>
> With regard to the first position, the apostle Paul argues the case so forcibly, and with such logical clearness, that I shall quote his words, both as the best arguments and the best authority, that can be adduced on the occasion.[31]

He set down, as a general principle: "An attention to the examples and precepts recorded in the Holy Scriptures . . . also justifies our [Quakers'] conduct."[32] Specifically, he had stated that, in Matthew 10:8-14, "We have directions for the conduct of the ministers of Christ."[33]

In a grand summary, Tuke proclaimed: "The holy Scriptures are the blessed means of introducing us to an acquaintance with the way of life and salvation, and of affording us much instruction in our various duties to God, and one to another."[34]

If Robert Barclay and William Penn took the first steps away from George Fox's, Margaret Fell's, and Edward Burrough's empathetic reading of the Bible by using Bible passages as steps in careful, logical arguments, or by seeing the Bible as a handbook, a collection of resources and guidelines for Christian faith and life, then Henry Tuke reached the destination of that path. The Bible has become the authoritative textbook, providing—sometimes by explicit example, but more characteristically in propositional form—the basic premises from which we can logically deduce the doctrines of a system of Christian theology and the principles of a system of Christian ethics.

In contrast, Job Scott, Abraham Shackleton, and Hannah Barnard had barely begun to venture out on the trail that had briefly been blazed by Samuel Fisher—the trail of bold questioning and careful analysis that we know today as biblical criticism.

Tuke had to account for situations or issues "where there is an apparent difference between one part of scripture and another."[35] He began with the principle "that scripture is the best interpreter of scripture."[36] We can see how he applied this principle in connection with the Quaker practice

> that we admit women, as well as men, to a participation and exercise of the gift of gospel ministry. We are aware of the objection which is made, from the prohibition laid upon women speaking and teaching in the church, and usurping authority over the man. [1 Tim. ii. 11-15][37]

Even though he referred to "John Locke's note on Cor. xi. 3,"[38] he made no attempt to follow either Josiah Martin or Benjamin Coole in their discussion of Locke's solution to the discrepancies. Instead, he referred to "the admission of the female sex, in early times, to the work and service of the gospel," and went on to his controlling passage:

> This was expressly foretold in such a manner, as would, if we had no precedent, fully warrant the practice: for on this subject we may use the words of the apostle Peter, and say: "This is that which was spoken by the prophet Joel: And it shall come to pass in the last days, saith God, I will pour out of my Spirit upon all flesh, and your sons and your *daughters* shall prophesy; and your young men shall see visions, and your old men shall dream dreams: and on my servants, and on my *handmaidens*, I will pour out in those days of my Spirit, and they shall prophesy." [Acts ii. 16 to 18][39]

Tuke also appealed to numerous women in the Old and New Testaments who were "engaged in the work of the ministry, . . . partakers of the effusions of the Holy Spirit, . . . prophetesses or fellow-labourers with the apostles in the Gospel of Christ," including, among others, Deborah,

> and Huldah, . . . Anna, a prophetess in the Jewish Church, publicly exercising her gift in the Temple; and hailing the recent birth of the Messiah. The Samaritan woman, with whom our Saviour held an interesting conversation at Jacob's Well, appears to have been the first of his disciples, who publicly preached the coming of Christ. . . . Women were the first witnesses of our Lord's resurrection, and were commissioned by him to proclaim this important truth to his disciples. . . .
>
> Philip the deacon . . . "had four daughters, which did prophesy." [Acts xxi. 9] . . . Phebe our sister, . . . Priscilla.[40]

Tuke appears to have gone back to George Fox's pamphlet, "The Woman Learning in Silence" for the starting point of his argument and for some examples, and may have taken some more examples from Margaret Fell's *Womens Speaking Justified*.

I find in Henry Tuke's book a continuation of the use of William Penn's idea that God has acted in history through a sequence of dispensations: "These writings are divided into two parts, the Old and the New Testaments. . . . Their object appears to be, to exhibit the various dispensations of God to mankind. . . ."[41] In the scriptures "you may be made acquainted with the dispensation of the law, the predictions of the prophets, the ministration of John, and the most glorious dispensation of the gospel."[42]

What at first looks extraordinary is his extended argument using the concept of dispensations to explain the apparent inconsistency between God commanding bloodthirsty warfare in some parts of the Old Testament and God forbidding violence in the New Testament:

> If some of those who, with myself, consider war altogether incon- sistent with the Christian dispensation, should argue from the unchangeableness of the Divine nature, that the Almighty could not allow of, or enjoin practices, in one age, which are inconsistent in another; it may and ought to be observed, that, in his dispensa- tions to mankind, great variety is evident; and many things which were not only allowed, but commanded, in former times, and under different circumstances, would now be improper.

It also appears, that when our blessed Lord set forth the peace-ableness of the gospel dispensation, he showed that a contrary conduct had been more than permitted in former times; and unless we intend to controvert the propriety of the manner, in which the Author of the Christian religion propagated it, we must allow, that there have been times, in which divers things were lawful that are now unlawful; and thus we may reconcile the consistency of the Jewish wars with the Divine will. "Ye have heard that it hath been said, an eye for an eye, and a tooth for a tooth; but I say unto you, resist not evil." Again, "Ye have heard that it hath been said, Thou shalt love thy neighbour, and hate thine enemy; but I say unto you, Love your enemies," &c. Now, when we consider the expressions just cited, and observe the obvious difference they make between the dispensations of the law and of the Gospel; we may find abundant reason to believe, that it was not inconsistent with the Divine nature and will, to command those things which are related respecting the wars of the Jews. . . .

Let us, therefore, be content with that evidence of the Divine will which is afforded us; and, rather than impugn the former dispensations of God to mankind, be thankful to Him for having introduced one so much more excellent, in which—"Glory to God in the highest," is peculiarly united with—"Peace on earth, and good will to men."

But whilst I have been endeavouring to remove these objections, I have regretted that there should be any necessity, thus to "justify the ways of God to men," as recorded in holy writ, and to endeavour to support the cause of that Omnipotent Being, whose prerogative alone it is—"That he giveth no account of any of his matters." He has, notwithstanding, as far as different circumstances will permit, condescended to adapt his dispensations towards mankind, to those principles of wisdom, justice, and mercy, which are the rules of our conduct towards each other. If, in some instances, we cannot perceive this consistency, the infinite disparity between the Divine Being and his creature man, might reasonably induce us to expect difficulties of this kind; and surely the wisdom, no more than the faith, of those is to be admired, who reject every thing respecting an Infinite Being, that does not comport with their finite capacities. "Canst thou, by searching, find out God? Canst thou find out the

Almighty to perfection? It is as high as heaven; what canst thou do? Deeper than hell; what canst thou know? The measure thereof is longer than the earth, and broader than the sea. If he cut off, and shut up, and gather together, then who can hinder him?" [Job xi. 7.][43]

There can be no doubt: Tuke's intention in these paragraphs was to demolish the arguments of Abraham Shackleton and Hannah Barnard and to justify their disownment. The concept of different divine commands in different dispensations should have answered their questions. But Shackleton, at least, was doubtless familiar with the dispensational explanation—even his friend Job Scott had appealed to this concept in his arguments against water baptism—and found it insufficient to solve his difficulties. The crux of Shackleton's and Barnard's rejection of the Old Testament wars was their conviction that the God revealed by and in Jesus is ultimately loving and merciful. Tuke simply bypassed that issue; his argument presupposed a God who is ultimately the all-powerful authority (a dictator?) and at best condescending toward humans. Tuke's final thrust was that the ultimate inscrutability of God rules out all questioning. In that day (assuming the book of Job was a seamless whole), an astute critic could have pointed out the context of the two quotations from Job that supported that position. Tuke's final quotation was from a speech by Job's friend Zophar, but in the last chapter of the book of Job, God said to their friend Eliphaz, "My wrath is kindled against thee, and against thy two friends: for ye have not spoken of me the thing that is right, as my servant Job hath" (Job 42:7 KJV)—God had directly repudiated Zophar's explanation. "He giveth no account of any of his matters" Job 33:13, is from the speech of Elihu, who had angrily stepped in to criticize Job after his three friends had given up their arguments—but if Job has indeed "spoken of me the thing that is right," this at least calls into question whether Elihu's speeches were to be accepted as the "truth" about God. Tuke's arguments may have satisfied his evangelically-inclined readers, but their effect could only have widened the rift between these Friends and those who supported the views of Shackleton and Barnard.

This rift continued to widen until the fateful years of 1827 and 1828 when it reached a crisis, and the Society of Friends split into two hostile groups. Members of each group refused to recognize that their antagonists even had a right to the name Friends. The events of 1827 and 1828 are usually called The Great Separation. One Friend's name has permanently and notoriously been most closely connected to this widening division and to this Separation: Elias Hicks (1748-1830).

Elias Hicks was born in Hempstead, Long Island, New York. In 1771 he was married to Jemima Seaman in a Quaker wedding at the Meeting House in Westbury, Long Island. Jemima and Elias had eleven sons and daughters; only five of them—all daughters—lived to adulthood. A few months after their marriage, Elias and Jemima moved to the farm belonging to her parents. They lived there where Elias worked as a farmer for the rest of his life.

From the time of their move to Jericho, Elias and Jemima Hicks regularly attended meetings at the Friends meeting house in Jericho—a house that Elias himself helped to build. Jericho Meeting was part of Westbury Monthly Meeting until 1789; that monthly meeting recorded Elias Hicks as a minister in 1778. In 1779 New York Yearly Meeting appointed Elias Hicks and another Friend to travel to Philadelphia Yearly Meeting to seek direction on a matter involving the use of the new meeting house in New York City by British troops occupying the city. During the rest of his life he traveled many times. Some of these trips were under the direction of the yearly meeting; New York Friends clearly valued his service and leadership. Most of the trips occurred when Elias Hicks believed that God had called him to visit specific areas after he sought the meeting's confirmation of his call to that service, and he was granted a traveling minute by Jericho Monthly Meeting.

As early as 1799, Elias Hicks noted that large crowds—sometimes a thousand or more—came when local Friends published the fact that he would attend a meeting specifically appointed for that purpose. He noted in his *Journal* that in 1813,

> we then returned in the evening to Philadelphia; and the next day being the first of the week, and the 6th of 6th month, were at Friends' meeting at Arch-street in the morning, and at the North meeting in the afternoon. Some previous notice having been given of my intention of attending them, they were unusually large; and many had to go away for want of room. It was supposed there were three thousand people at the beginning of the meeting, and toward the close many more than the rooms could contain.[44]

Within the next month, as he appointed meetings in the towns west of Philadelphia, he noted that "many were very large, more than the houses could contain."[45] He made similar reports about many of the meetings appointed in his travels during the remaining seventeen years of his life.

Elias Hicks's final appointed meeting was in Brooklyn, New York, in November, 1829. A ten-year-old boy attended that meeting with his parents.

Nearly sixty years later that boy—the poet Walt Whitman—recorded his vivid memory of the preaching of Elias Hicks:

> After a pause and stillness becoming almost painful, Elias rises and stands for a moment or two without a word. . . . A moment looking around the audience with those piercing eyes, amid the perfect stillness. (I can almost see him and the whole scene now.) Then the words come from his lips, very emphatically and slowly pronounc'd, in a resonant, grave, melodious voice. . . .
>
> The discourse . . . presently becomes very fervid, and in the midst of its fervor he takes the broad-brim hat from his head, and almost dashing it down with violence on the seat behind, continues with uninterrupted earnestness. . . . A pleading, tender, nearly agonizing conviction, and magnetic stream of natural eloquence, before which all minds and natures, all emotions, high or low, gentle or simple, yielded entirely without exception, was its cause, method, and effect. Many, very many were in tears.[46]

Hicks appears to have been a dynamic—perhaps even charismatic—preacher. No wonder he attracted such large crowds and won a devoted following among Friends, particularly younger and rural Friends, but also in a couple of large urban meetings: Wilmington, Delaware, and Green Street in Philadelphia. He carried on a wide-ranging correspondence. Many Friends wanted to know his views on theological issues; they were happy to find that he was adventurous in his thinking but did not insist that they agree with him on every point.

But he faced growing opposition. Many Friends, especially in London Yearly Meeting and among the elders and yearly meeting leadership in Philadelphia, suspected that his views threatened evangelical orthodoxy. They became increasingly alarmed that his popularity would threaten the theological unity that Friends had earlier preserved by disowning mavericks such as Abraham Shackleton and Hannah Barnard.

One of the first Friends to challenge Elias Hicks's orthodoxy was Stephen Grellet. In 1808 New York Yearly Meeting appointed a committee of six Friends to visit local meetings and encourage greater faithfulness in living up to Quaker practices and discipline. Two members of the committee were Elias Hicks (then sixty years old) and Stephen Grellet, a thirty-four-year-old minister. As they traveled together, they found that they differed on one issue of discipline. Grellet believed their obligation was to enforce strict observance of the Sabbath on Sundays; Hicks was a firm believer in the old Quaker tradition that no day should be treated as more holy than any other. Grellet became convinced that their differences ran even deeper:

> Elias Hicks, one of our Committee, frequently advanced sentiments repugnant to the Christian faith, tending to lessen the authority of the Holy Scriptures, to undervalue the sacred offices of our holy and blessed Redeemer, and to promote a disregard for the right observance of the first day of the week. . . . I frequently, fervently, and earnestly laboured with him. He promised that he would be more guarded; but vain promises they were, and several times I felt constrained publicly to disavow the unchristian doctrine that he advanced.[47]

Hicks gave a more optimistic report on these travels: "The faithful were strengthened, and made at times to rejoice together. . . . It was a season of renewed powerful visitation, and manifestation of the Lord's mercy to many."[48] In his *Journal* he did not name any of his traveling companions or refer to any differences among them; for him differences in theology were never vitally important.

The next confrontation came ten years later, in Hicks's own monthly meeting. Thomas Willis was a recorded minister and his wife, Phebe Willis, was an elder—both in Jericho Monthly Meeting. In 1818 they complained to Elias Hicks that he, in his "public communication, lowered down the character of Jesus and the Scriptures of truth." A committee appointed by the meeting tried unsuccessfully to deal with the couple's fears; when Thomas and Phebe Willis remained "persistent in their opposition, they were suspended from the meeting of ministers and elders, but were permitted to retain their membership in the Society."[49]

Between 1820 and 1823, some Friends in Wilmington, Delaware—close friends of Elias Hicks—carried on a controversy with a Presbyterian minister in the pages of a Presbyterian periodical. In their defense of Quakerism, they insisted (with George Fox) that terms such as "Trinity" were unscriptural. Some yearly meeting leaders in Philadelphia were alarmed: these Friends were not following correct procedure of having publications approved by the appropriate body, and they were presenting a view of Quakerism that the leaders believed was not sufficiently evangelical and orthodox. They suspected Elias Hicks of spearheading a movement that threatened the source of true Christianity.

In July 1822, Elias Hicks set out, with a minute from Jericho Monthly Meeting, to visit Friends in Philadelphia and Baltimore Yearly Meetings. On his trip south he went around to the west of Philadelphia. After he attended yearly meeting in Baltimore in October, he headed north, planning to travel through Wilmington and Philadelphia. A number of leading elders and yearly meeting officers in Philadelphia were determined "to prevent Hicks from spreading his message within the city."[50] (This group included Samuel Bettle, clerk of Philadelphia Yearly Meeting, and Jonathan Evans, a Philadelphia elder and former yearly meeting clerk.) Hicks, forewarned of these plans, arrived in Philadelphia December 7, 1822. He began a series of visits to families belonging to Green Street Meeting—a meeting in which he had many supporters. He at first refused a request that he meet with a group of Philadelphia elders; then, at the urging of his Green Street friends, he did agree to meet the elders at Green Street Meeting House on December 12. The elders arrived, intending to hold a private conference with Hicks and his traveling companion. Instead, Elias had a number of witnesses with him—Friends from Green Street and ministers and elders from several meetings outside of Philadelphia. No agreement could be reached on how many Friends should be present. As the elders rose to depart, one of them "flung out, 'The *ministers* are *answerable* to the *Elders*.' . . . Hicks retorted, . . . 'I have a certificate from my *friends at home* and I am *answerable* to them.'"[51] Hicks continued with his family visits and at least one large public meeting in Philadelphia, and left the city on December 25. As he finished his long journey, he reported: "We were favoured to reach our homes with feelings of thanksgiving to our gracious Preserver, and with the enjoyment of that precious peace, which is experienced by those whose minds are stayed on God."[52]

Friends in Great Britain continued to be solidly in the evangelical camp. During the 1820s the ministers from London Yearly Meeting who traveled to America increasingly spoke out in public against what they believed to be a growing tide of unbelief among American Quakers. One English Quaker minister referred to Elias Hicks as "that poor deluded old man." Another "publicly declared that Elias Hicks's teachings were '*diabolical* and *luciferian* and *damnable*.'"[53]

Hicks and his supporters were frequently accused of being deists. Deism is, strictly speaking, the belief that God created the universe but has never intervened in the course of nature or history since the moment of creation. More broadly, the term *deism* can be applied to any belief in God that does not also include a belief in divine revelation. In America, Thomas Paine was the person who most clearly and persuasively set forth the ideas of deism. The beliefs of other Founding Fathers, such as Benjamin Franklin, Thomas Jefferson, James Madison, include at least a modified form of deism. Quaker leaders had been wary of deism for some time. John Churchman in 1773 "had a concern to warn the youth to beware of Deism."[54]

Elias Hicks expressed very similar views; traveling in Virginia in 1798, he had a sense of the

> prevailing of a spirit of great infidelity and deism among the people, and darkness spreading over the minds of many as a thick veil. It was a time in which Thomas Paine's *Age of Reason* (falsely so called) was much attended to in those parts; and some, who were members in our society, as I was informed, were captivated by his dark insinuating address, and were ready almost to make shipwreck of faith and a good conscience.[55]

His view of deism showed up again in a sermon that he preached in 1817:

> All those who presume in their own wills and creaturely wisdom, independent of the teaching of the spirit of God, to know good and evil, do thereby desert God, and so become dead to the divine life; and this is man's fall, and leads to Deism and Atheism.[56]

In 1806 Hicks proposed the best defense against falling into deism or atheism:

> I was led, in a clear manner, to show the ground from whence all this darkness and unbelief proceeded; that it was from a want of due attention to, and right belief in, the *inward manifestation of divine light*, which reveals itself in the heart of man against sin and uncleanness; and at the same time shows what is right, and justifies for right doing. Therefore while men disregard this inward divine principle, of grace and truth, and do not believe in it, as *essential* and *sufficient to salvation;* they are in danger of becoming either Atheists, or Deists.[57]

In 1822 he was still emphasizing the light within as the basic foundation of Christianity,

> setting forth the great declension of the professed Christian Churches, from the simplicity and integrity of the primitive disciples; and showing that it was all brought about by a departure from the only sure foundation of true and real Christianity, the *light within*, or *spirit of truth, the immediate revelation of the spirit of God*, in the

immortal souls of men and women; the only and alone true teacher of the things of God under the gospel.[58]

Again, in an 1825 letter, he zeroed in on the inward gospel that he saw as being essential to salvation: We need to be

> always attentive to that gospel that the Scripture tells us is preached in every creature—not out of them, but in them—by the light and Spirit of God, and is the power of God unto salvation. A belief in, and obedience to this inward gospel and power of God, as all that is essential to our salvation; for this, and this only, can bring us to love God above all, and our neighbours as ourselves, and to love our enemies, and to pray to God for them, and to beat our swords into ploughshares, and spears into pruning hooks, and no more learn war, but be at peace with God, and with all men.[59]

Elias Hicks was deeply influenced by the Enlightenment's emphasis on reason in religion. He did not go to the deists' extreme of throwing out revelation and depending only on reason for our knowledge of God; he insisted rather on the harmony of revelation and reason: "The infinitely wise and perfect God, in creation, has seen fit to make man a rational being, hence all his communications and revelations to him, must and will be rational, and in a way to be rationally understood."[60] It followed, for Hicks, "that we *cannot*, and therefore *are not*, bound to believe what we cannot comprehend."[61] "We cannot believe what we do not understand."[62]

Since the inward light, revealed in the heart, is essential to salvation, and since all revelation must be rational and comprehensible, it followed for Hicks that "that which is essential to the salvation of the souls of the children of men, is certainly dispensed by our common Creator, to every rational creature under heaven."[63]

This conclusion led Hicks to what at first glance might have seemed an unusual twist in his thought: When asked, "Dost thou believe in the miraculous conception of Jesus in the womb of his mother Mary?" he answered, "I had believed it from my youth up to the present time, as far as history and tradition could give belief." He went on to insist that "a belief therein was not an essential to salvation."[64] This was clearly because many humans, even though they have rational minds, have never been acquainted with the biblical account of Jesus' virgin birth. Elias Hicks would have been convinced that this was only a logical conclusion to William Penn's argument that Socrates and Plato had reasoned their way to a true knowledge of God.

Although Hicks believed in the virgin birth of Jesus, he also believed that Jesus did not become the Son of God until the event that occurred at his baptism: "After having finished the law, John's water baptism being the last ritual he had to conform to, he immediately after this received the descendings of the Holy Spirit of God upon him, . . . and by this spiritual birth, became the Son of God with power."[65] This was a point on which he agreed with his closest Wilmington Friend, William Poole:

> As to what thou observes respecting Jesus not being the Son of God, spiritually, until after the baptism of John and descent of the Holy Spirit upon him, it is a subject that appears to be a very simple one, as all truths are, and does not admit of any speculation, as the whole rests upon matter of fact, as recorded in the Scriptures. . . .
>
> After the Holy Spirit descended upon him, and by which he was then more fully the Son of God, and filled with the Divine nature of his Heavenly Father.[66]

This position is very similar to the views of some second- and third-century Christians, often called Adoptionism. Interestingly, the earliest known Adoptionist, named Theodotus, also believed in the virgin birth of Jesus.[67]

Elias Hicks posed a question in his essay against slavery: "Were not the people of Africa . . . possessed of the same natural and unalienable rights, as the people of any other nation?" He replied: "They certainly were."[68] He was a strong and consistent opponent of slavery. He refused to buy or use anything that slaves grew or produced. He was also a strong advocate of the Quaker testimony against war; he refused to pay taxes raised to support the American Revolution and the War of 1812. Even though no Quaker yearly meeting required their members to go to that extent in their opposition to slavery or war, Elias Hicks sharply criticized Friends who did not boycott the products of slavery or withhold taxes for war.

Elias Hicks reported an incident in 1817, which helped him clarify for himself the relative unimportance of correct doctrine:

> We had the company of a Friend in the ministry. . . . He preached the truth to us in a pretty correct manner; but I thought I never saw, with greater clearness than at this time, that ministers might preach the literal truth, and yet not preach the real gospel: and herein is witnessed the truth of that saying of the apostle, that "the *letter*," however true, "*killeth;*" "but the *spirit*," and the spirit only: "*giveth*

life." And it is a great thing when ministers keep in remembrance that necessary caution of the divine Master, not to premeditate what they shall say; but carefully to wait in the nothingness and emptiness of self, that what they speak may be only what the Holy Spirit speaketh in them; then will they not only speak the truth, but the truth, accompanied with power, and thereby profit the hearers.[69]

Hicks was frequently concerned to point out the dangers of misusing scripture—particularly of interpreting them too literally and of depending on them as the *only* rule of faith and practice:

At divers times, when in conversation with hireling teachers, . . . I have given it as my opinion, that so long as they held the Scriptures to be the only rule of faith and practice, and by which they justify wars, hireling ministry, predestination, and what they call the ordinances, viz: water baptism and the passover supper, mere relics of the Jewish law, so long the Scriptures did such, more harm than good; but that the fault was not in the Scriptures, but in their literal and carnal interpretation of them—and that would always be the case until they came to the Spirit that gave them forth.[70]

He especially emphasized the harm that could come from conflicting interpretations of scripture:

When the professors of Christianity began to quarrel with and separate from each other, it all sprang from their different views and different interpretations of passages of Scripture, and to such a pitch did their quarrels arise, as that a recurrence to the sword was soon deemed necessary to settle those disputes.[71]

Hicks liked to contrast the harm done by the misuse of scripture with the good done by its right use:

It is my candid belief, that those that hold and believe the Scriptures to be the only rule of faith and practice, to those it does much more hurt than good. And has any thing tended more to divide Christendom into sects and parties, than the Scriptures? and by which so many cruel and bloody wars have been promulgated. And yet, at the same time, may it not be one of the best books, if rightly used under the guidance of the Holy Spirit?[72]

If the scriptures are not the ultimate rule of faith and practice, what is? Elias Hicks insisted that the Quaker answer is this:

What reproach and inconsistency must attach to every rational being, who makes the high profession that we do, of being led and guided by an unerring principle of light and truth in the mind, as a sufficient and only rule of faith and practice, when such turn back to the letter, and presume to establish a rule from the writings of men in former ages, and so contradict their profession. . . .

The blessed Jesus . . . in his last counsel and command to his immediate followers, turned their attention entirely away from placing any dependance on external evidence, even the best that was ever dispensed to the children of men.[73]

Not the Scriptures but the Spirit of Truth, which Jesus commanded his disciples to wait for, as their only rule, they would teach them all things, and guide them into all truth, is the primary and only rule of faith and practice, and is the only means by which our salvation is effected.[74]

"Principle of light and truth in the mind" and "Spirit of Truth" clearly are synonymous phrases to Hicks; this principle or Spirit is not only the final rule of faith and practice, but also the only way to salvation. Being guided by this principle, which he also called the "light within," is also the only way to properly understand and interpret scripture:

As to the Scriptures of truth; . . . I have always accounted them, when rightly understood, as the best of books extant. I have always delighted in reading them, in my serious moments, in preference to any other book, from my youth up, and have made more use of their contents to confirm and establish my ministerial labours in the gospel, than most other ministers that I am acquainted with. But at the same time, I prize that from which they have derived their origin, much higher than I do them. . . . No man, I conceive, can know or rightly profit by them, but by the opening of the same inspiring spirit, by which they were written, and, I apprehend, I have read them as much as most other men, and few, I believe, have derived more profit from them than I have.[75]

We all might, by faithful attention and adherence to the aforesaid divine principle, *the light within*, come to know and believe the certainty of those excellent scripture doctrines; of the coming, life, righteous works, sufferings, death, and resurrection of Jesus Christ, our blessed pattern: and that *it is by obedience to this inward light only*, that we are prepared for an admittance into the heavenly kingdom.[76]

As Bliss Forbush observed, from a careful reading of Elias Hicks's *Journal*: "The home journal records that he stimulated his spiritual life, in spite of material demands on his time, by spending many evenings in Bible reading."[77]

When Elias Hicks stated that the Holy Spirit or light within, not the Bible, is the primary rule of faith and practice, and when he claimed that we can correctly interpret scripture only through the guidance of the Holy Spirit, he was echoing what any eighteenth-century Friends minister or writer would have affirmed. Yet their togetherness in relying on the Holy Spirit did not result in uniformity in the ways in which these Friends actually read, understood, and interpreted the Bible. I therefore cannot move on from Elias Hicks before I give careful attention to how he in practice made use of the Bible.

Elias Hicks's essay against slavery, published in 1811, contained just two quotations from the Bible. The first was the "Golden Rule":

> I consider it a matter of fact, obviously clear to every rational, contemplative mind, that neither custom nor education, nor any law of men or nations, can alter the nature of justice and equity; which will and must, essentially and eternally, rest upon their own proper base, as laid down by the great Christian Lawgiver, viz. "Therefore, all things, whatsoever ye would that men should do to you, do ye even to them: for this is the law and the prophets."[78]

In making this single saying of Jesus the starting point for his whole argument, he was following the precedent set by John Hepburn in 1715—but with this remarkable difference: Hepburn argued totally within a Christian context; Hicks insisted that Jesus had pronounced a universal principle, obvious to any rational mind, as the foundation for all justice.

The second quotation was from Ezekiel 18, verses 4 and 20, connected by the phrase, "the soul that sinneth, it shall die," which occurs in both verses:

> It is generally acknowledged, by the people of every enlightened country, and particularly by those who believe in revelation, as testified of in the Scriptures of Truth, that man is a moral agent, (that is, free to act, with the restriction of accountability to his Creator,) agreeably to the declaration of the prophet Ezekiel; through whom, Jehovah, in his benignity and justice, claims the right of sovereignty over the children of men: "All souls are mine; as the soul of the father, so also the soul of the son is mine: the soul that sinneth, it

shall die: the son shall not bear the iniquity of the father, neither shall the father bear the iniquity of the son!" This Scripture testimony, perfectly consonant with reason and justice, not only proves, that every man is to bear his own iniquity, but that he also stands fully indemnified thereby, from all the iniquity of his predecessors; and likewise fully establishes man's free agency: and, of course, proves, that every moral agent born into the world, (whatever the conduct and situation of his parents may have been) is born FREE.[79]

John Woolman had already used Ezekiel 18:20 to make the point that Hicks summarized as being "indemnified from the iniquity of his predecessors." In the further conclusions that he drew from these verses, Hicks went boldly beyond Woolman.

In his letters, Elias Hicks used the Bible in an astonishing variety of ways. In an 1820 letter he tackled the problem of the inconsistencies in Paul's writings about the ministry of women:

In respect to what Paul says of women keeping silence in the churches, as also in some other respects; . . . I apprehend, if Paul hath said what we find recorded in 1st Corinthians, xiv. 34, 35, and 1st Timothy ii. 11, 12, that he had no allusion at all to their preaching or prophesying in the churches; and if he had, we have no right, nor reason, at all to admit it as sound doctrine, as it contradicts a number more of his own declarations on that point, (as also the general testimony of scripture,) which are much more rational, clear, and plain, as may be seen in his epistle to the Romans, xvi.; Philippians, iv. 3; 1st Corinthians, xi. 5-13; and Paul assures us, that male and female are one in Christ, that is, when they become real Christians, of whom Christ is the head. Also, under the law there were prophetesses as well as prophets, and the effusion of the spirit in the latter day, as prophesied by Joel, was to be equally on sons and daughters, servants and handmaids; and, to believe otherwise, is irrational and inconsistent with the Divine attributes, and would charge the Almighty with partiality and injustice to one-half of his rational creation. Therefore, in my belief, it would be wrong to admit it, although asserted in the most plain and positive manner by men or angels.[80]

The novelty in Hicks's interpretation lies in his using rationality, clearness, and plainness as criteria for determining which biblical verses are to be taken as primary or controlling. In his readiness to disregard any biblical passages or interpretations that seem inconsistent with God's justice and impartiality, he was following through on the course first charted by Abraham Shackleton and Hannah Barnard.

Hicks was, indeed, a bit more cautious than Shackleton and Barnard in that he recognized the finiteness and fallibility of human reason. He affirmed

the privilege of individual investigation and the equal right of withholding our assent to any proposition which we believe is not in accordance with truth and reason. . . .

I consider it impossible that a pure, just, and holy God could ever act arbitrarily, oppressively, or tyrannically towards his rational creation. Nevertheless, I believe that God, who is the author and preserver of all created existence, may and sometimes does act in a way so far beyond the investigation of finite man in his fallen state that in the darkness he is enveloped in, he accuses him of acting arbitrarily and oppressively.[81]

An example that Elias Hicks cited in making this point was one that Shackleton and Barnard had centered on as inconceivable to be the action of a loving and merciful God—the command to utterly destroy the Canaanites in war:

Many (some we know of) . . . do not assent to the record of the deluge as a truth, nor that Moses was commanded of God to slay the nations of Canaan, as recorded. [Deut. 7:1-2] But I see no difficulty in believing these accounts and, at the same time, exonerating the Almighty from doing anything repugnant or contrary to his excellent attributes of justice and mercy, for I cannot believe he does any act but such as his justice and mercy are united in the doing of it. . . .

The account given in the Scriptures concerning the covenant the Lord made with Abraham embraces a promise that he would give the land then possessed by the seven nations of Canaan to his children after him, but he also assured him that he could not give that land to them until four hundred years should expire, and gives as a reason that the sins of this people were not yet full. [Gen. 15:13, 16] Now, as we ought always to put the best construction on our neighbors words and actions that truth and justice will warrant, how much more ought we to do it as it respects the ways and works of Jehovah? . . . I consider the suspension that took place from the time the promise was made to the time it was fulfilled was in order to give that people a time of full and entire probation. And when he ordered their entire extirpation, it was the best possible act respecting them that his wisdom could devise and his justice and mercy unite in. . . .

The enlightened mind is brought to see that there is an overruling and gracious Providence, not bound entirely by any general laws, but is always free and at liberty to act as, in his infinite wisdom, he sees meet. And which, by his infinite power, he effects, but always in conformity to his justice, mercy, and truth.[82]

Elias Hicks was making a bold attempt to strike a fine line between Shackleton's and Barnard's rejection of the destruction of the Canaanites as a genuine command of God, and Henry Tuke's insistence that we dare not question the ultimate inscrutability of God's nature and actions. A key point in his argument was his implicit recognition that defining God's omnipotence as the ability to do *anything (period)* goes beyond the bounds of reason. ("Can God create a rock so big that he cannot move it?") On the other hand, Hicks was an absolute pacifist in his time, even questioning whether any Friends should pay war taxes, and yet his argument here came close to resting on anti-pacifist "lesser evil" reasoning.

In the 1820s modern biblical criticism was in its infancy, confined mainly to German university scholars. It is all the more remarkable, then, that Elias Hicks displayed a flash of critical insight in an 1822 letter to Gideon Seaman, a fellow New York Yearly Meeting Friend. Seaman was becoming increasingly doubtful of the soundness of Hicks's doctrine, and had charged him with a serious error on the basis of reports that he had heard. In responding, Hicks noted, "(Some have reported) that I have asserted as my belief that Jesus was really the son of Joseph and Mary—which, I assure thee, is an absolute falsehood."[83]

Elias Hicks went on to explain his view on a closely related question. He began with a point on which he agreed with Seaman: "Where thou mentions Matthew's genealogy of Jesus, thou says when it comes to Joseph, he alters his style. Surely he has so (or some other has done it for him)."[84] What Seaman and Hicks meant by Matthew's "altering his style" becomes clearer if we look at Matthew's genealogy in the King James Version, the translation in common use in their time. The first gospel began: "The book of the generation of Jesus Christ, the son of David, the son of Abraham"

(Matthew 1:1). What followed was one of the notorious and numerous lists of "begats" in that version of the Bible; this list began: "Abraham begat Isaac; and Isaac begat Jacob," (Matthew 1:2) and continued in similar "style," with occasional variations, such as "Jesse begat David the king; and David the king begat Solomon of her that had been the wife of Uriah," (Matthew 1:6) through to the final generations: "Matthan begat Jacob; and Jacob begat Joseph the husband of Mary, of whom was born Jesus, who is called Christ" (Matthew 1:15-16)—*not* "Jacob begat Joseph; and Joseph begat Jesus, who is called Christ, of Mary," as we might expect if the style had not been "altered." After agreeing that Matthew here "alters his style," Elias Hicks continued with this startling statement:

> By so doing, he has in my opinion entirely invalidated his whole testimony on that subject in the view of every sensible man. For of what use is his genealogy? And what did he intend to instruct his reader in by it? Was it not to prove the fulfillment of the prophesies concerning Jesus and that he was truly the son—or that he came through the loins—of Abraham and David, as was prophesied concerning him? And therefore, [he] begins his book with these remarkable words, "The book of the generation of Jesus Christ, the son of David, son of Abraham. And Abraham begat Isaac, etc." Carrying it down in a regular line to Joseph, and then throws it all away, and renders his genealogy abortive and worth nothing, and proves nothing of the fulfillment of the prophesies concerning him, which appears clearly to have been his design in his first setting out. Hence, I consider the testimony of such a history is of very little account. . . . I consider Matthew's account to be of but very little use, as he undoes his own work.[85]

Doubtless Gideon Seaman would have been scandalized by this statement, that a portion of the New Testament was "worth nothing" and "of but very little use," and would have found it even more disturbing than the slanderous "falsehood" that he had originally claimed Elias Hicks had spoken.

On the other hand, nearly every twentieth- or twenty-first-century critical scholar of the New Testament would agree with Hicks that the words of Matthew 1:16, which referred simply to "Joseph, the husband of Mary, who gave birth to Jesus called Messiah" (NEB), indeed "render [Matthew's] genealogy abortive." Many would suggest that this phrase was probably an editorial revision of the original genealogy, an attempt to harmonize that early Christian tradition with the contrasting tradition found immediately afterward in Matthew 1:18-25. That second tradition was the account and explanation of the virgin birth of Jesus, which claimed that Jesus had *no* human father. In his letter to Gideon Seaman, Elias Hicks had taken a significant step beyond Abraham Shackleton and Hannah Barnard in reclaiming Samuel Fisher's critical approach to biblical texts.

Going back to the issue of the equality of men and women in the people of God, Elias Hicks in an 1821 letter had tried out a unique approach:

> It is clear, from the history of Israel's redemption from Pharaoh's yoke, that this complete passive state of the will, was the principal requisite in effecting their deliverance. . . . When our first parents set up a will, and turned away from that passive state, they ought ever to have stood in to the divine will, God graciously ordained, that the woman should be subject to her husband, and he should rule over her, and this subjection ought to continue until both surrender their wills again to God, as in the beginning, and then male and female are one in him, and then man's sovereignty over the woman is entirely done away, and God's will becomes all in all.[86]

He was evidently taking off from George Fox's claim that men's domination over women was God's penalty for Eve's disobedience, and that this penalty was annulled when Christ came again to teach his people and brought the faithful into a renewed Eden, where the original equality between the sexes again prevailed:

> This Seed is come: . . . the Seed of the Woman, who suffered and tasted death for every man that was and is in death. So when Christ was risen, the woman that was first in the transgression, the women went first to declare the Resurrection out of death, out of the grave. . . . When they came into the belief of it, male and female believed: so both are one in Christ Jesus. . . .
>
> So here, in the resurrection and restoration of man up again into the image of God; . . . they come to be meet helps; Not as it was in the fall: the woman was first in transgression, then Adam was set over the woman; now here is unity, here is the headship in Christ Jesus.[87]

But Fox's "realizing eschatology" was a world-view that Elias Hicks would have found incomprehensible, and so he transformed it into the Quietist call to shut down our wills into total passiveness as the way to become fully obedient to God.

In 1822 Hicks wrote of "many false reports and unjust insinuations that have been spread concerning me, . . . terming me a deist, a seducer, Socinian, Unitarian, denying the divinity of Christ the Saviour, . . . and divesting him of his eternal God-head." In order to counter these charges, he wrote:

> The Proverbs, which as most agree intend Christ the Saviour, speak in this manner, (viii. 15, 20, 23); "By me kings reign, and princes decree justice." "I (wisdom) lead in the way of righteousness; in the midst of the paths of judgment, I was set up from everlasting." To which Paul alludes, (1 Cor. i. 24), "Unto them which are called," we preach "Christ the power of God, and the wisdom of God." Which doctrine, thousands can bear me witness, I have often held forth and urged on my hearers, in my public communications, and from whence I conclude, that if Christ is the power of God, and wisdom of God, then certainly Christ the Saviour is God, in as much as it is impossible God's power and wisdom should be distinct or divided from himself: Therefore Christ is not distinct from God, but entirely that same God, and which the Evangelist also asserts concerning Christ, the word, that was in the beginning with God and was God.[88]

In an 1827 letter he wrote in response to one of a series of queries:

> As to the divinity of Jesus Christ, the son of the virgin, when he had arrived to a full state of sonship in the spiritual generation, he was wholly swallowed up into the divinity of his heavenly Father, [2 Pet. i. 4.] and was one with his Father, with only this difference; his Father's divinity was underived, being self-existent, but the son's divinity was altogether derived from the Father; for otherwise he could not be the son of God, as in the moral relation to be a son of man, the son must be begotten by one father, and he must be in the same nature, spirit, and likeness of his father, so as to say, I and my father are one in all those respects. But this was not the case with Jesus in the spiritual relation, until he had gone through the last institute of the law dispensation, viz. John's watery baptism, and had received additional power [Luke ii. 52.] from on high, by the descending of the holy ghost upon him as he came up out of the water. [Matt. iii. 16.] He then witnessed the fulness of the second birth, being now born into the nature, spirit, and likeness of the heavenly Father, and God gave witness of it to John, saying, "This is my beloved son, in whom I am well pleased." And this agrees with Paul's testimony, where he assures us that as many as are led by the

spirit of God, do become the sons of God. [Rom. viii. 14.] So Jesus, by being faithful to the leading of the spirit of God, fulfilled all the righteousness of the Jewish law, [Matt. iii. 15.] and was then prepared to receive additional power from on high, by which he was qualified to enter upon his gospel mission, and introduce the new covenant, prophesied of long before by Jeremy the prophet, and by which he went far beyond all the former prophets, [Acts, iii. 22.] and witnessed in spirit the substance of all the shadows of their law and covenant, being the son of God with power, according to the spirit of holiness by the resurrection from the dead. [Rom. i. 4.] And all who come rightly into the new covenant, and are led by the spirit that Jesus commanded his disciples to wait for, [Luke, xxiv. 49.] become the sons of God, and joint heirs with Jesus Christ, [Rom. viii. 17.] and are made kings and priests unto God, [Rev. i. 6, and v. 10.] having overcome the world as Jesus did, and are preachers of righteousness both in word and deed.[89]

In these two letters Elias Hicks was drawing on the Bible as a sourcebook for propositions, from which doctrinal statements could be deduced.

In a January 1824 letter to a member of Green Street Meeting in Philadelphia, Elias Hicks reminded him of the confrontations that had taken place there the previous winter:

I often look back with pleasure on the time I spent with my dear friends at Philadelphia, and, in a particular manner, the near unity and fellowship witnessed with those of Green Street monthly meeting, whom I visited in the Gospel of Christ. And although the enemy of all good seemed busy in endeavouring to stir up opposition, yet, through the condescending goodness of Israel's Shepherd, the truth was raised so above him, and so bruised his head, that he had no power to bruise the heel, but was cast out into the earth, the habitation of beasts. And, dear friend, seeing the Lord, by his own right hand of power, hath been with us, and preserved us thus far, and hath enabled us to set up our Ebenezer, let us thank him and take courage, standing fast in the faith, without wavering or turning aside in the least degree, although all men may rise up against us; ever remembering, however we may be buffeted within or without, his grace is sufficient for us in the midst of all our tribulations; and as we continue faithful, without turning aside, to the right hand or to the left, through the fear or favour of man, he will carry us through and over all to his praise who is calling us to glory and virtue.[90]

I was able to tease quite a few biblical references out of this paragraph:

> The LORD God said unto the serpent, . . . I will put enmity between thee and the woman, and between thy seed and her seed; it shall bruise thy head, and thou shalt bruise his heel (Genesis 3:14-15).

> Thy right hand, O LORD, is become glorious in power (Exodus 15:6).

> Then Samuel took a stone, and set it between Mizpeh and Shen, and called the name of it Ebenezer, saying, Hitherto hath the LORD helped us (1 Samuel 7:12).

> Stand fast in the faith (1 Corinthians 16:13).

> Let us hold fast the profession of our faith without wavering (Hebrews 10:23).

> Through thy name will we tread them under that rise up against us (Psalm 44:5).

> My grace is sufficient for thee (2 Corinthians 12:9).

> Do therefore as the LORD your God hath commanded you: ye shall not turn aside to the right hand or to the left (Deuteronomy 5:32).

Hicks's words flowed out here in a cascade of biblical metaphors as he recalled the events they had gone through together.

I continue with a few biblical references from the *Journal* of Elias Hicks. He cited Romans 8:1-2 in his summary of a message he spoke in 1814 at Westbury (Long Island) Meeting:

> I was led to set forth the excellency of the state described by the apostle Paul, which is freed from condemnation, and is effected by a full submission and obedience to the law of the spirit of life in Christ Jesus, which sets free from the law of sin and death.[91]

In an 1815 message at Jericho Meeting, Elias Hicks drew together references from the first letter of John, Paul's letters to the Romans and the Corinthians, and the gospel of Matthew, as he developed the theme of his sermon:

> My mind was led into a consideration of the testimony of the apostle John, where he assures us, agreeably to truth and right reason, that God is love, and that they who dwell in love, dwell in God, and God in them. My mind was opened to set forth to the people

the excellency of this state and the certainty of its attainment, by all such as sincerely desire salvation; and in order therefore, are willing, through and by the leading and teaching of divine grace, which the apostle Paul assures us, agreeably to our own sensible experience, has appeared to all men, to forego all our selfish and creaturely inclinations, and to deny self; and by bearing our cross daily, come to a full crucifixion of the old man, with all his corrupt and ungodly deeds. We thereby come to know a putting on the new man, even Christ, or a salvation state, agreeably to another declaration of the same apostle, where he asserts: "Therefore, if any man be in Christ, he is a new creature; old things are passed away, behold all things are become new, and all things are of God" [2 Corinthians 5:17]. I was likewise led to show the good fruits that would be the natural result of such a state, as certain as good fruit is produced by a good tree; for we should no longer love as man loves in his fallen state, from a selfish motive, self being slain; but we should love as God loves, with a disinterested love, and then we should love, not our friends and neighbours only, but our greatest enemies also; and we should become qualified sincerely to pray to God for them.[92]

Michael Birkel first pointed out John Woolman's significant use of the phrase, "near sympathy." Elias Hicks also used this phrase. With help from the Digital Quaker Collection, I found fifteen occurrences of the phrase in his *Journal* and *Letters*. But he always used it when addressing or writing about fellow Quakers. Most characteristically, he used it in letters to his Quaker allies when they were under fire from evangelically oriented Friends. In writing about his relationship with biblical figures, the closest he came to "near sympathy" was in an 1817 sermon at his home meeting in Jericho:

Soon after I took my seat in our meeting today, my mind was quickened and led into a sympathetic feeling with the state of Elijah, when he fled from the wrath and persecution of Ahab and Jezebel. When under great discouragement and dismay, he bemoaned his condition—that they had pulled down the Lord's altars, slain his servants, and he only was left and they sought his life. But the Lord told him for his encouragement, that there were seven thousand yet left in Israel that had not bowed their knee to the image of Baal. But these, no doubt, were so scattered and dispersed among the people, that Elijah could scarcely find one to open his mind to, and therefore felt himself as one alone. And this, no doubt, is the lot of some of the Lord's most faithful servants in the present day. And was it not for the same divine help and succor that Elijah experienced, some of these at times would be altogether cast down and discouraged.[93]

Even at first glance, Hicks's sympathy hardly reached the depth of full empathy—his account was detached and analytical. As I look at the context of the biblical account, I am struck by a deeper problem: Elias Hicks totally ignored that context. Elijah had been in a contest with four hundred fifty prophets of Baal (1 Kings 18:19), who were on Queen Jezebel's payroll. After his victory in the contest, Elijah took the prophets of Baal "down to the brook Kishon, and slew them there" (1 Kings 18:40 KJV). Afterward, King

Ahab told Jezebel all that Elijah had done, and withal how he had slain all the prophets with the sword. Then Jezebel sent a messenger unto Elijah, saying, So let the gods do to me, and more also, if I make not thy life as the life of one of them by tomorrow about this time (1 Kings 19:1-2 KJV). ("The gods do the same to me and more, unless by this time tomorrow I have taken your life as you took theirs" [1 Kings 19:2 NEB].)

Elijah was a mass-murderer on the lam from the queen's justice (or revenge?)! Elias Hicks's failure to take note of this fact casts serious doubt on the depth—or even the genuineness—of his "sympathetic feeling with the state of Elijah."

Hicks continued his sermon:

The subject spread and enlarged and opened to a field of doctrine, wherein I was led to show to the people that the mystery of iniquity [Satan] had wrought in and under every dispensation of God to the Church through his varied transformations—always resembling as much as may be, an angel of light—by which he lies in wait to deceive, and has generally deceived, and still deceives, the greater part of the people of all the nations under heaven—setting up his post by God's post, and leading his votaries to perform their worship and works just like the Lord's servants, with only this difference—that it's done in a way and time of their own heart's devising. And there is no other distinguishing mark than that the Lord's children are all taught of the Lord. And they are made to know it, for in righteousness they are established, and great is the peace of these children.[94]

When his subject did "spread and enlarge," it became even more abstract than the preceding account, as he promptly moved into an exposition of doctrine.

Several times Elias Hicks made use of the Bible as a sourcebook for statements from which he could deduce doctrinal truths. He also used scriptural quotations and references in a variety of other ways. I find it difficult to fit them into any comprehensive or systematic pattern. The best I can do is to hazard a guess using Galatians 3:24-25 as a clue, even though I have not yet found evidence that Elias Hicks ever quoted or referred to these verses. Paul wrote: "The law was our schoolmaster to bring us unto Christ, that we might be justified by faith. But after that faith is come, we are no longer under a schoolmaster." The "law" that Paul referred to was, of course, the Torah—the heart of scripture for Jews and for first-century Christians alike. For Paul, then, we can say that scripture was a schoolmaster to bring us to Christ. Similarly, for Elias Hicks, scripture was a schoolmaster to bring us to the Spirit of Christ.

He could use scripture as a sourcebook for Christian doctrine. Doctrine was truth, but it was not saving truth. Saving truth came from the Spirit of Christ, the light within. Doctrine was of preliminary importance; far weightier matters were justice, peace, and love—including the testimonies against slavery and war, and the narrow path that was the traditional Quaker way of life. Scripture could point us toward all of these. But it was the "principle of light and truth in the mind" that was the "sufficient and only rule of faith and practice,"[95] and "It is by obedience to this inward light only, that we are prepared for an admittance into the heavenly kingdom."[96] And so scripture could be used in a variety of ways, but always to point beyond itself.

I will, in due course, review a few key events in the Great Separation of 1827 and 1828. For now, I jump ahead to note that in the following years those who came to be called Orthodox Friends carried out a number of notable publishing activities in their effort to prove that they were the true inheritors of the Quaker tradition. In 1831 they brought together for the first time the major published writings of George Fox in a single eight-volume printing. And in 1837 Jonathan Evans, the Philadelphia elder who had been one of the most outspoken opponents of Elias Hicks, published a journal of a noted Friends minister, William Savery. Savery had written copious notes on his travels in the ministry, but they had been scattered into the hands of various Friends. Evans brought them together, edited out some excess details, and added some biographical material to connect them into a single narrative. Savery's writings and Evans's notes are easy to distinguish, because Evans used quotation marks to separate out what Savery had written. The printed edition also includes several footnotes to the Savery text, whose origin is not at first glance made clear. However, internal evidence solves the problem. One note contained the phrase, "when our friend William Savery was here."[97] On another page, where Savery's text read, "Although the people behaved well in general, I did not think it so open as many others.*"[98] the asterisked footnote began: "It is not strange that our dear friend found so little openness."[99] I find it safe to conclude that the author of the footnotes was Jonathan Evans, not William Savery. (I will suggest later that some otherwise careful historians have stumbled because they failed to notice this point.)

William Savery (1750-1804) was the son of Quaker parents and grandson (possibly great-grandson?) of a Huguenot who had fled France when religious persecution broke out in that country in 1685. He lived his entire life in Philadelphia, except for a few years as an apprentice to a tanner in Goshen, Pennsylvania, several miles west of the city. In 1778 he married a Friend, Sarah Evans, and established a business as a master tanner. In 1781 he was recorded as a minister; in the following years he traveled several times in the ministry. He volunteered to join two delegations of Friends who traveled to the American frontier in 1793 and in 1794 to lend their presence to efforts to establish treaties between the American government and various Native American tribes. His final and most extensive trip in the ministry was to the British Isles and the continent of Europe, from 1796 to 1798. On this trip he joined a small party of Friends who visited scattered Friends meetings in Germany, the Netherlands, and France; he also visited Friends in England, Scotland, Wales, and Ireland.

Compared with other Quaker journalists, his own references to topics on which he preached or to his thoughts on religious subjects were rather sparse. In addition, two slim volumes of his sermons, prayers, and discourses were recorded in shorthand and later published.

In one sermon William Savery affirmed the traditional Quaker view of the scriptures as being secondary to the Spirit of God within:

> The Scriptures are excellent: they are much more so, and worthier to be held in greater estimation than all the books in the world. But the Scriptures point only to that holy all-powerful Word which indeed gave all the Scripture. The whole tenor of the Gospel doctrine is to bring men there—to settle them upon that foundation;

where they may build with safety—to the teachings of the holy and blessed spirit of God within them.[100]

In another sermon he exalted the scriptures to a height that had rarely been heard among Friends:

> Jesus Christ came . . . to enlighten the world with a greater degree of light than ever was before—to bring light and immortality more abundantly to life in the world. And a great and especial favour I account it to be. And I believe the more we are acquainted with the Scriptures, the more we shall be made to acknowledge, they are a special favour of God to mankind: containing, in the simplicity of their doctrine, the most deep and heavenly mysteries; and sublime beyond all the writings of any philosophers in the world, be they ever so great; or any that are called divines: yea, they are simply, and virtually in their doctrines, truly sublime beyond all the soaring opinions of men![101]

For Savery, the most sublime doctrines and heavenly mysteries were the biblical glimpses of the glories of eternity that open up beyond this present life:

> I most sincerely desire a higher degree of attainment, even the state of a perfect man in Christ Jesus—that I may be thoroughly washed in the laver of regeneration, until I am prepared, through adorable mercy, to be presented faultless before the throne of his glory with exceeding joy.[102]

> Our days are passing on, a few more years over many of our heads and our sun must set—the curtain of the evening will be drawed between us and all visible things. A day of prosperity is hastening on, a thousand times more glorious than the enjoyment of all temporal blessings.—A day is coming, when it will be said, time is no more, and then all these things which perish with the using, will be nothing more than a clod of earth, all the enjoyments of this earth having passed away. But if you are found at a throne of grace, the Lord Jesus Christ will give you a crown of glory for ever incorruptible and that will never fade away; where there will be no room for sorrow. And I am persuaded, that a true Christian passing from a state of mortality to a state of immortality, may be a little compared to passing out of a dark into a glorious dignified mansion. It is a light inconceivable and glory inexpressible.[103]

Perhaps Savery's favorite biblical verse was John 14:2: "In my Father's house are many mansions. . . . I go to prepare a place for you":

> This world and the fashion of it passeth away. O may we secure an inheritance through our Lord Jesus Christ in an ever-abiding mansion in the world to come.[104]

> Lord, teach us to aspire with increasing ardor, after that glory which is celestial and eternal, and those mansions of immutable felicity, which thou hast prepared in the riches of thy mercy, for all those who love thee and keep thy commandments.[105]

How did William Savery believe that God's "adorable mercy" might bring us into "those mansions of immutable felicity"? According to Jonathan Evans, Savery preached that it was through "the efficacy of [Christ's] propitiatory sacrifice, . . . who hath by his own blood obtained eternal redemption for all that come unto Him in true faith."[106] And yet I did not find words like "propitiatory sacrifice" in Savery's published sermons nor in his own words in his *Journal.* I find, rather, words like these:

> I believe that if those who are convinced of the ways of Truth and Righteousness, if they with simplicity of soul acknowledge the truth, and live in the truth of the divine law, they will not only have a gladdening hope of a glorious immortality in the world to come; but they will also be favoured with an hundred fold of peace and joy in this life. I think I know it with some degree of experience, I never knew what true and real enjoyment was in the Lord's temporal blessings, till it pleased him to touch my heart and bring me to a sense of my state, and of obedience to him.[107]

The TRUTH upon which glory, immortality, and eternal life depend, is plain, free, and simple: "*To know* THEE *the only true God, and* JESUS CHRIST *whom thou hast sent, is life eternal*" [John 17:3].

> Well, my friends, how shall we know this?—where shall we find it?—how shall we be assured that we are really in this knowledge—and in this faith? why, I think, if men—I speak now in much charity, for I do not boast of my own attainments, but what I feel and believe to be true from my own experience, and which appears to me to be consistent with the doctrines both of the Old and New Testament, that I am not ashamed to declare, though it were to thousands and ten thousands: for I say from the very beginning there was an

ETERNAL PRINCIPLE—there was an holy unflattering and unchangeable GUIDE placed in the souls of men, which if they had attended
to; all men would have been led safe. "It is shewn to thee, (says the
prophet) O man, what thou shouldst do, and what the Lord thy God
requireth at thy hands; to do justice, to love mercy, and to walk humbly with thy GOD."—It is shewn to thee what is good.—These are
the forcible expressions—to "DO JUSTICE, to LOVE MERCY, to WALK
HUMBLY WITH THY GOD."

And here I believe is the ground work and foundation of all
religion.[108]

For Savery, the words of Micah 6:8 were at the heart of the way to eternal
life. It is through our obedience to God and keeping his commandments that
his "adorable mercy" brings us into heavenly bliss. I believe that Jonathan
Evans was reading his own evangelical beliefs back into the message of his
"brother beloved,"[109] William Savery.

Apparently William Savery, like Elias Hicks, was an eloquent public
speaker. His biographer affirmed: "There can be no doubt that William
Savery was gifted with a wonderful voice."[110] In one respect, however,
Savery and Hicks were at opposite poles. Elias Hicks was convinced that true
Christian obedience can be attained only by being faithful to the strictest
Quaker discipline, and he often spoke out against the "hireling" ministers of
other churches. William Savery preached that Christians of all varieties can
be obedient to God within their own denominations:

Men may call themselves what they please: the world calls me a
Quaker—and thee a *Dissenter* in another form—and thee a member
of the *Established church*—But what is all this? My friends, these are
names, they are distinctions amongst men: but are they distinctions
with God? Does he know *high* church, and *low* church? Does he
descend to enquire whether thou art a *methodist* or a *presbyterian,* thou
a *baptist,* thou a *roman catholic*? No: But is thy *heart* right? Art thou
sincere in thy desires to know him and to serve him? This is the
great point: to know him, and to know thine ownself; the situation in
which he has placed thee, who is the Author of thy being; the reason
he has given to thee that *being,* and the glory which he proposes to
crown it with, if thou wilt with simplicity of heart live in his counsel,
and in his fear, and avoid those things that are repugnant to God's
purity, with a pure and truly enlightened mind.[111]

Perhaps the most significant legacies of William Savery's life have come through his encounters with three individuals during his journey through Europe, Great Britain, and Ireland.

In February 1797 William Savery and David Sands were traveling together in France, when they chanced upon Thomas Paine in a coffee house in Paris. Thomas Paine had been born a Friend in England; he was the most famous pamphleteer on behalf of the American Revolution, and had later written *The Age of Reason*, which popularized the philosophy of deism. Savery described their meeting:

> In the evening, David Sands and myself fell in with Thomas Paine, and spent about an hour and a half in conversation about his opinions and writings. He made many assertions against Moses, the prophets, Jesus Christ, &c., which had much more the appearance of passionate railing than argument; to all which we replied. I felt zealously opposed to him, and believe that nothing was said by my companion or myself that gave him the least occasion to exult: we bore our testimony against him firmly.[112]

William Savery was not the only Friend or Christian who believed that deism was a major threat. Francis Taylor, in his biography of Savery, nicely summed it up: "In a very real sense William Savery and David Sands thought they were standing at Armageddon to battle for the Lord."[113]

In May 1797 William Savery and David Sands sailed from France to England. Among his many stops in Great Britain and Ireland, Savery arrived in the city of Norwich, in England, on February 3, 1798. On Sunday morning, February 4, he was present at the Goats Lane Meeting in Norwich. He "thought it the gayest meeting of Friends I ever sat in, and was grieved to see it." He also spoke at a public meeting "in the evening, in a large meeting-house in another part of the town." Savery reacted:

> The marks of wealth and grandeur are too obvious in several families of Friends in this place, which made me sorrowful, yet saw but little opening to relieve my mind; several of the younger branches, though they are enabled, through Divine grace, to see what the Truth leads to, yet it is uncertain whether, with all the alluring things of this world around them, they will choose the simple, safe path of self-denial.[114]

"Gay Friends" was a term used at the time to describe members who attended meeting but were lax in following Quaker discipline; they enjoyed dancing, parties, and music, and wore fashionable, colorful clothing. Those who strictly followed Quaker discipline, particularly in the way they dressed, were known as "Plain Friends." One of the most prominent Gay Friends in Norwich was John Gurney, a wealthy banker and widower, who lived on a large country estate named Earlham Hall with his eleven children. Most of the family were present at the February 4 Goats Lane Meeting including his seventeen-year-old daughter, Betsy Gurney, resplendent in her purple boots with scarlet laces.

The lively Gurney sisters usually thought meeting at "Goats" was b.o.r.i.n.g, but this morning was different—especially for Betsy. That afternoon John Gurney's brother, Joseph Gurney, a Plain Friend, invited William Savery and a large group of Friends, including Betsy, to his home for a dinner party. Uncle Joseph arranged for Betsy to ride alone in the carriage with William Savery, to and from the evening meeting, at which he spoke. Monday morning William Savery visited John Gurney and his family at Earlham Hall. The entry in Betsy's diary for those days is so revealing and vulnerable that a number of historians and biographers have quoted from it:

> Today I have *felt* there is a *God*. I loved the man as if almost he were sent from heaven. We had much serious conversation, in short, what he said and what I felt was like a refreshing shower upon parched up earth that had been dried up for ages.[115]

From late February to the middle of April, Betsy visited Friends in London. She made a point of going to every meeting where William Savery was present; she visited several homes when Savery was visiting and had more conversations with him. It seems clear that Betsy had a crush on him, very like modern teen-age crushes on a favorite teacher or a celebrity rock musician. But her life was changing in more profound ways. A few days after their first meeting, she confided to her diary: "I should not be surprised to see myself a plain friend. Things do change so oddly in this motley world."[116] In September she wrote: "I know now what the mountain is I have to climb. *I am to be a quaker.*"[117] The change came slowly, in fits and starts. The biggest obstacles were within her own family; Betsy dearly loved her father and her sisters, and they were making every effort to persuade her not to give up her Gay Quaker lifestyle.

Within a couple of years, Betsy Gurney was fully committed to the strict Quaker way of life. This commitment was cemented when, at the age of twenty, she married Joseph Fry, a young, wealthy Plain Friend. In due time she found her life's vocation—ministering to women in prison and working ardently for prison reform. We remember her today as Elizabeth Fry. As historian John Punshon has observed: "Outside her Society she is probably the best known of all Quakers."[118]

When John Gurney's wife, Catherine, had died, their next-to-youngest son, Joseph John, was four years old. After his mother's death, when he felt nighttime terrors, it was usually his sister Betsy whom he ran to for comfort and safety. He was only nine when William Savery visited Earlham Hall. David Swift, in his biography of Joseph John Gurney, suggested

> that Elizabeth's dramatic conversion to plain Quakerism . . . may have been an influential prologue to her brother's later, less spectacular but equally decisive commitment to the way of life of Friends.[119]

> [Joseph John] Gurney became a strait Friend only after years of struggle. He had felt a strong pull in this direction as early as the fall of 1809, influenced by a visit to Earlham by Elizabeth Fry, who was by then a gifted minister in the Society.[120]

Quite a few other influences also made their impact on the spiritual development of young Joseph John Gurney. The outcome in his life was so remarkable that David Swift was on safe ground when he concluded, "In the impact of Evangelicalism upon Quakerism, Gurney was perhaps the single most important figure."[121] When William Savery left Norwich feeling uncertain whether any of the younger Friends there would "choose the simple, safe path of self-denial," he little dreamed that he had begun a connection that was to become his great Quaker legacy, lasting well into the nineteenth century.

Four weeks before his visit to Norwich, England, William Savery was in Waterford, Ireland. There, on January 8, 1798, he reported:

> At my lodgings in the evening came Robert Greer and Abraham Shackleton, the latter from Ballitore, who had come forty-two miles in order to see me. He holds opinions of a singular nature; objects "to the five first books of Moses in particular, but in general to the accounts of the Jews in the Old Testament." . . . For my part, I could not see as he did, nor unite with him in his erroneous expressions and opinions, and I feel a fear they will produce much hurt, if he and others in this nation are not brought into deep abasement; his

talents and morality making error in his hands more dangerous. We separated without much satisfaction, at least on my side.[122]

Over the next couple of days Savery and Shackleton had more discussions, with similar outcomes:

Went with Abraham Shackleton to a Friend's house, and opened to him more of my disapprobation than I had before. . . .

Received a letter from Abraham Shackleton, in which he *appears* lovingly disposed towards me, but evidently wrong, so far as I am able to judge, in many of his opinions.[123]

Finally, "Abraham Shackleton . . . has gone for his home, and I am not sorry for his leaving us; he has give me much exercise."[124]

Rufus Jones described Savery's reaction this way: "William Savery was plainly shocked at the radical views of the Irish Friend, and he concluded that the latter and his sympathizers were caught in 'the vortex of Deism' and were being carried on into atheism."[125] John Punshon's account included the same quotation:

William's resolute mind was unable to minister to Abraham's difficulties as it had to Elizabeth Gurney's, and he summarised their unhappy encounter with the celebrated and dramatic comment that Shackleton and his sympathisers were caught in the "vortex of deism."[126]

But the *text* of Savery's *Journal* does *not* contain that "celebrated and dramatic" phrase. The words "vortex of Deism" are in a *footnote* to Savery's text:

The deceitful, subtle spirit . . . carried away many unsuspecting souls into the vortex of Deism, and at length into Atheism. . . . This same insidious spirit having since got into America, lamentable desolation of a considerable number of meetings of Friends in different parts ensued.[127]

Jonathan Evans was the one who penned the phrase in order to tie Shackleton to Elias Hicks and the others who separated from the evangelical or orthodox Friends in 1827 and 1828.

Although Jones and Punshon were trapped into overstating the *rhetoric* of Savery's reaction to Shackleton, they failed to follow the clues that show how the depth of his reaction affected his *actions* in the next few months.

Back in England, in Chester on March 29, 1798, Savery wrote: "My mind to-day much exercised about right direction, when and how to move towards my dear home, desiring to be released as soon as the Lord may please to make way for it in peace."[128] On April 10 he was in Liverpool: "Low in mind, not seeing how to move for the best as respects my leaving this country. My natural feelings are strongly drawn towards home, but no light seems to shine upon it; and I never had more need to ask for patience than at present."[129] Although he was desperately homesick, a feeling of something not finished was gnawing at him. He sensed—through a glass, darkly—that God had work left for him to do before he could go back to Philadelphia. He returned to the port city of Liverpool on April 16; there on the twentieth his resolve was severely tested: "A ship is to sail in two days for Philadelphia, and my mind is much exercised, not feeling liberty to return to America."[130]

Savery went on to Wales and then sailed to Ireland, arriving in Dublin April 29, just in time for the yearly meeting of Irish Friends. In the business session the next day,

> in considering the reports from the different meetings, the subject of reading the Scriptures took up the attention of Friends. Some of the accounts being deficient, Friends could not easily get over it, but were not sufficiently clear and explicit in mentioning their painful apprehensions, and were about to pass it by. I pressed their closer attention to it, but Friends were not moving toward unity on whether to take any action: I now saw in part what brought me to Ireland again.[131]

Surely this was the time and place for which God had been preparing him. William Savery seized the moment:

> I urged it again, when Friends spoke their minds freely, and it appeared that a number in different parts of the nation were in a disposition to lay waste in great measure the Holy Scriptures, disputed the Divinity of Christ, . . . but yet professed to exalt the Divine Light and immediate revelation very highly. After several hours spent on the subject, a large committee was appointed to take the matter into consideration, and join with the women Friends in bringing in a report. David Sands and myself were requested to sit with them.[132]

On May 2 Abraham Shackleton and another Friend met with the committee:

Abraham Shackleton . . . was for mutilating the Scriptures, saying that many parts were unprofitable, and some things derogatory to the Divine Being . . . he did not deny that Jesus Christ was a Divine person, but it was not clear what his ideas of the Divinity were.[133]

On May 3, 1798:

A report drawn up by the sub-committee to be presented to the Yearly Meeting, was read, setting forth that there was reason to believe, that some members of Society held the Scriptures, particularly some parts of them, in very light estimation, and were also tinctured with unsound doctrines, and proposing it to be recommended, that such should be tenderly treated with by the Monthly Meetings, and if they could not be brought to condemn their errors, the Monthly Meetings should request the assistance of the Quarters to labor further with them, and if they still persisted to hold those pernicious opinions, Friends were then to declare their disunity with them. The [Yearly] meeting again assembling at five o'clock, the report of the committee, with some small alteration, was adopted.[134]

William Savery had his doubts, whether the yearly meeting would have taken this drastic and decisive action without his strong urging; he was satisfied that this was the work that the Lord had been holding him out to accomplish. He was now free to wind up his affairs in England and return home to Philadelphia.

Savery died in 1804. Henry Tuke published *The Principles of Religion* in 1805. In 1806 Philadelphia Yearly Meeting followed Ireland's example and revised its *Book of Discipline*: to "deny the divinity of our Lord and Saviour Jesus Christ, the immediate revelation of the Holy Spirit or the authenticity of the Scriptures"[135] was now grounds for disownment. Jonathan Evans may well have been inspired by William Savery's success, in drumming Abraham Shackleton and others out of the Society of Friends, as grounds for hope that similar firm steps in 1822 and 1823 might rid Quakerism of the dangerous ideas being promoted by Elias Hicks, William Poole, and their friends.

John Comly was born in November 1773 in Byberry, which was then a rural township in Philadelphia County, Pennsylvania. His father and mother were "members of the religious society of Friends. They were plain, frugal, and industrious people."[136] In 1794 he began working as a school teacher in Byberry. In 1799, Philadelphia Yearly Meeting had established a boarding school at Westtown, in Chester County, Pennsylvania. John Comly taught at Westtown School from April, 1801, until November, 1802. While at Westtown, he had "formed an acquaintance and marriage engagement with Rebecca Budd, one of the female teachers," and he left the school in order to make "the necessary arrangements preparatory to the contemplated event of marriage."[137] He purchased a farm in Byberry. John and Rebecca were married in June 1803, and they "settled in Byberry, on the farm purchased the spring preceding."[138]

John and Rebecca Comly opened their own school, Pleasant Hill Boarding School, in 1804. John was recorded as a minister in 1813. Rebecca and John "continued this boarding-school until the spring of 1815; when, apprehending the time had arrived for relinquishing the toils and care attendant on the business, we discontinued it."[139] John, in particular, "resigned his school in 1815 to devote his time to travel in the ministry and farming."[140] Soon after the boarding school was established, John Comly published an English grammar and a spelling book, which—as his children later reported—"through a long course of years, have received deservedly the approval of experienced instructors, and been adopted in a vast number of schools in the United States."[141] In his *Journal*, John Comly first mentioned his children in 1815. He and Rebecca had at least two daughters and one son.

In his first ministry trip outside of Philadelphia Yearly Meeting, Comly traveled in New York and New England in 1815. Early in that trip, he "called to see that dear and worthy Friend, Elias Hicks, at his own house, where simplicity and neatness prevail."[142] The next day he appointed a meeting three miles from Jericho: "Dear Elias Hicks, who was present, rode with us after meeting, and was kind and tender as a father in experience, and his meek and upright deportment was that of a humble follower of Christ."[143]

By 1822, John Comly was assistant clerk of Philadelphia men's yearly meeting and a member of the yearly meeting's Meeting for Sufferings. He was one of the Friends whom Elias Hicks took along as witnesses for his December 1822 confrontation with some of that yearly meeting's elders.

Meeting for Sufferings met in January 1823. A pamphlet was brought forward entitled, *Extracts from the Writings of Primitive Friends concerning the Divinity of our Lord and Saviour Jesus Christ.* "The authors of the excerpts were not listed, nor were the sources from which they came, although the compilers relied heavily on Robert Barclay's *Apology*."[144] Quotations included:

The Holy Scriptures were written by divine inspiration. . . . They

211

are not or cannot be subjected to the fallen, corrupt reason of man.
. . . We receive and believe in the testimony of the Scriptures simply
as it stands in the text. . . . By the propitiatory sacrifice of Christ
without us we, truly repenting and believing, . . . [are] justified from
the imputation of sins and transgressions that are past."[145]

At the meeting,

> a Friend suggested that the Extracts be printed for general circula-
> tion. . . . John Comly and others objected to the publication on the
> grounds that the document was an effort "to palm off a creed on
> the society," that the pamphlet "would be used to abridge the right
> of private judgement," and "that something was about to be got
> up calculated to trammel our conscientious rights." These Quakers
> held that if such a document were issued over the signature of the
> Clerk of the Meeting for Sufferings, it would have the appearance
> of a definite creed drawn up and approved by the chief committee
> of the Yearly Meeting. If adopted by the Yearly Meeting the docu-
> ment would stand as an official declaration of faith. Although the
> objectors were overruled and 10,000 copies of the Extracts printed,
> there was some uneasiness about broadcasting them over the exist-
> ing opposition. It was decided to wait until after the coming Yearly
> Meeting.[146]

Yearly meeting met in April. One Friend present was John Comfort, a
relative of John Woolman. Some Friends described him as a "pretty substantial and solid old Friend from the country;"[147] to others he was "a man of no
religious weight."[148] The session opened with the reading of the minutes of
Meeting for Sufferings, including the full text of the *Extracts*. John Comfort
cried out: "Who hath required this at your hands?" Arguments boiled on
for several hours on the first two days of yearly meeting. Finally the clerk,
Samuel Bettle, "proposed that the pamphlet not be published but that its
text remain in the minutes. Late into the second day and after a bit more
debate, the meeting approved this solution."[149]

During the next few years, John Comly grew increasingly concerned
about what he viewed as a "spirit or image of jealousy,"[150] first in New
England and then in Philadelphia Yearly Meeting—or, as he later named
it, "this dominant, inquisitorial spirit."[151] Elders and leaders in the yearly
meeting, especially in Philadelphia Quarterly Meeting, seemed to be determined to suppress vocal ministry that did not conform to their evangelical

interpretation of sound Quaker theology. By the autumn and winter of 1826,

> a long struggle had been maintained against the usurpations of power; and to more distant and dispassionate observers, it was evident this scene could not long endure. The feelings of Christian love appeared to be withering, and the spirit of warfare was evidently gaining strength.[152]

In February 1827 he wrote:

> My mind was opened to see more clearly that this contest would result in a separation of the two conflicting parts of society, as the only means of saving the whole from a total wreck; and the way and manner of this separation was clearly unfolded to my mental vision; that on the part of Friends it must be effected in the peaceable spirit of the non-resisting Lamb—first, by ceasing from the spirit of contention and strife, and then uniting together in the support of the order and discipline of the Society of Friends, separate and apart from those who had introduced the difficulties, and who claimed to be the orthodox part of society.[153]

He began to propose this plan privately to friends who were chafing under increasing control by evangelicals.

Philadelphia Yearly Meeting met in April at the large Arch Street meeting house. Tempers were hot, and arguments broke out over a number of issues. Perhaps the most contentious issue was a proposal to appoint a committee to visit local and quarterly meetings of ministers and elders "on the subject of unsoundness in the ministry. . . . They are to sit in judgment on the ministry of their brethren; to form, of course, a standard of soundness, and to judge down what they may deem unsound."[154] At one point in the sessions, John Comly proposed:

> It was a fact unquestionable, that in the present Yearly Meeting of the Society of Friends there existed two distinct parties. . . . Love and unity do not subsist between these two parties as become the followers of Christ, or as brethren. . . . I proposed that as we were evidently at the present time in such a state that we were not qualified to transact any business to profit as a Yearly Meeting—that the meeting suspend all further prosecution of its business, and adjourn till we can come together in more harmony, love, and unity one with and toward another.[155]

It was time for Comly to bring others together to put his proposal for a separation into effect: "Meetings of conference on the subject of a peaceful, quiet retreat from the present state of confusion, were held by a number of exercised Friends at two or three times."[156] On the last three days of yearly meeting, in the evenings large groups of Friends met at Green Street meeting house to consider what to do. At the final session of yearly meeting, John Comly "saw that the Yearly Meeting was now usurped by orthodox power, and henceforth to be under their control and direction."[157] That evening, after yearly meeting closed, the third meeting at Green Street was held—"A conference of seven or eight hundred Friends, resulting in a mild, pacific address to Friends, in order to prepare their minds for 'a quiet retreat from these scenes of confusion' and disorder."[158] In addition to issuing this "Green Street Address," signed by John Comly and seven other Friends, the conference agreed to meet again in early June.

The Green Street conference met again on June 4 and 5. "It was thought upward of a thousand were in attendance. . . . Believing that there would be a propriety in looking toward re-organizing the yearly meeting, an epistle was addressed to our absent members."[159] The epistle called on quarterly and monthly meetings to appoint representatives to meet and hold a yearly meeting in mid-October 1827. The reorganized yearly meeting did meet in October; it concluded by sending an epistle to meetings within the yearly meeting. The epistle was signed by Benjamin Ferris as clerk of the men's yearly meeting and by Rebecca Comly as clerk of the women's yearly meeting.

John Comly's expectation, that the separation would be a peaceful retreat from the scene of confusion, was doomed. As the separation took place within each local meeting, conflicts broke out over possession of property and minute books. Arguments grew fierce; disputing parties locked their opponents out of meeting houses or sued in court for legal ownership of the property; in some meetings, tussles over keeping the monthly meeting minute books became physical. Hopes vanished that the separation might be temporary. In April 1828, the separatist yearly meeting was held at Green Street one week before the orthodox yearly meeting at Arch Street.

In the next few years, John Comly visited Friends meetings in New York, Maryland, Virginia, and Ohio. An epistle from the 1830 Philadelphia Yearly Meeting was signed by John Comly as clerk of the men's yearly meeting and by Lucretia Mott as clerk of the women's yearly meeting. John's wife, Rebecca Comly, died in August 1832. His final travel in the ministry took place in 1845. "The few remaining years were spent chiefly at home, with the infirmities of age and disease increasing upon him, but with a mind unimpaired, sensitive, and alive in concern for the welfare of the human family, and particularly that of his own religious society."[160]

John Comly "edited the writings of John Woolman and Job Scott, and, with his brother, edited the twelve-volume *Friends Miscellany*, which provided for Hicksites the writings of early Quakers."[161] In August 1850 John Comly "was attacked with a violent pain in the chest, and difficulty of respiration"[162] and died within a few hours. Two and a half years later, his children published his *Journal*, adding brief narratives of the periods in his life that he had not himself written about.

During his first summer as a teacher at Westtown School, John Comly recorded in his *Journal* a series of passages that sensitively reveal his inward life and growth. The first two show a deep hunger and thirst for righteousness:

> Humbly hope that Divine Goodness has not forsaken me; but I feel the need of more inwardness and stayedness on that Rock which cannot be shaken, that so I may feel an anchor to my soul in times of trial. O Holy One! preserve me little and low with the seed of life; having no dependence but on Thee, whom I desire to serve.[163]

> Oh! when shall I learn wisdom? when shall I acquire stability and a humble reliance on Divine Guidance in all my ways? Father of Light and Life, forsake me not.[164]

The second of these passages was dated July 5, 1801. Beginning eleven days later, and continuing through the end of August, came an outpouring of outstanding depth and lyrical beauty:

> A pleasant morning. the enlivening scenes of nature are displayed around me in the beautiful landscapes, which are rendered more delightful by a clear sky and the gentle breezes which fan them; the notes of birds warbling on the branches, hymning their great Creator's praise, add a pleasing sensation to the contemplative mind. O my soul! what does all this impress on the understanding? What instruction canst thou derive from the Divine works thus opened to thy view? Meditate and adore.[165]

Toward the close, light again broke forth in feeling intercession to the Father of Mercies, and humble adoration of that great name which is a strong tower to those who trust therein. Thus, in extremity, he is sometimes pleased to appear with healing in his wings. O my soul! reverence and adore, and still trust in him. . . .

At times through the day I have witnessed a comfortable feeling, as under my own vine and fig-tree, where nothing can make afraid. Thus day and night, seed-time and harvest, summer and winter, succeed each other. May I learn in times of refreshing to labour after an increase of faith, and trust in God, so as to have oil in my vessel when darkness or wintry seasons are allotted me.[166]

Alas! what a trifle will discompose me. Ah! where is the meekness and patience of the *Lamb!*—that evenness of temper which the gospel inspires. . . .

In wonderful mercy and loving-kindness, the great Parent of Love was pleased to manifest himself toward the close in a sweet, comfortable visitation of his love to my soul. "Can a maid forget her ornaments, or a bride her attire? Yet Zion said, My Lord hath forsaken me, and my God hath forgotten me. Yea, they may forget, yet will not I forget thee—thou art graven upon the *palms* of my hands. Thy walls are *continually* before me." Such was the comfortable language that revived upon my mind, inspiring earnest breathings that his protecting care might continue to be over me; and in a grateful sense of his watchful providence, my soul was made to adore him whom I have desired to serve.

Thus in extremity the gracious Master is pleased to extend his arm of power, and to reach forth to the fainting mind the wine of his kingdom. Learn, O my soul, by this day's experience, to put thy trust in Omnipotence, and never despair of his mercy. Whatever trials may attend thee, look unto him with steadfastness, and in humble confidence that he will never forget those who desire to love and serve him, but will, in his own time arise with healing in his wings.[167]

The biblical quotation, enclosed in quotation marks, was Jeremiah 2:32, followed by Isaiah 49:14-16 KJV.

I have felt much like a vessel or dam of water, full, as if, were the gate only rightly opened, my heart could pour out much of a stream of Divine love to my fellow-creatures, so very desirous do I feel for their everlasting well-being.[168]

These words and phrases from John Comly's first Westtown summer show forth a spirituality that is spontaneous, imaginative, emotional, sensual—very like George Fox's "affective spirituality."

George Fox, Edward Burrough, Margaret Fell, and other early Friends had often expressed their affective spirituality through the use of biblical metaphors, figures of speech, and symbols. Unlike these forbears, John Comly was an experienced grammarian: he knew what metaphors and figures of speech were, he recognized their presence in the Bible, and he self-consciously made use of them in expressing his spiritual condition and in interpreting biblical passages. Thus, he described the beginning of his first journey in the ministry:

> I was fully persuaded that J. W. ought to have accompanied me in this arduous and important concern. . . . Had human prudence been less consulted by Friends, and he properly encouraged, no doubt he would have united with me as a true yoke-fellow in the work and in the concern I felt to visit the seed of life in the Eastern States.

> I now felt as if I had no outward staff to lean upon, and the whole figure was realized—no money, no purse, no scrip, and only the single coat or clothing of humble confidence in the Shepherd of Israel remained. The seraphim, with covered face, covered feet, and simply the wings of faith and hope to fly on the Lord's errands, was presented to my view, and appeared to be the motto for me. I felt in a degree the awful majesty of Heaven, high and lifted up in immaculate purity, to whom the anthem of Holy, Holy, Holy was ascribed, sitting on his throne; and I felt that he justly claimed all the powers of my body, soul, and spirit, to be devoted to his work and service, and in deep prostration of soul the language was felt, "Lord, here am I, send me," and this is all I can do or offer.

> This state of resignation being attained after a hard struggle, and my mind calm and composed, we set forward on the journey.[169]

In an essay on the first chapter of the gospel of John, Comly wrote:

> John says, "And the light shineth in darkness, and the darkness comprehended it not." This figurative expression must refer to mind and not to matter, or the word *comprehended* would not be used. . . .

> "He (the Light, the Life, the Word, God) was in the world, and the world was made by him, and the world knew him not."

This metaphor of *the world* may represent the state of the soul or mind of man, otherwise called "darkness," before the faculties of perception and understanding are unfolded, or it may be produced, after their development, by inattention to the light, yet God is in the soul, by him it exists, as it was made by him, yet it knows him not till awakened, quickened, enlightened by his renewed visitation and the manifestation of himself.[170]

And John Comly wrote, in an essay on the transfiguration of Jesus:

Now of this transcendent vision, or transfiguration, it might be said of the disciples who were the witnesses of it, as was said on the occasion of Jesus riding into Jerusalem on a young ass, amid the acclamations of the people—"These things understood not his disciples *at the first*; but when Jesus was glorified," then opened he their understandings, and they remembered his words. But so it is with man in his natural state, as Paul said of the Israelites when they read Moses—"the vail is upon their hearts." But when Christ is risen in the soul, and becomes the light and leader thereof, the "vail is done away in Christ, the resurrection and the life" of the soul. Then, and not till then, is this striking figure and just emblem or representation of the Divine harmony of the transfiguration, or conference of Moses, Elias, and Jesus Christ, the representatives of the three dispensations of the law given from Sinai, the prophets, and Christ, understood and to be testified of.[171]

With all of his affective spirituality and grasp of biblical metaphors and figures of speech, I find John Comly to be a bit detached in his approach to biblical passages. He came up just short of the deep empathy with biblical people and times that I found in Fox, Fell, and Burrough.

In his essay on the first chapter of John, Comly suggested that the text could be understood in two very different senses:

"In the beginning was the Word, and the Word was with God, and the Word was God.". . .

If *"the beginning"* is considered in relation to time, and the production of the visible creation, then, in the beginning of time, God, by the putting forth of his power, wisdom, and goodness, created the material world, or universe. By his *word* he produced light, and order, and harmony in the works of Creation.

But if more importantly applying the terms and declaration to inward and spiritual light, order, and peace, we understand "the beginning" to be of the Divine operations in the soul of man, of every man. Then we ascribe all good, all light, all knowledge, all power, that is divine and spiritual, to God only. Thus it is, that "all things are made by" the power, wisdom, and goodness of God, *that are made*, formed, or produced in the mind of the enlightened, quickened man; "and without him," the Word, the Divine power, wisdom, and goodness operating in the soul, there is not any thing made that is made.[172]

The second, "more important" interpretation is close to John Churchman's "spiritualizing" interpretation of many biblical texts. Comly did not go as far as Churchman did toward allegorical interpretations, although one extended passage came close:

In the progression of the Divine work in man, God says, "Let there be a firmament in the midst of the waters, and let it divide the waters from the waters." Man is again addressed as having a part, and an important part, to act in this separation between what is of the earth earthy, carnal, material, sensual, and what is above the reach of all his earthly powers and faculties to investigate or comprehend: for so are all spiritual realities, all real heavenly views, feelings, and impressions. Thus the evidence of Divine revelation is in itself, and hence he that believeth hath the witness of his faith in himself. The firmament is placed in his mind which separates the waters, the instability of human opinions, the fluctuations of the mind, that are and ever ought to be *under* and in subjection to the certain evidence of Divine Truth—the firmament—from the waters, the living refreshing waters of life, which are always above the firmament, divided distinctly, and with a certain calming evidence in themselves from all the imaginations, willings, and runnings of creaturely activity. God called the firmament heaven. And in every obedient mind he makes this firmament, this heaven within; but it is by and with the consent and co-operation of that mind. Hence is understood the expression, "My sheep know my voice and they follow me, and I give unto them eternal life." The dedicated mind learns to know and distinguish between the Divine voice or revelation, and every resemblance of it that may arise in the imagination. A separation is made between the motions or movings of the Spirit and the notions of the creature. The mind acquires stability, firmness, calmness, deliberation, which constitutes the firmament, and God sees and man feels that *it is so*, and that it is good. Then the work goes on in order, the new creation progresses in the soul, the waters under the firmament or government of heavenly power and light are gathered together, and the dry land appears; firm ground and settlement ensues, even in earthly or temporal concerns; for the mind acknowledges and owns the Divine law as its guide in all things, and knows it to direct all its paths both in things earthly and heavenly, and each is kept in its proper place.[173]

When Churchman resorted to allegory, he gave clear, crisp "spiritual" meanings to each term in the text; Comly's spiritualizing here was tentative and sometimes unclear. He identified "firmament" once as "Divine Truth," later as "this heaven within," and third as the "government of heavenly power and light."

In his essay on the transfiguration of Jesus, John Comly re-echoed William Penn's idea of a series of dispensations in which God's requirements for human action had differed:

As the Divine harmony of all the dispensations of God to his creature man, in the progressive work of the new creation, is revealed when the vail is done away in Christ, so the cloud is removed; and the ministration of death, with all the sanguinary laws and their death-penalties, and all the wars and judgments that were commanded by God himself under that typical dispensation, and of which he made the Israelites his executioners—with all the rituals, ceremonies, outward sacrifices and ordinances, oaths and circumcisions, as well as outward washings of that shadowy and figurative dispensation, together with the prophetic or foreseeing dispensation, and the watery baptism of John, under the representation of the prophet Elias—passes away as of no further obligation or use, (however glorious and real in their day,) and Jesus is left alone, with the Divine command to every disciple *to hear him*. Thus Christ, the Light, the Spirit of Truth, the Divine Anointing, the unerring Lawgiver, as well as Saviour of the soul of man, becomes all in all; and our whole and undivided attention is directed *to hear him*, and obey him in all things. Thus, also, we come to witness the new creation; a new heaven and a new earth, wherein dwelleth righteousness, peace, and joy in the Holy Spirit.[174]

I do not find this dispensational language elsewhere in Comly's *Journal*. Indeed, in an 1831 essay he gave an entirely different explanation of the differences between New Testament ethics and Old Testament law. He took the phrase "for the hardness of your heart" (Mark 10:5 KJV), which Jesus had used in forbidding divorce, and generalized it to contrast the imperfections of the law of Moses with the more perfect law of Jesus:

> If we look at the circumstances and state of the Israelites, when Moses delivered to them the law which perfect Wisdom and Goodness adapted to their *low, weak*, and even *hardened* condition, we may see a wise reason in the administration of Providence for suffering or bearing with many things in that people, and giving them ordinances accordingly; which, as they gradually advanced under the tuition of that schoolmaster, they afterward would have no need of, and their obligations would consequently cease. The law would be repealed because fulfilled, and therefore obsolete.

> Thus when Christ, the great Prophet, came, he referred to the law given through Moses, and owned and honoured it by his fulfilling it; but showed the people, in various instances, that it was not adapted to an advanced state of greater perfection and light, which through obedience to that law, as a schoolmaster, they were capable of attaining, and which he instructed them in. Thus, he says, "Ye have heard that it was said by them of old time, Thou shalt not kill"—a positive law, contained in what is called the Decalogue, or laws written by the finger of God himself, on tables of stone. Now let us mark the advanced state of the human mind which Jesus addressed, when he not only confirmed this law but referred to the causes or feelings that would induce a violation of it, and taught the necessity of subduing those passions or lusts which occasioned killing; that thus the root being taken away, the fruit would cease; that the gospel principle of love being embraced, would effectually eradicate hatred; the law of mercy and forgiveness of injuries would supersede the *lex talionis*, which, because of the hardness of their hearts, had been suffered in their low, dark, and carnal state; when it was said, "Thou shall love thy neighbour and hate thy enemy;" and when, for the same reason, they were permitted to exact an eye for an eye, a tooth for a tooth, &c. How different the benign principles that qualify men to "*Love* their enemies, *bless* them that curse, *do good* to them that hate, and *pray* for them that despitefully use and

persecute." And yet these latter are the *positive laws* of Christ, him who we call Master and Lord, and who himself says, "Why call ye me Master and Lord, and do not the things which I say?" . . .

Moses delivered to the Israelites positive and plain precepts, adapted to their understandings, respecting the use of language, in their intercourse one with another. The most obvious principle inculcated is the *speaking of truth*. Hence, all deception and falsehood were forbidden. And here, again, the low, weak, and darkened state of that people was considered and permitted for a season, in suffering them to use oaths for the confirmation of what was asserted for truth. This would be natural in a state of distrust and jealousy. For where mutual confidence is wanting suspicion arises, and the fear of imposition or falsehood instead of sincerity and truth. "For the hardness of your hearts, Moses gave you that precept," might be applied to many parts of that system of government; and among the rest *swearing* was suffered to remain, "until the times of reformation," but the law guarded carefully against deception and fraud by perjury, which it would seem that people were prone to in the selfishness of their dark state.

When Jesus Christ, the Divine Lawgiver, came, he adverted particularly to this subject, as it stood in the statute book of Moses. Perjury or false swearing had been expressly forbidden by Moses, and Jesus forbids *all* swearing. The darkness and hardness of their hearts being removed by light and knowledge, the people, or at least some of them, were prepared to understand, that speaking the truth in sincerity precluded the necessity of oaths.[175]

I can't help speculating whether such an explanation could have helped Abraham Shackleton in his perplexities over reconciling some of the harsh divine commands in the Old Testament with the character of a loving God.

In November 1828, a few months after the separation took place in New York Yearly Meeting, John Comly was visiting Friends in New York state. He proposed to a Friend from Brookfield that he visit the meeting in that town; the Friend "wanted to ask me some questions, . . . to gain information"— presumably to decide whether Comly was orthodox enough to be welcome at that meeting:

His first interrogation was, "Whether I believed in the divinity of our Saviour, and that we had remission of sins through his blood?"

Certainly, said I. I never entertained a doubt on the subject. But it is possible my views may differ from those entertained by some other professors in relation to the meaning and application of the term "blood." Some appear to suppose it is the outward blood that was shed on the outward cross at Jerusalem, more than eighteen hundred years ago. My belief is, that, according to the explanation given by Moses in the law, "the blood is the life," and that we have remission of sins through the life of Christ being raised in us and becoming our life, by our obedience to the light of Christ in us. Thus, through the cross and the denial of self, we come to know a ceasing to do evil and a turning away from all iniquity, and then learning to do well, or to live righteously and godly in this present world; our iniquities are forgiven, and "remembered no more against us," agreeable to the declaration of the Almighty by the mouth of his prophet Ezekiel. Thus we are reconciled by his death, the death of the cross, and saved by his life in us. "For in that he died, he died unto sin once, but in that he liveth, he liveth unto God;" and "because" (or, for the very cause that) "he liveth, we shall live also," with more of like import. To which he fully assented, but wanted to know my views of the propitiatory sacrifice on the cross, as an atonement for the sins of the world; though he said "it was only the body that died; the spirit could not die or be killed." I told him I could not find the term a "propitiatory sacrifice" in the Scriptures, and the application of such a term to the death of Jesus on the cross I thought unwarrantable. The apostle John said, "He is the propitiation for our sins," which I fully believed in; but this did not allude to the body, the manhood that died on the outward cross. It was the Spirit of Truth operating in us, to produce, by our uniting with it, a state of acceptance or reconciliation with God. But he still turned to the outward body, that he said ascended up into heaven. I told him the Scriptures nowhere said the outward body ascended into heaven, though it declared that he was taken up, and a *cloud* received him out of the sight of his gazing disciples; that the cloud still hid his spiritual manifestation from all those who were gazing after the outward body; and this was an instructive figure or parable to such who could not discover his spiritual appearance, but through the dispelling of the cloud in their own minds.[176]

Here he resorted to the approach used by evangelical Friend, Henry

Tuke—using the Bible as an authoritative textbook, from which Christian doctrines were to be deduced—in order to disprove some of the doctrinal positions on which the evangelicals were insisting.

John Comly used the Bible in a variety of ways as did Elias Hicks. He did not venture out into new or unusual doctrinal positions, nor point out the dangers of misusing scripture, as Hicks did. He *was* clearly opposed to any attempt to impose a single set of doctrinal beliefs as a criterion of sound ministry or as a requirement for membership in the Society of Friends.

In November 1773—less than three weeks before the birth of John Comly—Etienne de Grellet du Mabillier was born in Limoges, France. His parents were wealthy members of the French nobility; they were Roman Catholics. He was educated by private tutors and then in several schools and finally at a Catholic college in Lyon. After the French Revolution broke out in 1789, Etienne's parents were sent to prison. In 1791 Etienne and some of his brothers joined the royalist army that was gathering in Germany. After being taken as prisoners of war, the brothers escaped and fled to Amsterdam. Etienne and his brother Joseph sailed in 1793 to French Guiana, in South America, and then in 1795 to New York. By that time, Etienne had given up any faith in God and had become a disciple of the deist philosopher, Voltaire. In America, he anglicized his name to Stephen Grellet.

The brothers arrived in America with no knowledge of English; they spent the summer of 1795 on Long Island. Stephen had heard of the political writings and influence of William Penn and obtaining a volume of Penn's works, dictionary in hand, he began to read it.

> One evening as I was walking in the fields, alone, my mind being under no kind of religious concern, nor in the least excited by any thing I had heard or thought of, I was suddenly arrested by what seemed to be an awful voice proclaiming the words, "Eternity! Eternity! Eternity!" It reached my very soul,—my whole man shook—it brought me, like Saul, to the ground. The great depravity and sinfulness of my heart were set open before me, and the gulf of everlasting destruction to which I was verging. I was made bitterly to cry out, "If there is no God—doubtless there is a hell." I found myself as in the midst of it. . . .
>
> I now took up again the works of William Penn, and opened upon "No Cross, No Crown." The title alone reached to my heart. I proceeded to read it with the help of my dictionary, having to look

for the meaning of nearly every word. . . . I had never met with anything of the kind; neither had I felt the Divine witness in me operating so powerfully before.

I now withdrew from company, and spent most of my time in retirement, and in silent waiting upon God. I began to read the Bible, with the aid of my dictionary.[177]

One day Joseph and Stephen Grellet

heard that a meeting for Divine Worship was appointed to be held next day in the Friends' Meeting House, by two English women on a religious visit to this land, to which we were invited. We felt inclined to go. The Friends were Deborah Darby and Rebecca Young. The sight of them brought solemn feelings over me; . . . in an inward silent frame of mind, seeking for the Divine presence, I was favored to find *in* me, what I had so long, and with so many tears, sought for *without* me. . . . I felt the Lord's power in such a manner, that my inner man was prostrated before my blessed Redeemer. A secret joy filled me, in that I had found Him after whom my soul had longed . . .

My brother and myself were invited to dine in the company of these Friends. . . . I could hardly understand a word of what was said, but, as D. D. began to address my brother and myself, it seemed as if the Lord opened my outward ear, and my heart. Her words partook of the efficacy of that "word" which is "quick and powerful, and sharper than any two-edged sword, piercing even to the dividing asunder of soul and spirit, and of the joints and marrow, and is a discerner of the thoughts and intents of the heart." She seemed like one reading the pages of my heart, with clearness describing how it had been, and how it was with me. . . . My heart was opened. . . . O what sweetness did I then feel! It was indeed a memorable day. I was like one introduced into a new world; the creation, and all things around me, bore a different aspect—my heart glowed with love to all. The awfulness of that day of God's visitation can never cease to be remembered with peculiar interest and gratitude, as long as I have the use of my mental faculties. I have been as one plucked from the burning—rescued from the brink of an horrible pit. O how can the extent of the Lord's love, mercy, pity, and tender compassion be fathomed![178]

Three years later Deborah Darby was to make a significant impact on Betsy Gurney. Not long after William Savery's visit, Deborah Darby also came to Norwich: At a family "opportunity" Deborah Darby suddenly addressed Elizabeth, declaring that the latter was under the hand of God to be "a light to the blind; speech to the dumb; and feet to the lame." . . . From this time on, Elizabeth Gurney became interested in the condition of the poor and was a frequent visitor in their homes.[179]

Soon after his encounter with Deborah Darby, Stephen Grellet began to attend Friends meetings, and then gradually to adopt the plain clothes and speech of Friends. His brother Joseph found work in New York City. Stephen moved to Philadelphia in December 1795. He began to work as a teacher of French, and to attend the North Meeting in Philadelphia—William Savery's meeting. He became a member of that meeting in 1796.

In France, Stephen Grellet's parents were several times at the point of being executed; instead, they were released from prison in 1796. Stephen was recorded as a minister in March, 1798, and in 1799 he moved to New York and became a partner in business with his brother Joseph. Joseph moved back to France in 1802, in order to be with his parents. Their father died late in 1803. Stephen Grellet married Rebecca Collins, a New York Friend, in January, 1804. They had one daughter. About 1815, he formed a business partnership with Robert Pearsall, his brother-in-law.

Stephen Grellet traveled frequently in the ministry—in many parts of North America; to the island nation of Haiti in 1816; and most memorably, four times to Europe. On his first European trip, from June 1807 to March 1808, he went only to France. His second trip, May 1811 to November 1814, took him to the British Isles, France, northern Italy, Switzerland, Germany, and the Netherlands. On his third trip, June 1818 to August 1820, he traveled through England, Norway, Sweden, Finland, Russia, Turkey, Greece, Italy—where he had an audience with the Pope—Switzerland, Germany, France, and Ireland.

In March 1823, Stephen Grellet and his family moved from New York to Burlington, New Jersey, where he again became a member of Philadelphia Yearly Meeting. At the time of the separation in 1827, he was an active leader of the orthodox party. His fourth trip to Europe, June 1831 to July 1834, was to England, Netherlands, Germany, Bohemia, Austria, Hungary, Switzerland, northern Italy, France, Spain, Scotland, and Ireland.

On all four of his European trips, Stephen Grellet visited his mother and other close relatives. He always spent some time with the small group of Friends in southern France. On his second and fourth trips, he also visited the small body of Friends in Germany. He spent much time with monarchs and members of the nobility, and regularly visited prisons, hospitals, and homes for the poor. Frequently, when he found dreadful living conditions in prisons, he would report these in detail to the king or some other government leader; often this led to significant reforms in the management of the prisons.

Stephen Grellet continued to travel in the ministry until 1846. After that, recurring illness kept him increasingly close to home until his death at home in Burlington in November 1855. He had written extensive notes about his travels in the ministry. His accounts of trips to Europe and to Haiti were long and fully detailed. His notes on travels in the United States and Canada were much briefer. In 1860 a German-British Friend, Benjamin Seebohm, gathered these notes, along with some of Grellet's letters and his own narratives of periods not covered by Grellet's writings, and published them as the two-volume *Memoirs* of Stephen Grellet.

Given the brevity of Grellet's account of times when he was in the United States, I found it significant that he mentioned Elias Hicks more than half a dozen times. The first was in an account of the work of a visiting committee appointed by New York Yearly Meeting in 1808:

> Elias Hicks, one of our Committee, frequently advanced sentiments repugnant to the Christian faith, tending to lessen the authority of the Holy Scriptures, to undervalue the sacred offices of our holy and blessed Redeemer. . . . I felt constrained publicly to disavow the unchristian doctrine that he advanced.[180]

In 1816, after his second trip to Europe, he "deeply lamented" developments in New York Yearly Meeting: "Some are carried away by a worldly spirit—others by that of Anti-Christ, under a specious appearance of sanctity. . . . I have felt it to be my duty to labour in love with individuals, and particularly with E. H----."[181] In August 1820, two days after returning from his third European trip, he wrote:

> Attended our meeting. How mingled were my feelings! . . . I find the adversary has sown his seed of enmity to the Truth, and enmity to those that love the Truth; that spirit has spread wide its roots. On sitting in the meeting, . . . I wept bitterly. Elias Hicks has led many to imbibe his anti-christian errors.[182]

In 1822, at the conclusion of a religious visit to Friends in New York, Vermont, and Ontario:

> We then proceeded to Long Island, where I attended all the meetings; but here my soul's distress exceeded all I had known during the preceding months, though my baptisms had been deep. I found that the greatest part of the members of our Society, and many of the Ministers and Elders, are carried away by the principles which Elias Hicks has so assiduously promulgated among them; he now speaks out boldly, disguising his sentiments no longer; he seeks to invalidate the Holy Scriptures, and sets up man's reason as his only guide, openly denying the Divinity of Christ.[183]

In October 1823, a few months after he moved to Burlington, New Jersey, and attended Philadelphia Yearly Meeting, he lamented: "I feel peaceful in having come here; but my sadness is not lessened; the little dark cloud, which years past, rested chiefly over a small spot at Jericho, on Long Island, is now like a thick darkness over the land."[184] In 1829, the year after the separation took place in New York Yearly Meeting, Stephen Grellet was holding meetings in upstate New York: "Elias Hicks was travelling in these parts. . . . I had meetings in places where he had been one or two days before. The people had been brought under great excitement by the anti-christian doctrines he had delivered."[185]

On his final European trip, Grellet was visiting scattered Waldensian communities in northern Italy in November 1832. Even as he marveled at the faithfulness with which these Christians had endured centuries of persecution,

> My soul did yearn towards those in America who have been subverted from the faith and the hope of that salvation which is through Jesus Christ, by Elias Hicks and his coadjutors; yet I entertain a hope that the Lord's faithful messengers will, in days to come, when those who have been active in sowing the evil seed are laid in the silent grave, be sent and commissioned to preach unto their children the glad tidings of salvation, and the word of reconciliation with God through Jesus Christ.[186]

Stephen Grellet's attitudes toward Elias Hicks and those Friends who were to become Hicksites seem to me to have been so harsh and unrelenting that John Comly's hopes that a separation could be peaceable and that it might be temporary until an accommodation could be found, were doomed from the start.

Carole Spencer has offered a more sympathetic reading of Grellet on this matter:

> Grellet, who was known for his compassion and spiritual sensitivity, and not his polemic, nevertheless found himself painfully swept into the storm of the Hicksite-Orthodox separation. . . . His darkest "dark night of the soul" was the Orthodox-Hicksite split, which plunged him into the "deepest baptisms" of his spiritual life.[187]

In truth, we all see through a glass darkly. Going back to the argument between Larry Ingle and Doug Gwyn about facts and interpretation in history, I note that Ingle was honest enough in his Preface to the second edition of *Quakers in Conflict*, to confess "that I found (and find) the Hicksites' commitment to doctrinal tolerance more appealing than the heavy-handedness practiced by their opponents."[188] I am convinced that recognizing the lens through which he read the events of the Hicksite-Orthodox Separation enhanced the value of this masterful study for our understanding of those events. One of my own goals, in reading not only the Bible but any other writings, is to achieve an empathy that makes it possible for me to interpret the author's views from within, or at least as a close friend. I must confess that I find it singularly difficult to empathize with Stephen Grellet. My interpretation of his writings is perforce as an outsider, puzzled about what makes him tick, and sometimes offended by what he says. I will try to achieve some balance here by quoting occasionally from Carole Spencer and other writers who read him more sympathetically.

Stephen Grellet recorded his thoughts while attending a Friends meeting for worship, during that first summer in 1795—an early expression of his Christian spirituality:

> My misery was great; my cry was not unlike that of Isaiah, "*Woe is me, for I am undone!*" The nearer I was then favoured to approach to Him "who dwelleth in the light," the more I saw my uncleanness and my wretchedness. But how can I set forth the fulness of heavenly joy that filled me, when the hope was again raised that there was One, even He whom I had pierced, Jesus Christ the Redeemer, that was able to save me? I saw him to be the Lamb of God that taketh away the sins of the world; who was delivered for our offences, and raised again for our justification; who is our propitiatory sacrifice, our advocate with the Father, our intercessor with God. I felt faith in His atoning blood quickening my soul, giving me to believe, that it was

He who could wash me from my many pollutions, and deliver me from death and destruction.[189]

A number of biblical quotations are clear in this passage:

Woe is me, for I am undone!—Isaiah 6:5

the Lamb of God that taketh away the sin of the world—John 1:29

raised again for our justification—Romans 4:25

advocate with the Father—1 John 2:1

Two phrases are more problematic: "our propitiatory sacrifice" and "His atoning blood." Their absence from Cruden's Concordance confirms that these are *not* biblical quotations. Could they reflect the spirituality of early Friends?

A word search, using the Digital Quaker Collection, turned up zero occurrences of the phrase "atoning blood" in the writings of George Fox, Francis Howgill, Edward Burrough, Margaret Fell, Isaac Penington, Samuel Fisher, William Penn, and Robert Barclay. Earlier in this chapter, I reported on the use of the phrase "propitiatory sacrifice" in Fox, Penn, and Barclay (p. 172). Burrough, Fell, and Fisher did not use that phrase. Howgill used it only in a quotation from a Roman Catholic opponent (where it referred to the Eucharist). The phrase appeared in the extended title of one epistle by Isaac Penington, addressed "to all Serious Professors of the Christian Religion"; Penington also wrote "propitiatory sacrifice" once in the text of that epistle. At most, clearly, the phrases "atoning blood" and "propitiatory sacrifice" played an extremely insignificant part in the thought or spirituality of seventeenth-century Friends.

A much later expression of Grellet's spirituality was penned in 1831, shortly after his arrival in England, on his final European journey. Friends at Coventry Meeting, he wrote,

worship before the throne of God, joining with angels and arch-angels in singing the song of Moses and of the Lamb. May I so keep under the guidance of the Holy Spirit, and under the baptizing and purifying influences thereof, that at the end of my earthly race, I may, through redeeming love and mercy, be admitted into that blessed and glorious company, and join them in the endless song of glory and praise to the Lord God Almighty and to the Lamb, my Saviour and Redeemer. Earnest were my prayers, that my beloved wife and daughter, from whom I am now separated for the service of the Lord in his militant church, may be admitted also with me into those mansions of everlasting felicity.[190]

The phrase, "the endless song of glory and praise to the Lord God Almighty and to the Lamb, my Saviour and Redeemer," is characteristic of Stephen Grellet's tendency to bring biblical words and brief phrases together into a combination that is not found in any single biblical context. Brief phrases, such as "blessed Redeemer" and "the Lord's mercy," are scattered frequently through his narratives.

At a meeting in Ontario in 1829,

I proceeded to state what kind of doctrine ought to be preached by a minister of the Gospel of Jesus Christ, unto whom the word of reconciliation is committed, as the Apostle goes on to say, "Now then we are ambassadors for Christ, as though God did beseech you by us; we pray you in Christ's stead, be ye reconciled to God." I entreated, most fervently, all present not to reject such great salvation as was offered to all through the tender mercies of God and the love of the Redeemer. . . . A meeting for Divine worship was held afterwards, and a great crowd attended it; for Christian professors of various denominations felt much for Friends on the occasion; they consider that the doctrines promulgated by the separatists are attacks upon vital Christianity.[191]

He clearly approved the position taken by those "Christian professors." Stephen Grellet was convinced that correct doctrine was essential to "vital Christianity" and that incorrect doctrine amounted to a rejection of the Christian gospel of salvation.

I conclude that Stephen Grellet drew on the Bible as a source book of texts for doctrines that he considered essential to salvation and to true Christian faith. The following passage written in 1822 can serve as an example:

The concern that laid with great weight upon me, during my religious engagement, was that Friends generally, and the dear young people particularly, might be deeply rooted and established in the saving knowledge of God and our Lord Jesus Christ; for "to know him, the true God and Jesus Christ, whom he hath sent, is life eternal." My commission day by day, and from place to place, was renewed, to preach Christ and him crucified, unto the Jews a stumbling block, and unto the Greeks foolishness, but to them that believe the power of God and the wisdom of God, who also is made to them of God wisdom and righteousness, sanctification, and redemption. He was delivered for our offences, and was raised again for our justification, and ever liveth to make intercession for them that come unto God by him. I directed them to him who is the Lamb of God that taketh away the sin of the world, and the author of eternal salvation unto all that obey him. I rehearsed the words of the apostle Peter; "Be it known unto you all and to all the people of Israel, that by the name of Jesus Christ of Nazareth, whom ye crucified, whom God raised from the dead, even by Him doth this man stand here before you whole. This is the stone which was set at nought of you builders, which is become the head of the corner, neither is there salvation in any other: for there is none other name under heaven given among men, whereby you must be saved."[192]

For Grellet, the Bible also served as a textbook for Christian ethics. He believed that the standards for Christian behavior were based on the fundamental doctrines of the Christian faith. An example of his thought on ethics can be found in this passage, written in France in 1833:

I found among the chief magistrates present a good deal of seriousness, and a desire to obtain information on Friends' Christian principles and peaceable testimonies. The subject of war is one of peculiar inquiry and interest to some of them. Very nearly connected with this is faith in God, and in our Lord Jesus Christ, the Prince of Peace. If we believe truly in Him, we must necessarily keep his commandments. This is his commandment, that we love one another as he has loved us. How can then the servants of the Lord Jesus fight? Their weapons are not carnal, but spiritual; their sword is that of the Spirit; their whole armour is that of Light. Many will assent to these Gospel truths, but the obedience of faith is lacking in them.[193]

I see an important difference between Stephen Grellet's preaching and the preaching of early Friends. In the middle of the seventeenth century, Friends primarily attempted to draw their hearers into a gathered people, through which God would act to accomplish his redemptive purposes in history. Grellet's chief aim was to save souls, to convert individuals to the true faith so that they would go to heaven, not hell, after their death. (He did add to this a clear concern for social outreach, particularly prison reform.)

Carole Spencer focused more on Grellet's continuity with early Friends: "Grellet's experience contains many of the same elements as found in the conversion narratives of early Quakers."[194] She summarized her assessment of Stephen Grellet:

> This later period, 1775-1830, can be identified as "Evangelical Quietism." . . . Perhaps the greatest "Public Friend" in the Quietist period was Stephen Grellet, one of a group of evangelical Quietist ministers—though not revivalists—with their deep concern for spiritual nurture of the Quaker community, and a passion for outreach, both evangelistic and social.[195]

Rufus Jones also believed that Stephen Grellet shared the central values of his Quaker heritage: "There is no doubt whatever that Grellet appreciated at its full value the inner way of worship and the direct influence of the Holy Spirit." Although Jones was critical of Grellet's theology and his "evangelical temper," he expressed this deep appreciation of Stephen Grellet:

> He had an unmistakable unction from above, and he often seemed carried beyond himself with an inspiration which none who heard him at such times could doubt. He felt intensely the burden of the world's suffering, and he yearned with apostolic zeal over those who were astray in the deeps of sin. He was a tender prophet, appealing in love rather than moving by emotions of fear and terror.[196]

William Wistar Comfort, in his biography of Stephen Grellet, summed up his evaluation of Grellet's preaching: "The secret of his appeal must have been in a personality and a delivery that both attracted and held the hearer."[197] Comfort emphasized that Stephen Grellet "left behind him a luminous trail of accomplishment. No other Quaker in modern times can be said in reality to have been an international figure. . . . Grellet was in first place . . . as an evangelist and as a humanitarian."[198]

The separation that began in Philadelphia in 1827 spread to several other yearly meetings in 1828. When New York Yearly Meeting convened in May, quite a few visiting Friends were present—including Thomas Shillitoe, a recorded minister from London Yearly Meeting, and a considerable number of Hicksite Friends from Philadelphia. Shillitoe objected to the presence of the latter group, pointing out that they had been disowned by their (orthodox) meetings. Two hours of debate grew raucous in spite of Elias Hicks's attempts to quiet the crowd. Finally, the orthodox minority tried to move downstairs and reconvene in the basement, only to find themselves locked out.

In July 1828 Elias Hicks headed west on a religious visit to Friends in Ohio and Indiana, including attendance at both Ohio and Indiana Yearly Meetings:

> Meanwhile Thomas Shillitoe was also driving towards Ohio Yearly Meeting. . . . In western Pennsylvania the two opponents came face to face. At Westland, after Elias finished speaking, Thomas Shillitoe greatly disturbed the gathering by his pointed opposition. A little later he called Elias an imposter. . . . On several occasions, in business sessions, the English minister opposed the reading of Elias' certificate, and once declared he would rather not have his own certificate read if the certificate of the Jericho minister was to be minuted.[199]

The separation at Ohio Yearly Meeting was the most disorderly of all, with one session degenerating into a near-riot.

In spite of their complaints about Orthodox attempts to impose a creed, Hicksite Friends had their own limits. In 1829 Wilmington Monthly Meeting (one of the strongholds of the Hicksite dissent) disowned several members, led by Benjamin Webb, because they "'denied . . . *certain parts of the Scripture*'"[200] and reprinted the writings of some of the more extreme religious skeptics of their day.

Epilogue

Through a close reading of portions of the writings of George Fox, Edward Burrough, and Margaret Fell, I made the discovery that at least these three, first-generation Friends, were reading the Bible with empathy. They stood within the thought and life-world of the earliest Christians and looked at the world through the window of biblical faith. For them the heart of the Bible lay in its personal narratives—the stories of living men, women, and communities; unlike many Christians, then and now, they did not look at the Bible as a legal constitution. They reveled in the poetic language of the Bible's rich symbol and metaphor. Out of this empathetic reading emerged not only some of their strange behaviors, such as going naked in public "as a sign," but also their innovative understanding of the Christian way of life—their anti-war testimony and commitment to social justice (through their empathetic "Lamb's War" reading of The Book of Revelation), their insistence on the full equality of women and men in preaching and declaring the Christian message.

I have argued that Fox's method of reading and interpreting the Bible was indeed "the linchpin of George Fox's understanding of Quakerism."[1] But Fox and nearly all the earliest Friends were unsophisticated in linguistics, rhetoric, and philosophy. They never used the term "empathy" themselves; the closest they could come to recognizing symbol and metaphor was to say that they were reading the Bible "spiritually." So Fox failed to notice that second-generation Friends were using the Bible quite differently; William Penn looked on the Bible primarily as a handbook, a collection of rules and guidelines, or a series of "dispensations" within the history of God's dealings with humanity. For Penn, the linchpin of Friends had become "The Light of Christ within, as God's gift for man's salvation."[2] For Robert Barclay, the linchpin had apparently become the Spirit as primary authority, with scripture as "a secondary rule, subordinate to the Spirit. . . . The fact that early Friends were unable to recognize that they were reading the Bible empathetically and metaphorically may be one reason why this way of reading and understanding the Bible almost disappeared after the first generation of Quakerism."[3]

In the eighteenth century a series of (sometimes marginal) Friends developed a variety of biblical arguments in their efforts to influence Friends to give up slaveholding. During this period many Friends were deeply influenced by a French Roman Catholic mystical movement known as Quietism. After the middle of the century, leading Quietist Friends became active in efforts to reform the Society of Friends. They were determined to enforce discipline by strengthening a "hedge" to prevent outside influences from diluting Quakerism's core traditions; they also saw the need to deepen Quaker ethical practice by gradually eliminating the holding of slaves by Friends and by getting rid of compromises to the peace testimony involved in continuing Quakers' political control of the Pennsylvania colony.

I have noted astonishing differences in the ways these reformers made use of the Bible. Even John Woolman used varying approaches, tailored to his specific audiences. In his antislavery essays he made principles the starting point: biblical principles such as love, justice, and universality, and philosophical principles such as natural human rights. Then he used sophisticated arguments in making other specific biblical precepts or practices secondary. At points in his *Journal* he confessed to a "near sympathy" with biblical prophets as well as with oppressed persons and groups in his own day. Woolman, unlike George Fox and Edward Burrough, showed conscious awareness that he was reading the Bible with empathy. But the empathetic reading of the Bible was a grace note in his spirituality and not the center of his understanding of Quaker and Christian faith.

In spite of their differing ways of reading the Bible, George Fox and William Penn had been close friends and allies on controversial issues among Friends, such as the establishment of women's meetings for business. In like manner, Woolman, Anthony Benezet, John Churchman, and Samuel Fothergill, despite their differences in interpreting the Bible, had also been close friends and allies in the antislavery struggle. They were united in openly refusing to pay war taxes to the Pennsylvania colonial government during the French and Indian War, and in their successful struggle to have Philadelphia Yearly Meeting approve this action as an acceptable expression of the Quaker testimony against war.

By the end of the eighteenth century, the reformers' "hedge" of strict Quaker discipline was clearly failing in its primary goal—to keep outside influences from having a major impact on Quaker thinking and spirituality. Two major worldviews were sweeping through Western society—the Enlightenment and the Evangelical Movement. Many Friends found in Evangelicalism a depth of Christian enthusiasm and commitment to social justice that seemed to echo the fervor and testimonies of the earliest Friends. Many others found in the Enlightenment an emphasis on reason in religion that reminded them of the writings of Penn and Robert Barclay, and a commitment to religious and political freedom that matched the struggles of the first Friends. Friends on both sides failed to notice the ways in which the movements they espoused differed profoundly from the spirituality, community life, and thought of the founders of Quakerism.

The idea and practice of reading the Bible with empathy had long since been forgotten. Evangelical Friends, such as Henry Tuke and Stephen Grellet, openly turned to the Bible as a legal constitution, providing clear, consistent, not-to-be-questioned rules for Christian thought and behavior. If there seemed to be inconsistencies in the Bible, this was simply the inability to comprehend the depths of God's inscrutable wisdom. Enlightenment Friends, including John Comly and Elias Hicks, were more free in their approach to the Bible. Comly, a teacher and grammarian, recognized the importance of figurative speech, symbolism, and metaphors in biblical narratives. Elias Hicks insisted on the Bible as a secondary rule, subordinate to the "principle of light and truth in the mind,"[4] and that "we cannot believe what we do not understand."[5] He was quite prepared to accept the reality of inconsistencies within the Bible, and that some passages, such as Matthew's genealogy of Jesus, were therefore "of very little use."[6]

A pair of incidents stand out as signposts of the growing conflict between these two Quaker groups. In December 1822 Elias Hicks, who was returning from a traveling ministry in the Baltimore area to his home in Long Island, New York, arrived in Philadelphia. A number of Philadelphia elders had heard reports that Hicks was spreading unscriptural ideas that threatened the true Christian faith; they were determined to prevent him from preaching these ideas in the city of Philadelphia. These elders requested a meeting, intending to meet privately with Hicks and his traveling companion. Hicks had been forewarned of their intentions and brought a number of supporters with him, including John Comly, as witnesses. No agreement could be reached on how many Friends could be present. As the meeting broke up, one elder "flung out, 'The *ministers* are *answerable* to the *Elders.*' . . . Hicks retorted, . . . 'I have a certificate from my *friends at home* and I am *answerable* to them.'"[7] Hicks continued his public ministry in Philadelphia for nearly two weeks before heading home.

During the sessions of New York Yearly Meeting in June 1826, Elias Hicks was one of more than two thousand Friends who attended meeting for worship at Rose Street Meeting in New York City. Visiting ministers present included Elizabeth Robson and Anna Braithwaite from London Yearly Meeting, and Thomas Wetherald from Alexandria, Virginia. Evidently many New York Friends were hoping to hear messages from Wetherald and Hicks. But early in the meeting, Elizabeth Robson rose and gave an evangelical-sounding sermon that lasted "for more than an hour."[8] "As soon as she sat down Anna Braithwaite kneeled [and prayed vocally]. And almost as soon as she arose,"[9] two Friends on the facing bench shook hands, as a signal that the meeting was closed. But a Friend sitting close by "and Thomas Wetherald sat still"[10] refused to shake hands—breaking the chain. Every Friend continued sitting in silence until Wetherald rose and spoke; Elias Hicks then briefly continued Wetherald's train of thought, concluding with the words:

> Christ, which is the Saviour of the world, . . . never was crucified by the sons of men. They crucified only the outward part, the flesh. . . .
>
> This Christ never was crucified outwardly. But the children of men have an opportunity of crucifying him in their own hearts.[11]

Then "a short pause ensued—when Mr. Hicks and Mr. Wetherald shook hands, and the meeting quietly dispersed."[12]

To expand the context of John Comly's 1827 phrase, Quakerism in America had truly become (with some stirring of the pot by visiting Quaker ministers from London Yearly Meeting) a "scene of confusion." This confusion was complicated by the fact that disagreement over how to understand and use the Bible was only part of the controversy. For many Evangelicals the core of the "horribly blasphemous preaching" of Hicks was that he "denied the Atonement."[13] John Comly was among those who charged that leading Evangelical Friends were trying to impose a creed on their yearly meeting.

In chapter one I dealt with the theme of eschatology. In the following chapters I concentrated on the primary theme of this work: how Friends have looked at and used the Bible. In the second volume I will introduce two important new themes: the place of creeds among Friends, and the ways Friends have understood Christ's atonement. In the opening chapter of that volume, I will examine how Hicksite and Orthodox Friends not only sharply deviated from each other, but also deviated significantly from early Quaker thinking on these two issues.

Notes

Introduction

1. Robert Barclay, *An Apology for the True Christian Divinity: being an explanation and vindication of the principles and doctrines of the people called Quakers*, stereotype ed. (Philadelphia: Friends Book Store, 1908), 72.
2. Northwest Yearly Meeting of Friends, *Faith and Practice* (Newberg, Oregon: Barclay Press, Inc., 1987), 23-24.
3. Lucretia C. Mott, *Selected Letters of Lucretia Coffin Mott*, ed. Beverly Wilson Palmer (Urbana: University of Illinois Press, 2002), 175-6.
4. Lucretia Mott, *Lucretia Mott: Her Complete Speeches and Sermons*, ed. with Introduction by Dana Greene (New York and Toronto: Edwin Mellen Press, 1980), 111.
5. Ibid., 129.
6. Thomas R. Kelly, *A Testament of Devotion* (New York: Harper & Row, 1941), 82.
7. Kenneth Boulding, *The Practice of the Love of God*, Pendle Hill Pamphlet 374 (Wallingford, PA: Pendle Hill Publications, 2004), 31.

8. T. Vail Palmer Jr., "Deeds and Rules in Quaker Ethics," *Quaker Religious Thought* 13, no. 2 (Winter 1971-72): 6.

9. Bernhard W. Anderson, *Understanding the Old Testament*, 3rd ed. (Englewood Cliffs, NJ: Prentice-Hall, 1975), 13-14.

10. Bernhard W. Anderson, *The Unfolding Drama of the Bible* (New York: Association Press, 1957), 12.

11. G. Ernest Wright, *God Who Acts: Biblical Theology as Recital*, vol. 8, Studies in Biblical Theology (London: SCM Press, 1952), 28.

12. Margaret Fell, *Womens Speaking Justified.* . . . (1666; repr., Amherst, MA: Mosher Book & Tract Committee, New England Yearly Meeting of Friends, 1980), 9.

13. John Calvin, *The First Epistle of Paul the Apostle to the Corinthians*, trans. John W. Fraser, Calvin's New Testament Commentaries (1960; repr., Grand Rapids: William B. Eerdmans, 1976), 9:306.

14. George Fox, *The Works of George Fox*, 8 vols. New Foundation Publication (1831; repr., State College, PA: George Fox Fund, 1990), 4:106.

15. Ibid., 4:107.

16. Ibid., 4:109.

17. Fell, *Womens Speaking Justified*, 6-7.

18. Ibid., 13.

19. George Fox, *The Journal of George Fox*, rev. ed. by John L. Nickalls (Cambridge: Cambridge University Press, 1952), 71.

20. Barclay, *Apology*, 88.

21. John Woolman, *The Journal and Major Essays of John Woolman*, ed. Phillips P. Moulton (1971; 7th repr., Richmond, IN: Friends United Press, 2001), 60.

22. Michael L. Birkel, *A Near Sympathy: The Timeless Quaker Wisdom of John Woolman* (Richmond, IN: Friends United Press, 2003), 81.

23. Woolman, *Journal*, 133-4.

24. Thomas R. Kelly, *Reality of the Spiritual World*, Pendle Hill Pamphlet 21 (Wallingford, PA: Pendle Hill, 1942), 33.

25. Alan Kolp, "Fox Loved the Apostle Paul," *Quaker Religious Thought* 25, no. 2 (October 1991): 24.

26. Lonnie Valentine, "War and War Resistance in the Old Testament," in *The Quaker Bible Reader*, eds. Paul Buckley and Stephen W. Angell (Richmond, IN: Earlham School of Religion Publications, 2006), 78-79.

27. John Punshon, "Miss Wilson's Legacy: How My Early Schooling Taught Me to Read the Letter to the Hebrews," in *The Quaker Bible Reader*, eds. Paul Buckley and Stephen W. Angell (Richmond, IN: Earlham School of Religion Publications, 2006), 266.
28. Carole Dale Spencer, *Holiness: The Soul of Quakerism: An Historical Analysis of the Theology of Holiness in the Quaker Tradition*, Studies in Christian History and Thought (Eugene, OR: Wipf & Stock, 2008), 16.
29. Ibid., 16, n. 25.
30. Gerard Guiton, *The Early Quakers and the "Kingdom of God": Peace, Testimony and Revolution* (San Francisco: Inner Light Books, 2012), 4.
31. Michael Birkel, "Reading Scripture with Dorothy White," *Quaker Religious Thought* 30, no. 3 (September 2001): 58.
32. Ibid., 60-61.
33. Michael L. Birkel, *Engaging Scripture: Reading the Bible with Early Friends* (Richmond, IN: Friends United Press, 2005), xxi.
34. Ibid., 1-2.
35. Ibid., 10.
36. Ibid., 71-72.
37. Daniel L. Smith-Christopher, *A Biblical Theology of Exile*, Overtures to Biblical Theology (Minneapolis: Fortress Press, 2002), 54.
38. Daniel L. Smith-Christopher, *Jonah, Jesus, and Other Good Coyotes: Speaking Peace to Power in the Bible* (Nashville: Abingdon Press, 2007), 2.
39. Ibid., 4.
40. Ibid., 172.

Chapter One

1. H. Larry Ingle, "On the Folly of Seeking the Quaker Holy Grail," *Quaker Religious Thought* 25, no. 1 (May 1991): 25.
2. Douglas Gwyn, "Response" [to H. Larry Ingle, "On the Folly of Seeking the Quaker Holy Grail"], *Quaker Religious Thought* 25, no. 1 (May 1991): 31.
3. Ibid., 32.
4. Alfred North Whitehead, *Process and Reality: An Essay in Cosmology*, First Harper Torchbook Edition (New York: Harper & Brothers, 1960), 22.
5. William Penn, *Rise and Progress of the People Called Quakers* (1694; repr., Philadelphia: Friends Book Store, 1947), 7.

6.   Ibid., 9.
7.   Ibid., 15.
8.   Ibid., 11.
9.   D. M. Baillie, *God Was in Christ: An Essay on Incarnation and Atonement* (New York: Charles Scribner's Sons, 1948), 126.
10.   Albert Schweitzer, *The Quest of the Historical Jesus: A Critical Study of Its Progress from Reimarus to Wrede,* trans. W. Montgomery (1910; repr., New York: Macmillan, 1950), 403.
11.   Karl Barth, *The Epistle to the Romans*, trans. Edwin C. Hoskyns from 6th ed. (1933; repr., London: Oxford University Press, 1968), 17.
12.   Bernhard W. Anderson, *Understanding the Old Testament*, 3rd ed. (Englewood Cliffs, NJ: Prentice-Hall, 1975), 13-14.
13.   Bernard W. Anderson, *The Unfolding Drama of the Bible* (New York: Association Press, 1957), 12.
14.   G. Ernest Wright, *God Who Acts: Biblical Theology as Recital*, vol. 8, Studies in Biblical Theology (London: SCM Press, 1952), 28.
15.   Karl Barth, *The Word of God and the Word of Man*, trans. Douglas Horton (1928; New York: Harper & Brothers, 1957), 33.
16.   Ibid., 45.
17.   Ibid., 49.
18.   Ibid., 50.
19.   T. Vail Palmer Jr., "Deeds and Rules in Quaker Ethics," *Quaker Religious Thought* 13, no. 2 (Winter 1971-72): 6-7.
20.   Melvin Endy, "George Fox and William Penn: Their Relationship and Their Roles within the Quaker Movement," *Quaker History* 93, no. 1 (Spring 2004): 34.
21.   T. Canby Jones, *Triumph Through Obedience*, Quaker Lecture (Indianapolis: John Woolman Press, 1964), 40.
22.   R. W. Tucker, "Revolutionary Faithfulness," *Quaker Religious Thought* 9, no. 2 (Winter 1967-68): 28-29.
23.   Ibid., 23.
24.   Ibid., 4.
25.   Douglas Gwyn, *The Covenant Crucified: Quakers and the Rise of Capitalism* (Wallingford, PA: Pendle Hill Publications, 1995), 106.
26.   Hugh S. Barbour, "Protestant Quakerism," *Quaker Religious Thought* 11, no. 2 (Autumn 1969): 2.
27.   Maurice A. Creasey, "Radical Christianity and Christian Radicalism," in *Collected Essays of Maurice Creasey, 1912-2004: The Social Thought of a Quaker Thinker,* ed. David L. Johns, Quaker Studies 8 (Lewiston, NY: Edwin Mellen Press, 2011), 32.

28. Ibid., 34.
29. John Howard Yoder, *The Politics of Jesus: vicit agnus noster* (Grand Rapids: William B. Eerdmans, 1972), 46-47.
30. Tucker, "Revolutionary Faithfulness," 6-8.
31. T. Vail Palmer Jr., "The Radical-Reformation Tradition and Emergent Christian Ethics," (presentation, Annual Meeting of the American Academy of Religion, Newton, MA, 1969), 10.
32. Douglas Gwyn, *Seekers Found: Atonement in Early Quaker Experience* (Wallingford, PA: Pendle Hill Publications, 2000), 121.
33. Francis Howgill, "The inheritance of Jacob discovered. . . .," in *The Book of Francis Howgill*, comp. Will Hayes (1656; Meopham Green, Kent: The Order of the Great Companions, 1942), 63.
34. George Fox, *The Journal of George Fox*, rev. ed. by John L. Nickalls (Cambridge: Cambridge University Press, 1952), 107-9.
35. Francis Howgill, "Francis Howgil's Testimony Concerning the Life, Death, Tryals and Labours of Edward Burrough. . . ." in *The memorable Works of a Son of Thunder and Consolation. . . .*, by Edward Burrough (London: Ellis Hooks, 1672).
36. Fox, *Journal*, 1-2.
37. Elbert Russell, *The History of Quakerism* (Richmond, IN: Friends United Press, 1979), 22.
38. Fox, *Journal*, 11.
39. Ibid., 3.
40. Ibid., 12.
41. Ibid., 13.
42. Ibid., 14.
43. Ibid., 123.
44. Ibid., 3.
45. Ibid., 103-4.
46. Ibid., 104.
47. Ibid., 106.
48. Ibid., 104.
49. George Fox, *The Works of George Fox*, 8 vols. New Foundation Publication (1831; repr., State College, PA: George Fox Fund, 1990), 8:93.
50. Fox, *Journal*, 236.
51. Fox, *Works of George Fox*, 4:180.
52. Edward Burrough, *The memorable Works of a Son of Thunder and Consolation. . . .* (London: Ellis Hooks, 1672), 494.

53. T. Vail Palmer Jr., "Quaker Peace Witness: The Biblical and Historical Roots," *Quaker Religious Thought* 23, no. 2-3 (Summer 1988): 40-44.

54. Burrough, *Memorable Works*, 12.

55. Ibid., 18.

56. Pink Dandelion, *The Liturgies of Quakerism*, Liturgy, Worship and Society (Aldershot, Hampshire: Ashgate Publishing, 2005), 12.

57. Ibid., 42.

58. Ibid., 41.

59. Maurice A. Creasey, "Quakers and the Sacraments," *Quaker Religious Thought* 5, no. 1 (Spring 1963): 14.

60. Daniel Smith-Christopher, *A Biblical Theology of Exile*, Overtures to Biblical Theology (Minneapolis: Fortress Press, 2002), 66-73.

61. Anderson, *Understanding the Old Testament*, 462.

62. Ibid., 447.

63. Fox, *Journal*, 27.

64. C. H. Dodd, *Christianity and the Reconciliation of the Nations*, The Burge Memorial Lecture, November 1951 (London: SCM Press, 1952), 6.

65. Karl Barth, *Evangelical Theology: An Introduction*, trans. Grover Foley (Garden City, NY: Doubleday, 1964), 29-30.

66. Burrough, *Memorable Works*, 844.

67. Gwyn, *Covenant Crucified*, 109.

68. Ibid., 108.

69. William James, *The Varieties of Religious Experience: A Study in Human Nature*, The Modern Library (1902; New York: Random House, 1929), 8.

Chapter Two

1. T. Vail Palmer Jr., "Early Friends and the Bible," *Quaker Religious Thought* 23, no. 5 (1992).

2. George Fox, *The Works of George Fox*, 8 vols. New Foundation Publication (1831; repr., State College, PA: George Fox Fund, 1990), 7:16-17.

3. Edward Burrough, *An Epistle To all the Saints whom God hath called* (n.p., 1657), 1-2.

4. Edward Burrough, *The memorable Works of a Son of Thunder and Consolation. . . .* (London: Ellis Hooks, 1672), 64.

5. Fox, *Works of George Fox*, 4:306.

6. Ibid.
7. Ibid., 4:307-8.
8. Ibid., 4:309.
9. Ibid., 4:309-11.
10. Margaret Fell, *Womens Speaking Justified.* . . . (1666; repr., Amherst, MA: Mosher Book & Tract Committee, New England Yearly Meeting of Friends, 1980), 7-8.
11. Ibid., 9.
12. Ibid., 5.
13. Ibid., 6.
14. Ibid., 7.
15. Ibid., 11.
16. Ibid., 13.
17. Ibid., 4-5.
18. Ibid., 9.
19. George Fox, *The Journal of George Fox,* rev. ed. by John L. Nickalls (Cambridge: Cambridge University Press, 1952), 33.
20. Ibid., 71.
21. Alan Kolp, *Fresh Winds of the Spirit* (Richmond, IN: Friends United Press, 1991), 42.
22. Fell, *Womens Speaking Justified,* 4.
23. Kolp, *Fresh Winds,* 42.
24. Bruce C. Birch and Larry L. Rasmussen, *Bible and Ethics in the Christian Life* (Minneapolis: Augsburg, 1976), 104.
25. Carol D. Spencer, "Holiness: The Quaker Way of Perfection," *Quaker History* 93, no. 1 (Spring 2004): 143.
26. Michael L. Birkel, *Engaging Scripture: Reading the Bible with Early Friends* (Richmond, IN: Friends United Press, 2005), xx-xxi.
27. Michael L. Birkel, *A Near Sympathy: The Timeless Quaker Wisdom of John Woolman* (Richmond, IN: Friends United Press, 2003), 43.
28. Peter J. Gomes, *The Good Book: Reading the Bible with Mind and Heart* (1996; New York: Avon Books, 1998), 340-41.
29. T. Vann, *The Social Development of English Quakerism: 1655-1755* (Cambridge, MA: Harvard University Press, 1969), 84-85.
30. Ibid., 199.
31. T. Vail Palmer Jr., "A Revisionist Revised: A New Look at Bernstein's *Cromwell and Communism,*" in *Practiced in the Presence: Essays in Honor of T. Canby Jones,* eds. D. Neil Snarr and Daniel L. Smith-Christopher (Richmond, IN: Friends United Press, 1994), 43.

32. Samuel Fisher, "Rusticus ad Academicos," in *The Testimony of Truth Exalted. . . .*, by Samuel Fisher (n.p., 1679), 335.
33. Ibid., 404.
34. Ibid., 419.
35. Ibid., 415.
36. Ibid.
37. Ibid., 416-17.

Chapter Three

1. Maurice A. Creasey, *"Inward" and "Outward": A study in early Quaker language*, Supplement No. 30 to the *Journal of the Friends' Historical Society* (London: Friends' Historical Society, 1962): 11.
2. John Punshon, *Portrait in Grey: A short history of the Quakers* (London: Quaker Home Service, 1984), 125.
3. Robert Barclay, *An Apology for the True Christian Divinity: being an explanation and vindication of the principles and doctrines of the people called Quakers*, stereotype ed. (Philadelphia: Friends Book Store, 1908), 118-19.
4. Ibid., 306.
5. Ibid., 313-14.
6. Ibid., 313.
7. Ibid., Sect. 5.
8. Michael L. Birkel, *A Near Sympathy: The Timeless Quaker Wisdom of John Woolman* (Richmond, IN: Friends United Press, 2003), 42-43; Barclay, *Apology*, 88.
9. William Penn, *The Select Works of William Penn*, 4th ed., 3 vols. (1825; repr., New York: Kraus, 1971), 1:335-37.
10. George Fox, *The Works of George Fox*, 8 vols. New Foundation Publication (1831; repr., State College, PA: George Fox Fund, 1990), 8:232-33.
11. Penn, *Select Works*, 1:337.
12. Carole D. Spencer, "Holiness: The Quaker Way of Perfection," *Quaker History* 93, no. 1 (Spring 2004): 129.
13. Fox, *Works of George Fox*, 4:91.
14. Ibid., 3:145.
15. Ibid., 3:58-59.
16. Samuel Fisher, "Rusticus ad Academicos," in *The Testimony of Truth Exalted. . . .*, by Samuel Fisher (n.p., 1679), 414.

17. Ibid., 487-88.
18. Ibid., 453.
19. Barclay, *Apology*, 72.
20. Douglas Gwyn, *Apocalypse of the Word: the life and message of George Fox (1624-1691)* (Richmond, IN: Friends United Press, 1986), 193-97.
21. Hugh Barbour, *The Quakers in Puritan England*, Yale Publications in Religion 7 (New Haven: Yale University Press, 1964), 1.
22. T. Vail Palmer Jr., "Quaker Peace Witness: The Biblical and Historical Roots," *Quaker Religious Thought* 23, no. 2-3 (Summer 1988): 42; citing Edward Burrough, *The memorable Works of a Son of Thunder and Consolation.* . . . (London: Ellis Hooks, 1672), 625.
23. T. Canby Jones, *George Fox's Attitude Toward War: a documentary study* (Annapolis, MD: Academic Fellowship, 1972), 97-107.
24. Palmer, "Quaker Peace Witness," 41.
25. Edward Burrough, *The memorable Works of a Son of Thunder and Consolation.* . . . (London: Ellis Hooks, 1672), 9th (unnumbered) page.
26. Ibid., 665.
27. Palmer, "Quaker Peace Witness," 43.
28. Burrough, *Memorable Works*, 626.
29. Palmer, "Quaker Peace Witness," 46-47.
30. T. Vail Palmer Jr., "Religion and Ethics in the Thought of John Bellers," in *Truth's Bright Embrace: Essays and Poems in Honor of Arthur O. Roberts*, eds. Paul N. Anderson and Howard R. Macy (Newberg, OR: George Fox University Press, 1996), 68.
31. Ibid., 69.
32. John Calvin, *The First Epistle of Paul the Apostle to the Corinthians*, trans. John W. Fraser, Calvin's New Testament Commentaries, vol. 9 (1960; repr., Grand Rapids: William B. Eerdmans, 1976), 229.
33. Ibid., 230.
34. Ibid., 229.
35. Ibid., 230.
36. Ibid., 231.
37. Ibid., 271.
38. Ibid., 306.
39. Elbert Russell, *The History of Quakerism* (1942; Richmond, IN: Friends United Press, 1979), 30.
40. Fox, *Works of George Fox*, 4:104-10.
41. Ibid., 4:104.
42. Ibid., 4:106.

43. Ibid.
44. Ibid., 4:107.
45. Ibid., 4:108.
46. Ibid., 4:109.
47. Ibid.
48. Margaret Fell, *Womens Speaking Justified*. . . . (1666; repr., Amherst, MA: Mosher Book & Tract Committee, New England Yearly Meeting of Friends, 1980), 3.
49. Ibid., 12.
50. John Locke, *A Paraphrase and Notes on the Epistles of St. Paul to the Galatians, 1 and 2 Corinthians, Romans, Ephesians*, ed. Arthur W. Wainwright, 2 vols., The Clarendon Edition of the Works of John Locke (1707; Oxford: Clarendon Press, 1987), 221.
51. Ibid.
52. Ibid., 245.
53. Ibid., 222.
54. Peter A. Huff, "John Locke and the Prophecy of Quaker Women," *Quaker History* 86, no. 2 (Fall 1997).
55. Ibid., 27.
56. Ibid., 32.
57. Ibid., 34-35.
58. Benjamin Coole, *Some Brief Observations . . . John Locke. . . .*, quoted in "John Locke and the Prophecy of Quaker Women," by Peter A. Huff, *Quaker History* 89, no. 2 (Fall 1997): 35.
59. Ibid.
60. Josiah Martin, *A Vindication of Women's Preaching*, quoted in "John Locke and the Prophecy of Quaker Women," by Peter A. Huff, *Quaker History* 86, no. 2 (Fall 1997): 32.
61. Huff, "John Locke," 33.
62. Martin, *Vindication*, 35.
63. Ibid., 36.
64. Benjamin Lay, *All Slave-Keepers that Keep the Innocent in Bondage* (1737; repr., New York: Arno Press, 1969), 145-47.

Chapter Four

1. J. William Frost, ed., *The Quaker Origins of Antislavery* (Norwood, PA: Norwood Editions, 1980), 33.

2. John Hepburn, *The American Defence of the Christian Golden Rule. . . .*, (1715), repr. in *The Quaker Origins of Antislavery*, ed. J. William Frost (Norwood, PA: Norwood Editions, 1980), 89.
3. Thomas E. Drake, *Quakers and Slavery in America* (1950; repr., Gloucester, MA: Peter Smith, 1965), 39.
4. Ralph Sandiford, *A Brief Examination of the Practice of the Times*, (1729; repr., New York: Arno Press, 1969), unnumbered title page.
5. Ibid., 46-50.
6. Ibid., 10.
7. Ibid., 11-12.
8. Ibid., 13-14.
9. Ibid., 53-54.
10. William Penn, *Rise and Progress of the People Called Quakers*, (1694; repr., Philadelphia: Friends Book Store, 1947), 5.
11. Ibid., 7-8.
12. Ibid., 9.
13. Sandiford, *Brief Examination*, Preface: 4th and 5th (unnumbered) pages.
14. Ibid., 35-36.
15. Ibid., 51-52.
16. Drake, *Quakers and Slavery*, 43.
17. Maris Corbin, "An Old Quaker Burial Ground in Barbados," *Friends World Committee for Consultation/Section of the Americas Newsletter* (Summer 2004): 8.
18. John G. Whittier, introduction to *The Journal of John Woolman: with an introduction by John G. Whittier*, by John Woolman (Philadelphia: Friends Book Store, 1871), 13.
19. Benjamin Lay, *All Slave-Keepers that Keep the Innocent in Bondage*, (1737; repr., New York: Arno Press, 1969), 10.
20. Ibid., 27.
21. Ibid., 46.
22. Ibid., 47-48.
23. Ibid., 91-92.
24. Ibid., 10.
25. Ibid., 32-33.
26. Ibid., 36-37.
27. Ibid., 44.
28. Ibid., 56-57.

29. Phillips P. Moulton, introduction to *The Journal and Major Essays of John Woolman*, ed. Phillips P. Moulton (1971; 7th repr., Richmond, IN: Friends United Press, 2001), 5.

30. John Woolman, *The Journal and Major Essays of John Woolman*, ed. Phillips P. Moulton (1971; 7th repr., Richmond, IN: Friends United Press, 2001), 199-210.

31. Ibid., 214.

32. J. William Frost, "John Woolman and the Enlightenment," in *The Tendering Presence: Essays on John Woolman*, ed. Mike Heller (Wallingford, PA: Pendle Hill Publications, 2003), 185.

33. Michael L. Birkel, "Preparing the Heart for Sympathy: John Woolman Reading Scripture," in *The Tendering Presence: Essays on John Woolman*, ed. Mike Heller (Wallingford, PA: Pendle Hill Publications, 2003), 90-91.

34. Woolman, *Journal*, 60.

35. Michael L. Birkel, *A Near Sympathy: The Timeless Quaker Wisdom of John Woolman* (Richmond, IN: Friends United Press, 2003), 81.

36. Woolman, *Journal*, 133-34.

37. Birkel, *Near Sympathy*, 81.

38. Birkel, "Preparing the Heart," 99.

39. John Woolman, *John Woolman and the Affairs of Truth: The Journalist's Essays, Epistles, and Ephemera*, ed., James Proud (San Francisco: Inner Light Books, 2010), 103.

40. Woolman, *Journal*, 174-79.

41. Alan Kolp, *Fresh Winds of the Spirit* (Richmond, IN: Friends United Press, 1991), 42.

42. George S. Brookes, *Friend Anthony Benezet* (Philadelphia: University of Pennsylvania Press, 1937), 19.

43. Ibid., 23.

44. Ibid., 27.

45. Drake, *Quakers and Slavery*, 13-14.

46. Brookes, *Friend Anthony Benezet*, 26.

47. Anthony Benezet, Benezet Letters, repr. in *Friend Anthony Benezet*, by George S. Brookes (Philadelphia: University of Pennsylvania Press, 1937), 207.

48. Howard H. Brinton, introduction to *A Guide to True Peace, or the Excellency of Inward and Spiritual Prayer. . . .* (1839; repr., New York: Harper & Brothers, 1946), xi-xii.

49. Elbert Russell, *The History of Quakerism* (1942; Richmond, IN: Friends United Press, 1979), 229.
50. Ibid., 232.
51. Drake, *Quakers and Slavery*, 94.
52. Irv A. Brendlinger, *To Be Silent . . . Would Be Criminal: The Antislavery Influence and Writings of Anthony Benezet*, Pietist and Wesleyan Studies 20 (Lanham, MD: Scarecrow Press, 2007), 28.
53. Anthony Benezet, *Observations On the Inslaving, importing and purchasing of Negros. . . .*, 2nd ed. (Germantown, PA: Christopher Sower, 1760), repr. in *The Quaker Origins of Antislavery*, ed. J. William Frost (Norwood, PA: Norwood Editions, 1980), 201.
54. Benezet, Benezet Letters in *Friend Anthony Benezet*, 241.
55. Ibid., 360-62.
56. Anthony Benezet, Letters, repr. in *To Be Silent . . . Would Be Criminal: The Antislavery Influence and Writings of Anthony Benezet*, by Irv A. Brendlinger (Lanham, MD: Scarecrow Press, 2007), 86.
57. Benezet, Benezet Letters in *Friend Anthony Benezet*, 315-16.
58. Ibid., 330.
59. Hugh Barbour and J. William Frost, *The Quakers*, Denominations in America 3 (Westport, CT: Greenwood Press, 1988), 101.
60. Ibid., 102.
61. John Churchman, *An Account of the Gospel Labours and Christian Experiences. . . .* (Philadelphia: Joseph Crukshank, 1779), 11.
62. Ibid., 21.
63. Ibid., 106.
64. Ibid., 26.
65. Ibid., 64-65.
66. William P. Taber, "The Theology of the Inward Imperative: Traveling Quaker Ministry of the Middle Period," *Quaker Religious Thought* 18, no. 4 (Autumn, 1980): 10.
67. Churchman, *Account of the Gospel Labours*, 118-19.
68. Ibid., 127-29.
69. Ibid., 217-18.
70. M. Lucetta Mowry, "Allegory," in *The Interpreter's Dictionary of the Bible*, eds. George A. Buttrick et al., (Nashville: Abingdon Press, 1962), 1:82.
71. Churchman, *Account of the Gospel Labours*, 24.
72. Ibid., 67.
73. Ibid., 148.

74.   Ibid., 149.
75.   Ibid., 101.
76.   Ibid., 9.
77.   Ibid., 44.
78.   Ibid., 187-88.
79.   Ibid., 92.
80.   Ibid., 149-50.
81.   Ibid., 175-76.
82.   Ibid., 199.
83.   Jack D. Marietta, *The Reformation of American Quakerism, 1748-1783* (1984; Philadelphia: University of Pennsylvania Press, 2007), 137.
84.   Churchman, *Account of the Gospel Labours*, 69.
85.   Ibid.
86.   Ibid., 71-73.
87.   Woolman, *Journal*, 75.
88.   Marietta, *Reformation*, 152.
89.   Churchman, *Account of the Gospel Labours*, 169.
90.   Ibid.
91.   Ibid.,170.
92.   Ibid., 171.
93.   Woolman, *Journal*, 84-85.
94.   Churchman, *Account of the Gospel Labours*, 172.
95.   Woolman, *Journal*, 85; Churchman, *Account of the Gospel Labours*, 173.
96.   Churchman, *Account of the Gospel Labours*, 110-11.
97.   Ibid., 166.
98.   George Crosfield, *Memoirs of the Life and Gospel Labours of Samuel Fothergill. . . .*, 2nd ed. (1843; London: William and Frederick G. Cash, 1857), 180.
99.   Ibid., 189.
100.   Ibid., 198.
101.   Marietta, *Reformation*, 156.
102.   Ibid.
103.   Ibid., 163.
104.   Ibid., 162.
105.   Ibid., 166.
106.   Woolman, *Journal*, 87.
107.   Marietta, *Reformation*, 174.
108.   Woolman, *Journal*, 87.
109.   Marietta, *Reformation*, 174.

110. Ibid., 259.
111. Crosfield, *Memoirs.*
112. Ibid., 232-33.
113. Ibid., 82.
114. Ibid., 285-86.
115. Ibid., 94.
116. Ibid., 131.
117. Ibid., 179-80.
118. Ibid., 208.
119. Ibid., 253.
120. Ibid., 410.
121. Ibid., 78.
122. Ibid., 97.
123. Ibid., 324.
124. Ibid., 312-13.
125. Ibid., 158.
126. Ibid., 26.
127. Ibid., 147.
128. Job Scott, *Journal of the Life, Travels, and Gospel Labours, of that Faithful Servant, and Minister of Christ, Job Scott* (1798; repr., n.p.: Kessinger Publishing, 2007), 2.
129. Ibid., 12-13.
130. Ibid., 227.
131. Ibid., 47.
132. Ibid., 42.
133. Ibid., 43.
134. Ibid., 50-51.
135. Ibid., 51.
136. Ibid., 56.
137. Ibid., 2.
138. Ibid., 69.
139. Ibid., 163.
140. Ibid., 40-41.
141. Job Scott, *Baptism of Christ a Gospel Ordinance: Being altogether Inward and Spiritual. . . .* (Providence: J. Carter, 1793), 8-9. Digital Quaker Collection, Earlham School of Religion, http://esr.earlham.edu/dqc.
142. Ibid., 37-38.
143. Scott, *Journal of the Life,* 24.

144. Ibid., 262.
145. James Nayler, "James Nayler's Answer, and declaration, touching some things charged upon him, by the men aforesaid," in *Saul's Errand to Damascus: With his packet of letters. . . .* by George Fox and James Nayler (London: Giles Calvert, 1654) repr. in *Early Quaker Writings 1650-1700*, ed. Hugh Barbour and Arthur O. Roberts (Grand Rapids, MI: William B. Eerdmans, 1973), 258.
146. Job Scott, *The Knowledge of the Lord, the Only True God. . . .* (Philadelphia: Emmor Kimber, 1824), 32. Digital Quaker Collection, Earlham School of Religion, http://esr.earlham.edu/dqc.
147. Scott, *Journal of the Life*, 75.
148. Ibid., 74.
149. Ibid., 82.
150. Samuel Fisher, "Rusticus ad Academicos," in *The Testimony of Truth Exalted. . . .*, by Samuel Fisher (n.p., 1679), 592.
151. Scott, *Journal of the Life*, 76.
152. Ibid., 77.
153. Ibid., 80-81.
154. Ibid., 91.
155. Ibid., 84.
156. Ibid., 18.
157. Ibid., 83.
158. Scott, *Knowledge of the Lord*, 48.

Chapter Five

1. Robert Barclay, *An Apology for the True Christian Divinity: being an explanation and vindication of the principles and doctrines of the people called Quakers*, stereotype ed. (Philadelphia: Friends Book Store, 1908), 53.
2. Ibid., 52.
3. Ibid., 62.
4. Ibid., 68.
5. William Penn, *The Christian-Quaker, and his Divine Testimony, Stated and Vindicated, from Scripture, Reason and Authority* (London: J. Sowle), in *A Collection of the Works of William Penn. . . .* by William Penn, (n.p., 1726), 544 Digital Quaker Collection, Earlham School of Religion, http://esr.earlham.edu/dqc.
6. Ibid., 545.

7. Caroline Nicholson Jacob, *The Shackletons of Ballitore: The story of a Quaker family in Ireland and the school they founded and ran from 1726 to 1836* (Philadelphia: Friends General Conference, 1984), 19.

8. Ibid., 14.

9. Rufus M. Jones, *The Later Periods of Quakerism* (1921; repr., London: Macmillan, 1921), 1:294.

10. Ibid., 1:293-94.

11. Ibid., 1:293.

12. Jacob, *The Shackletons*, 19.

13. David Sands, *Journal of the Life and Gospel Labors of David Sands: with extracts from his correspondence* (1848; repr., London: Forgotten Books, 2015), 260.

14. George Fox, "The Man Christ Jesus The Head Of the Church. . . ." in *Works of George Fox*, by George Fox (no publisher, 1831), 5:448. Digital Quaker Collection, Earlham School of Religion, http://esr.earlham.edu/dqc.

15. William Penn, *A Brief Answer to a False and Foolish Libel. . . .*, in *A collection of the Works of William Penn. . . .*, by William Penn (no publisher, 1726), 2:675. Digital Quaker Collection, Earlham School of Religion, http://esr.earlham.edu/dqc.

16. Sands, *Journal of the Life*, 224.

17. Ibid., 242.

18. Jones, *Later Periods of Quakerism*, 1:295.

19. H. Larry Ingle, *Quakers in Conflict: The Hicksite Reformation*, 2nd ed. (1986; Wallingford, PA: Pendle Hill Publications, 1998), 9.

20. Jones, *Later Periods of Quakerism*, 1:302.

21. John Punshon, *Portrait in Grey: A short history of the Quakers* (London: Quaker Home Service, 1984), 114.

22. Walter R. Williams, *The Rich Heritage of Quakerism* (1962; ed. repr. with Epilogue by Paul Anderson, Newberg, OR: Barclay Press, 1987), 145.

23. Henry Tuke, *The Principles of Religion, as Professed by The Society of Christians, Usually Called Quakers. . . .* (1805; repr., n.p., Kessinger Publishing, 2005), iii.

24. Ibid., v.

25. Williams, *Rich Heritage*, 145-46.

26. Tuke, *Principles of Religion*, 19.

27. Ibid., 42.

28. Ibid., 54.

29. Ibid., 61.
30. Ibid., 64.
31. Ibid., 66.
32. Ibid., 159.
33. Ibid., 103.
34. Ibid., 179.
35. Ibid., 99.
36. Ibid.
37. Ibid.
38. Ibid., 100, Locke's note.
39. Ibid., 102.
40. Ibid., 100-101.
41. Ibid., 18.
42. Ibid., 179-80.
43. Ibid., 37-40.
44. Elias Hicks, *Journal of the Life and Religious Labours of Elias Hicks*, 3rd ed. (New York: Isaac T. Hopper, 1832), 143.
45. Ibid., 145.
46. Walt Whitman, *The Complete Poetry and Prose of Walt Whitman, as prepared by him for the Deathbed edition*, 2 vols. (New York: Pellegrini & Cudahy, 1948), 2:478-79.
47. Stephen Grellet, *Memoirs of the Life and Gospel Labours of Stephen Grellet*, ed. Benjamin Seebohm, 2 vols. in 1 (Philadelphia: Henry Longstreth, 1874), 1:142.
48. Hicks, *Journal of the Life*, 127-28.
49. Henry W. Wilbur, *The Life and Labors of Elias Hicks* (Philadelphia: Friends General Conference Advancement Committee, 1910), 125.
50. Ingle, *Quakers in Conflict*, 106.
51. Ibid., 111.
52. Hicks, *Journal of the Life*, 394.
53. Bliss Forbush, *Elias Hicks: Quaker Liberal* (New York: Columbia University Press, 1956), 224-25.
54. John Churchman, *An Account of the Gospel Labours and Christian Experiences. . . .* (Philadelphia: Joseph Crukshank, 1779), 238.
55. Hicks, *Journal of the Life*, 70.
56. Ibid., 298.
57. Ibid., 122.
58. Ibid., 411-12.
59. Elias Hicks, *Letters of Elias Hicks. Including also Observations. . . .* (Philadelphia: T. Ellwood Chapman, 1861), 178.

60. Ibid., 212.
61. Ibid., 150.
62. Wilbur, *Life and Labors*, 231.
63. Hicks, *Letters of Elias Hicks*, 178.
64. Ibid., 177-78.
65. Ibid., 84.
66. Ibid., 116-18.
67. J. N. D. Kelly, *Early Christian Doctrines*, rev. ed. (1960; San Francisco: HarperSanFrancisco, 1978), 116.
68. Hicks, *Letters of Elias Hicks*, 10.
69. Hicks, *Journal of the Life*, 295-96.
70. Wilbur, *Life and Labors*, 230-31.
71. Hicks, *Letters of Elias Hicks*, 45.
72. Ibid., 175.
73. Ibid., 121.
74. Wilbur, *Life and Labors*, 231.
75. Hicks, *Letters of Elias Hicks*, 215.
76. Hicks, *Journal of the Life*, 122-23.
77. Forbush, *Elias Hicks*, 158.
78. Hicks, *Letters of Elias Hicks*, 9.
79. Ibid., 9-10.
80. Ibid., 57.
81. Elias Hicks, *Dear Friend: Letters and Essays of Elias Hicks*, ed. Paul Buckley (San Francisco: Inner Light Books, 2011), 187.
82. Ibid., 187-88.
83. Ibid., 156.
84. Ibid., 158.
85. Ibid.
86. Hicks, *Letters of Elias Hicks*, 74-75.
87. George Fox, *George Fox's Sermon at Wheeler Street, London, at the General Meeting of 1st of 4th Month 1680*, repr. in *Early Quaker Writings 1650-1700*, eds. Hugh Barbour and Arthur O. Roberts (Grand Rapids, MI: William B. Eerdmans, 1973), 505.
88. Hicks, *Letters of Elias Hicks*, 98-99.
89. Ibid., 203-4.
90. Ibid., 146-47.
91. Hicks, *Journal of the Life*, 196.
92. Ibid., 225-26.
93. Elias Hicks, *The Journal of Elias Hicks*, ed. Paul Buckley (San Francisco: Inner Light Books, 2009), 295.

94. Ibid., 295-96.
95. Hicks, *Letters of Elias Hicks,* 121.
96. Hicks, *Journal of the Life,* 123.
97. Jonathan Evans, comp., *A Journal of the Life, Travels, and Religious Labors of William Savery.* . . . stereotype ed. (1873; repr., n.p.: Hard Press, 2007), 395n.
98. Ibid., 381.
99. Ibid., 381n.
100. William Savery, *Discourses Delivered by William Savery.* . . . (London: Darton and Harvey, 1806), 77-78.
101. William Savery, *Seven Sermons and a Prayer.* . . . (Philadelphia: Joseph Rakestraw, 1808), 63-64.
102. Evans, *Journal of the Life,* 276.
103. Savery, *Discourses Delivered,* 104.
104. Evans, *Journal of the Life,* 244.
105. Ibid., 324.
106. Ibid., v.
107. Savery, *Discourses Delivered,* 23-24.
108. Ibid., 69-70.
109. Evans, *Journal of the Life,* iv.
110. Francis R. Taylor, *Life of William Savery of Philadelphia, 1750-1804* (New York: Macmillan, 1925), 414.
111. Savery, *Discourses Delivered,* 37.
112. Evans, *Journal of the Life,* 287.
113. Taylor, *Life of William Savery,* 248.
114. Evans, *Journal of the Life,* 416-17.
115. Taylor, *Life of William Savery,* 430; David E. Swift, *Joseph John Gurney: Banker, Reformer, and Quaker* (Middletown, CT: Wesleyan University Press, 1962), 25. See also Janet Whitney, *Elizabeth Fry: Quaker Heroine,* reissue (1937; New York: Benjamin Blom, 1972), 49; June Rose, *Elizabeth Fry* (New York: St. Martins Press, 1981), 19; Rufus Jones, *Later Periods of Quakerism,* 354.
116. Swift, *Joseph John Gurney,* 25.
117. Whitney, *Elizabeth Fry,* 72.
118. Punshon, *Portrait in Grey,* 170.
119. Swift, *Joseph John Gurney,* 22.
120. Ibid., 43.
121. Ibid., 254.
122. Evans, *Journal of the Life,* 404-5.

123. Ibid., 406.
124. Ibid., 407.
125. Jones, *Later Periods of Quakerism*, 295.
126. Punshon, *Portrait in Grey*, 158.
127. Evans, *Journal of the Life*, 405n.
128. Ibid., 427-28.
129. Ibid., 431.
130. Ibid., 432.
131. Ibid., 436-37.
132. Ibid., 437.
133. Ibid., 438-39.
134. Ibid., 439-40.
135. Elbert Russell, *The History of Quakerism* (1942; Richmond, IN: Friends United Press, 1979), 296; Ingle, *Quakers in Conflict*, 68.
136. John Comly, *Journal of the Life and Religious Labours of John Comly late of Byberry, Pennsylvania* (Philadelphia: T. Ellwood Chapman, 1853), 3.
137. Ibid., 132.
138. Ibid., 142.
139. Ibid.
140. Hugh Barbour and William J. Frost, *The Quakers*, Denominations in America 3 (Westport, CT: Greenwood Press, 1988), 307.
141. Comly, *Journal of the Life*, 143.
142. Ibid., 158.
143. Ibid., 159.
144. Ingle, *Quakers in Conflict*, 120.
145. Wilbur, *Life and Labors*, 140-43.
146. Forbush, *Elias Hicks*, 218-19.
147. Ibid., 219.
148. Ingle, *Quakers in Conflict*, 124.
149. Ibid., 125.
150. Comly, *Journal of the Life*, 303.
151. Ibid., 318.
152. Ibid., 306.
153. Ibid., 309.
154. Ibid., 318.
155. Ibid., 322-23.
156. Ibid., 328.
157. Ibid., 332.
158. Ibid., 333.

159. Ibid., 338.
160. Ibid., 554.
161. Barbour and Frost, *The Quakers*, 308.
162. Comly, *Journal of the Life*, 556.
163. Ibid., 97.
164. Ibid., 98.
165. Ibid.
166. Ibid., 99-100.
167. Ibid., 100-101.
168. Ibid., 102.
169. Ibid., 150-51.
170. Ibid., 582-83.
171. Ibid., 587.
172. Ibid., 581.
173. Ibid., 563-64.
174. Ibid., 588.
175. Ibid., 569-71.
176. Ibid., 395-96.
177. Grellet, *Memoirs of the Life*, 1:19-20.
178. Ibid., 1:20-22.
179. Jones, *Later Periods of Quakerism*, 356-57.
180. Grellet, *Memoirs of the Life*, 1:142.
181. Ibid., 1:330.
182. Ibid., 2:140-41.
183. Ibid., 2:148.
184. Ibid., 2:150.
185. Ibid., 2:222.
186. Ibid., 2:356.
187. Carole Dale Spencer, *Holiness: The Soul of Quakerism: An Historical Analysis of the Theology of Holiness in the Quaker Tradition*, Studies in Christian History and Thought (Eugene, OR: Wipf & Stock, 2008), 106, 116.
188. Ingle, *Quakers in Conflict*, xiii.
189. Grellet, *Memoirs of the Life*, 1:24-25.
190. Ibid., 2:231.
191. Ibid., 2:219.
192. Ibid., 2:145.
193. Ibid., 2:370.
194. Spencer, *Holiness the Soul of Quakerism*, 108.

195. Ibid., 119.

196. Jones, *Later Periods of Quakerism*, 284-85.

197. William Wistar Comfort, *Stephen Grellet, 1773-1855* (New York: Macmillan, 1942), 196.

198. Ibid., 198.

199. Forbush, *Elias Hicks*, 266.

200. Thomas D. Hamm, "'A Protest against Protestantism': Hicksite Friends and the Bible in the Nineteenth Century," *Quaker Studies* 6, vol. 2 (March 2002): 183.

Epilogue

1. T. Vail Palmer, Jr., "Did William Penn Diverge Significantly from George Fox in His Understanding of the Quaker Message?" *Quaker Studies* 11, vol. 1 (September 2006): 63.

2. William Penn, *Rise and Progress of the People Called Quakers* (1694; repr., Philadelphia: Friends Book Store, 1947), 22.

3. Palmer, "Did William Penn Diverge," 69.

4. Elias Hicks, *Letters of Elias Hicks. Including also Observations. . . .* (Philadelphia: T. Ellwood Chapman, 1861), 121.

5. Henry W. Wilbur, *The Life and Labors of Elias Hicks* (Philadelphia: Friends General Conference Advancement Committee, 1910), 231.

6. Elias Hicks, *Dear Friend: Letters and Essays of Elias Hicks*, ed. Paul Buckley (San Francisco: Inner Light Books, 2011), 158.

7. H. Larry Ingle, *Quakers in Conflict: The Hicksite Reformation*, 2nd ed. (1986; Wallingford, PA: Pendle Hill Publications, 1998), 111.

8. Marcus T. C. Gould, extended footnote in *Sermons by Thomas Wetherald, and Elias Hicks. . . .* (Philadelphia: Marcus T. C. Gould, 1826), 185.

9. Elias Hicks, *Dear Friend*, 211.

10. Ibid., 212.

11. Elias Hicks, "Elias Hicks in Continuation," in *Sermons by Thomas Wetherald, and Elias Hicks. . . .* (Philadelphia: Marcus T. C. Gould, 1826), 200.

12. Gould, *Sermons*, 185.

13. Ingle, *Quakers in Conflict*, 30.

Bibliography

Anderson, Bernhard W. *Understanding the Old Testament*. 3rd ed. Englewood Cliffs, NJ: Prentice-Hall, 1975.

———. *The Unfolding Drama of the Bible*. New York: Association Press, 1957.

Baillie, D. M. *God Was in Christ: An Essay on Incarnation and Atonement*. New York: Charles Scribner's Sons, 1948.

Barbour, Hugh. *The Quakers in Puritan England*. Yale Publications in Religion 7. New Haven: Yale University Press, 1964.

Barbour, Hugh S. "Protestant Quakerism." *Quaker Religious Thought* 11, no. 2 (Autumn 1969): 2-33.

Barbour, Hugh and William J. Frost. *The Quakers*. Denominations in America 3. Westport, CT: Greenwood Press, 1988.

Barclay, Robert. *An Apology for the True Christian Divinity: being an explanation and vindication of the principles and doctrines of the people called Quakers*. Stereotype ed. 1678. Philadelphia: Friends Book Store, 1908.

Barth, Karl. *The Epistle to the Romans*. Translated from the 6th edition by Edwin C. Hoskyns. 1933. Reprint, London: Oxford University Press, 1968.

————. *Evangelical Theology: An Introduction.* Translated by Grover Foley. Garden City, NY: Doubleday, 1964.

————. *The Word of God and the Word of Man.* Translated by Douglas Horton. 1928. New York: Harper & Brothers, 1957.

Benezet, Anthony. Benezet Letters. Reprinted in *Friend Anthony Benezet* by George S. Brookes, 207-411. Philadelphia: University of Pennsylvania Press, 1937.

————. *A Caution and Warning to Great Britain and Her Colonies.* . . . Philadelphia: Henry Miller, 1766. Reprinted in *The Quaker Origins of Antislavery*, edited by J. William Frost, 204-237. Norwood, PA: Norwood Editions, 1980.

————. Letters. Reprinted in *To Be Silent . . . Would Be Criminal: The Antislavery Influence and Writings of Anthony Benezet* by Irv A. Brendlinger, 49-114. Pietist and Wesleyan Studies 20. Lanham, MD: Scarecrow Press, 2007.

————. Minor writings of Benezet. Reprinted in *Friend Anthony Benezet* by George S. Brookes, 475-500. Philadelphia: University of Pennsylvania Press, 1937.

————. *Observations On the Inslaving, importing and purchasing of Negroes.* . . . 2nd ed. Germantown, PA: Christopher Sower, 1760. Reprinted in *The Quaker Origins of Antislavery* edited by J. William Frost, 193-203. Norwood, PA: Norwood Editions, 1980.

————. *Some Historical Account of Guinea: Its Situation, Produce And The General Disposition Of Its Inhabitants.* 1772. Reprint, n.p.: Kessinger Publishing, 2004.

————. Tracts of Anthony Benezet. Reprinted in *To Be Silent . . . Would Be Criminal: The Antislavery Influence and Writings of Anthony Benezet* by Irv A. Brendlinger, 118-220. Pietist and Wesleyan Studies 20. Lanham, MD: Scarecrow Press, 2007.

Birch, Bruce C. and Larry L. Rasmussen. *Bible and Ethics in the Christian Life.* Minneapolis: Augsburg Publishing House, 1976.

Birkel, Michael L. *Engaging Scripture: Reading the Bible with Early Friends.* Richmond, IN: Friends United Press, 2005.

————. *A Near Sympathy: The Timeless Quaker Wisdom of John Woolman.* Richmond, IN: Friends United Press, 2003.

————. "Preparing the Heart for Sympathy: John Woolman Reading Scripture." In *The Tendering Presence: Essays on John Woolman*, edited by Mike Heller, 88-104. Wallingford, PA: Pendle Hill Publications, 2003.

———. "Reading Scripture with Dorothy White." *Quaker Religious Thought* 30, no. 3 (September 2001): 55-62.

Boulding, Kenneth. *The Practice of the Love of God.* Pendle Hill Pamphlet 374. Reprint with an introduction by Elise Boulding. Wallingford, PA: Pendle Hill Publications, 2004.

Brendlinger, Irv A. *To Be Silent . . . Would Be Criminal: The Antislavery Influence and Writings of Anthony Benezet.* Pietist and Wesleyan Studies 20. Lanham, MD: Scarecrow Press, 2007.

Brinton, Howard H. Introduction to *A Guide to True Peace, or the Excellency of Inward and Spiritual Prayer. . . .*, vii-xiii. 1839. Reprint, New York: Harper & Brothers, 1946.

Brookes, George S. *Friend Anthony Benezet.* Philadelphia: University of Pennsylvania Press, 1937.

Burrough, Edward. *An Epistle To all the Saints whom God hath called.* N.p. 1657.

———. *The memorable Works of a Son of Thunder and Consolation. . . .* London: Ellis Hooks, 1672.

Calvin, John. *The First Epistle of Paul the Apostle to the Corinthians.* Translated by John W. Fraser. Vol. 9, Calvin's New Testament Commentaries. 1960. Reprint, Grand Rapids, MI: William B. Eerdmans, 1976.

Churchman, John. *An Account of the Gospel Labours and Christian Experiences of a Faithful Minister of Christ, John Churchman. . . .* Philadelphia: Joseph Crukshank, 1779.

Comfort, William Wistar. *Stephen Grellet, 1773-1855.* New York: MacMillan, 1942.

Comly, John. *Journal of the Life and Religious Labours of John Comly, late of Byberry, Pennsylvania.* Philadelphia: T. Ellwood Chapman, 1853.

Coole, Benjamin. *Some Brief Observations on the Paraphrase and Notes of the Judicious John Locke. . . .* London: P. Gwillim, 1716. Quoted in "John Locke and the Prophecy of Quaker Women" by Peter A. Huff. *Quaker History* 86, no. 2 (Fall 1997): 27-35.

Corbin, Maris. "An Old Quaker Burial Ground in Barbados." *Friends World Committee for Consultation/Section of the Americas Newsletter* (Summer 2004): 8.

Creasey, Maurice A. *"Inward" and "Outward": A study in early Quaker language.* Supplement no. 30 to the *Journal of the Friends' Historical Society.* London: Friends' Historical Society, 1962.

———. "Quakers and the Sacraments." *Quaker Religious Thought* 5 no. 1 (Spring 1963): 2-25.

————. "Radical Christianity and Christian Radicalism." Paper read at the London Society for the Study of Religion, 1973. Reprinted in *Collected Essays of Maurice Creasey, 1912-2004: The Social Thought of a Quaker Thinker*, edited by David L. Johns, 23-54. Quaker Studies 8. Lewiston, NY: Edwin Mellen Press, 2011.

Crosfield, George. *Memoirs of the Life and Gospel Labours of Samuel Fothergill with Selections from his Correspondence. . . .* 2nd ed. 1843. London: William and Frederick G. Cash, 1857.

Dandelion, Pink. *The Liturgies of Quakerism.* Liturgy, Worship and Society. Aldershot, Hampshire: Ashgate Publishing, 2005.

Dodd, C. H. *Christianity and the Reconciliation of the Nations.* The Burge Memorial Lecture, November 1951. London: SCM Press, 1952.

Drake, Thomas E. *Quakers and Slavery in America.* 1950. Reprint, Gloucester, MA: Peter Smith, 1965.

Endy, Melvin. "George Fox and William Penn: Their Relationship and Their Roles within the Quaker Movement." *Quaker History* 93, no. 1 (Spring 2004): 1-39.

Evans, Jonathan, comp. *A Journal of the Life, Travels, and Religious Labors of William Savery. . . .* Stereotype ed. 1873. Reprint, n.p.: Hard Press, 2007.

Fell, Margaret. *Womens Speaking Justified, Proved and Allowed of by The Scriptures. . . .* 1666. Reprint, Amherst, MA: Mosher Book & Tract Committee, New England Yearly Meeting of Friends, 1980.

Fisher, Samuel. "Rusticus ad Academicos." In *The Testimony of Truth Exalted, by the Collected Labours of . . . Samuel Fisher. . . .*, by Samuel Fisher, 27-774. N.p., 1679.

Forbush, Bliss. *Elias Hicks: Quaker Liberal.* New York: Columbia University Press, 1956.

Fox, George. *George Fox's Sermon at Wheeler Street, London, at the General Meeting of 1st of 4th Month, 1680.* In *Early Quaker Writings, 1650-1700*, edited by Hugh Barbour and Arthur O. Roberts, 502-12. Grand Rapids, MI: Eerdmans, 1973.

————. *The Journal of George Fox.* Rev. ed. by John L. Nickalls. Cambridge: Cambridge University Press, 1952.

————. "The Man Christ Jesus The Head Of The Church, And True Mediator. . . ." In *Works of George Fox* by George Fox, 421-55. Vol. 5. N.p., 1831. Digital Quaker Collection, Earlham School of Religion, http://esr.earlham.edu/dqc.

————. *The Works of George Fox.* 8 vols. New Foundation Publication. 1831. Reprint, State College, PA: George Fox Fund, 1990.

Frost, J. William. "John Woolman and the Enlightenment." In *The Tendering Presence: Essays on John Woolman*, edited by Mike Heller, 167-89. Wallingford, PA: Pendle Hill Publications, 2003.

————, ed. with introduction. *The Quaker Origins of Antislavery.* Norwood, PA: Norwood Editions, 1980.

Gomes, Peter J. *The Good Book: Reading the Bible with Mind and Heart.* New York: Avon Books, 1998.

Gould, Marcus T. C. *Sermons by Thomas Wetherald, and Elias Hicks. . . .* Philadelphia: Marcus T. C. Gould, 1826.

Grellet, Stephen. *Memoirs of the Life and Gospel Labours of Stephen Grellet.* Edited by Benjamin Seebohm. 2 vols. in 1. Philadelphia: Henry Longstreth, 1874.

Guiton, Gerard. *The Early Quakers and the "Kingdom of God": Peace, Testimony and Revolution.* San Francisco: Inner Light Books, 2012.

Gwyn, Douglas. *Apocalypse of the Word: the life and message of George Fox (1624-1691).* Richmond, IN: Friends United Press, 1986.

————. *The Covenant Crucified: Quakers and the Rise of Capitalism.* Wallingford, PA: Pendle Hill Publications, 1995.

————. "Response" [to H. Larry Ingle, "On the Folly of Seeking the Quaker Holy Grail"]. *Quaker Religious Thought* 25, vol. 1 (May 1991): 31-33.

————. *Seekers Found: Atonement in Early Quaker Experience.* Wallingford, PA: Pendle Hill Publications, 2000.

Hamm, Thomas D. "'A Protest against Protestantism': Hicksite Friends and the Bible in the Nineteenth Century." *Quaker Studies* 6 no. 2 (March 2002): 175-94.

Heller, Mike, ed. *The Tendering Presence: Essays on John Woolman.* Wallingford, PA: Pendle Hill Publications, 2003.

Hepburn, John. *The American Defence of the Christian Golden Rule, Or An Essay to prove the Unlawfulness of making Slaves of Men.* 1715. Reprinted in *The Quaker Origins of Antislavery*, edited by J. William Frost, 82-122. Norwood, PA: Norwood Editions, 1980.

Hicks, Elias. *Dear Friend: Letters and Essays of Elias Hicks.* Edited by Paul Buckley. San Francisco: Inner Light Books, 2011.

————. "Elias Hicks in Continuation." In *Sermons by Thomas Wetherald, and Elias Hicks. . . .* by Marcus T. C. Gould. Philadelphia: Marcus T. C. Gould, 1826.

―――――. *The Journal of Elias Hicks*. Edited by Paul Buckley. San Francisco: Inner Light Books, 2009.

―――――. *Journal of the Life and Religious Labours of Elias Hicks*. 3rd ed. New York: Isaac T. Hopper, 1832.

―――――. *Letters of Elias Hicks. Including also Observations on the Slavery of the Africans*. . . . Philadelphia: T. Ellwood Chapman, 1861.

Howgill, Francis. "Francis Howgill's Testimony Concerning the Life, Death, Tryals, and Labours of Edward Burrough. . . . In *The memorable Works of a Son of Thunder and Consolation*. . . . by Edward Burrough, unnumbered pages. London: Ellis Hooks, 1672.

―――――. "The inheritance of Jacob discovered, after his return out of Egypt. . . . London: Giles Calvert, 1656. Quoted in *The Book of Francis Howgill*, written and compiled by Will Hayes. Meopham Green, Kent: The Order of the Great Companions, 1942.

Huff, Peter A. "John Locke and the Prophecy of Quaker Women." *Quaker History* 86, no. 2 (Fall 1997): 26-40.

Ingle, H. Larry. "On the Folly of Seeking the Quaker Holy Grail." *Quaker Religious Thought* 25, no. 1 (May 1991): 17-29.

―――――. *Quakers in Conflict: The Hicksite Reformation*. 2nd ed. 1986. Wallingford, PA: Pendle Hill Publications, 1998.

Jacob, Caroline Nicholson. *The Shackletons of Ballitore: The story of a Quaker family in Ireland and the school they founded and ran from 1726 to 1836*. Philadelphia: Friends General Conference, 1984.

James, William. *The Varieties of Religious Experience: A Study in Human Nature*. Gifford Lectures on Natural Religion, 1902. The Modern Library. New York: Random House, 1929.

Jones, Rufus M. *The Later Periods of Quakerism*. 2 vols. London: Macmillan, 1921.

―――――. *The Later Periods of Quakerism*. Vol. 1. 1921. Reprint, Westport, CT: Greenwood Press, 1970.

Jones, T. Canby. *George Fox's Attitude Toward War: a documentary study*. Annapolis, MD: Academic Fellowship, 1972.

―――――. *Triumph Through Obedience*. Quaker Lecture. Indianapolis: John Woolman Press, 1964.

Kelly, J. N. D. *Early Christian Doctrines*. Rev. ed. 1960. San Francisco: HarperSanFrancisco, 1978.

Kelly, Thomas R. *Reality of the Spiritual World*. Pendle Hill Pamphlet 21. Wallingford, PA: Pendle Hill, 1942.

————. *A Testament of Devotion*. With a biographical memoir by Douglas V. Steere. New York: Harper & Row, 1941.

Kolp, Alan. "Fox Loved the Apostle Paul." *Quaker Religious Thought* 25, no. 2 (October 1991): 7-26.

————. *Fresh Winds of the Spirit*. Richmond, IN: Friends United Press, 1991.

Lay, Benjamin. *All Slave-Keepers that Keep the Innocent in Bondage*. 1737. Reprint, New York: Arno Press, 1969.

Locke, John. *A Paraphrase and Notes on the Epistles of St. Paul to the Galatians, 1 and 2 Corinthians, Romans, Ephesians*. Edited by Arthur W. Wainwright. The Clarendon Edition of the Works of John Locke. 2 vols. 1707. Oxford, England: Clarendon Press, 1987.

Macy, Howard R. *The Shalom of God*. Dublin, IN: Friends United Press, 1972.

Marietta, Jack D. *The Reformation of American Quakerism, 1748-1783*. 1st paperback edition. 1984. Philadelphia: University of Pennsylvania Press, 2007.

Martin, Josiah. *A Vindication of Women's Preaching*. London: J. Sowle, 1717. Quoted in "John Locke and the Prophecy of Quaker Women" by Peter A. Huff. *Quaker History* 86, no. 2 (Fall 1997): 32-36.

Mott, Lucretia. *Lucretia Mott: Her Complete Speeches and Sermons*. Edited with an introduction by Dana Greene. Studies in Women and Religion 4. New York and Toronto: Edwin Mellen Press, 1980.

Mott, Lucretia C. *Selected Letters of Lucretia Coffin Mott*. Edited by Beverly Wilson Palmer. Urbana, IL: University of Illinois Press, 2002.

Moulton, Phillips P. Introduction to *The Journal and Major Essays of John Woolman*, by John Woolman, 3-16. Edited by Phillips P. Moulton. 1971. Richmond, IN: Friends United Press, 2001.

Mowry, M. Lucetta. "Allegory." In *The Interpreter's Dictionary of the Bible*, edited by George A. Buttrick et al., 82-84. Vol. 1. Nashville: Abingdon Press, 1962.

Nayler, James. "James Nayler's Answer, and declaration, touching some things charged upon him, by the men aforesaid." In *Saul's Errand to Damascus: With his packet of letters. . . .* by George Fox and James Nayler. 1654. Reprinted in *Early Quaker Writings, 1650-1700*, edited by Hugh Barbour and Arthur O. Roberts, 257-59. Grand Rapids: William B. Eerdmans, 1973.

Northwest Yearly Meeting of Friends Church. *Faith and Practice: A Book of Christian Discipline*. Newberg, OR: Barclay Press, 1987.

Palmer, T. Vail, Jr. "Deeds and Rules in Quaker Ethics." *Quaker Religious Thought* 13, vol. 2 (Winter 1971-72): 2-18.

————. "Did William Penn Diverge Significantly from George Fox in His Understanding of the Quaker Message?" *Quaker Studies* 11, vol. 1 (September 2006): 59-70.

————. "Early Friends and the Bible." *Quaker Religious Thought* 23 no. 5 (1992).

————. "Quaker Peace Witness: The Biblical and Historical Roots." *Quaker Religious Thought* 23, vols. 2 and 3 (Summer 1988): 36-55.

————. "The Radical-Reformation Tradition and Emergent Christian Ethics." Paper presented at the Annual Meeting of the American Academy of Religion, Newton, MA, 1969.

————. "Religion and Ethics in the Thought of John Bellers." In *Truth's Bright Embrace: Essays and Poems in Honor of Arthur O. Roberts*, edited by Paul N. Anderson and Howard R. Macy, 61-74. Newberg, OR: George Fox University Press, 1996.

————. "A Revisionist Revised: A New Look at Bernstein's *Cromwell and Communism*." In *Practiced in the Presence, Essays in Honor of T. Canby Jones*, edited by D. Neil Snarr and Daniel L. Smith-Christopher, 36-59. Richmond, IN: Friends United Press, 1994.

Penn, William. *A Brief Answer to a False and Foolish Libel. . . .* In *A Collection of the Works of William Penn. To which is Prefixed a Journal of his Life, with many Original Letters and Papers not before Published* by William Penn, 668-75. Vol. 2. N.p. 1726. Digital Quaker Collection, Earlham School of Religion, http://esr.earlham.edu/dqc.

————. *The Christian-Quaker, and his Divine Testimony, Stated and Vindicated, from Scripture, Reason and Authority.* In *A Collection of the Works of William Penn. To which is Prefixed a Journal of his Life, with many Original Letters and Papers not before Published* by William Penn, 522-90. Vol. 1. N.p., 1726. Digital Quaker Collection, Earlham School of Religion, http://esr.earlham.edu/dqc.

————. *Rise and Progress of the People Called Quakers.* 1694. Reprint, Philadelphia: Friends Book Store, 1947.

————. *The Select Works of William Penn.* 4th ed. 3 vols. 1825. Reprint, New York: Kraus Reprint, 1971.

Punshon, John. "Miss Wilson's Legacy: How My Early Schooling Taught Me to Read the Letter to the Hebrews." In *The Quaker Bible Reader*, edited by Paul Buckley and Stephen W. Angell, 251-71. Richmond, IN: Earlham School of Religion Publications, 2006.

————. *Portrait in Grey: A short history of the Quakers*. London: Quaker Home Service, 1984.

Rose, June. *Elizabeth Fry*. 1st U.S. ed. 1980. New York: St. Martin's Press, 1981.

Russell, Elbert. *The History of Quakerism*. 1942. Richmond, IN: Friends United Press, 1979.

Sandiford, Ralph. *A Brief Examination of the Practice of the Times*. 1729. Reprint, New York: Arno Press, 1969.

Sands, David. *Journal of the Life and Gospel Labors of David Sands: With extracts from his correspondence*. 1848. Reprint, London: Forgotten Books, 2015.

Savery, William. *Discourses Delivered by William Savery, of North America, at Several Meetings of the People Called Quakers, and Others*. London: Darton and Harvey, 1806.

————. *Seven Sermons and a Prayer, Preached at the Meetings of the Religious Society of Friends*. Philadelphia: Joseph Rakestraw, 1808.

Schweitzer, Albert. *The Quest of the Historical Jesus: A Critical Study of Its Progress from Reimarus to Wrede*. Translated by W. Montgomery. 1910. Reprint, New York: Macmillan, 1950.

Scott, Job. *Baptism of Christ a Gospel Ordinance: Being altogether Inward and Spiritual. . . .* Providence: J. Carter, 1793. Digital Quaker Collection, Earlham School of Religion, http://esr.earlham.edu/dqc.

————. *Journal of the Life, Travels, and Gospel Labours, of that Faithful Servant and Minister of Christ, Job Scott*. 1798. Reprint, n.p.: Kessinger Publishing, 2007.

————. *The Knowledge of the Lord, the Only True God. To Which Is Added, Remarks upon the Doctrine of Perseverance*. Philadelphia: Emmor Kimber, 1824. Digital Quaker Collection, Earlham School of Religion, http://esr.earlham.edu/dqc.

Smith, Daniel L. *The Religion of the Landless: The Social Context of the Babylonian Exile*. Bloomington, IN: Meyer-Stone Books, 1989.

Smith-Christopher, Daniel L. *A Biblical Theology of Exile*. Overtures to Biblical Theology. Minneapolis: Fortress Press, 2002.

————. *Jonah, Jesus, and Other Good Coyotes: Speaking Peace to Power in the Bible*. Nashville: Abingdon Press, 2007.

Spencer, Carole D. "Holiness: The Quaker Way of Perfection." *Quaker History* 93, vol. 1 (Spring 2004): 123-47.

Spencer, Carole Dale. *Holiness: The Soul of Quakerism: An Historical Analysis of the Theology of Holiness in the Quaker Tradition.* Studies in Christian History and Thought. Eugene, OR: Wipf & Stock, 2008.

Swift, David E. *Joseph John Gurney: Banker, Reformer, and Quaker.* Middletown, CT: Wesleyan University Press, 1962.

Taber, William P. "The Theology of the Inward Imperative: Traveling Quaker Ministry of the Middle Period." *Quaker Religious Thought* 18, no. 4 (Autumn 1980): 3-19.

Taylor, Francis R. *Life of William Savery of Philadelphia, 1750-1804.* New York: Macmillan, 1925.

Tucker, R. W. "Revolutionary Faithfulness." *Quaker Religious Thought* 9, vol. 2 (Winter 1967-68): 3-29.

Tuke, Henry. *The Principles of Religion, as Professed by The Society of Christians, Usually Called Quakers.* . . . 1805. Reprint, n.p.: Kessinger Publishing, 2005.

Valentine, Lonnie. "War and War Resistance in the Old Testament." In *The Quaker Bible Reader*, edited by Paul Buckley and Stephen W. Angell, 61-81. Richmond, IN: Earlham School of Religion Publications, 2006.

Vann, Richard T. *The Social Development of English Quakerism: 1655-1755.* Cambridge, MA: Harvard University Press, 1969.

Whitehead, Alfred North. *Process and Reality: An Essay in Cosmology.* 1929. New York: Harper & Brothers, 1960.

Whitman, Walt. *The Complete Poetry and Prose of Walt Whitman, as prepared by him for the Deathbed edition.* Introduction by Malcolm Cowley. 2 vols. New York: Pellegrini & Cudahy, 1948.

Whitney, Janet. *Elizabeth Fry: Quaker Heroine.* 1937. Reissue, New York: Benjamin Blom, 1972.

Whittier, John G. Introduction to *The Journal of John Woolman: with an introduction by John G. Whittier*, by John Woolman, 1-49. Philadelphia: Friends Book Store, 1871.

Wilbur, Henry W. *The Life and Labors of Elias Hicks.* Philadelphia: Friends General Conference Advancement Committee, 1910.

Williams, Walter. *The Rich Heritage of Quakerism.* 1962. Edited reprint with Epilogue by Paul Anderson. Newberg, OR: Barclay Press, 1987.

Woolman, John. *John Woolman and the Affairs of Truth: The Journalist's Essays, Epistles, and Ephemera.* Edited by James Proud. San Francisco: Inner Light Books, 2010.

————. *The Journal and Major Essays of John Woolman.* Edited by Phillips P. Moulton. 1971. 7th reprint, Richmond, IN: Friends United Press, 2001.

Wright, G. Ernest. *God Who Acts: Biblical Theology as Recital.* Studies in Biblical Theology 8. London: SCM Press, 1952.

Yoder, John Howard. *The Politics of Jesus: vicit agnus noster.* Grand Rapids: William B. Eerdmans, 1972.

Index

Old Testament

New Testament

Subject Index

A

Abingdon, Pennsylvania, 115

adoptionism, 186–187

African American, 19–20, 79–80

agnosticism, 9, 27

allegory, 91, 94, 138, 219–220

American Revolution, 159, 186, 205

Anabaptist, 36–37

Anderson, Bernhard W., 10, 31–32, 50, 78

Anthony, Eunice, 159

Anthonys, Daniel, 159

Audland, John, 40–41

Austria, 226

B

Baillie, Donald M., 29, 30

Ballitore, Ireland, 159, 171, 207

Baltimore, Maryland, 183, 238

Baltimore Yearly Meeting, 183

baptism, 163, 167, 179, 186–187, 195, 220, 228, 229

Baptist, 28, 40, 159, 166, 204

Barbados, 113–117

Barbour, Hugh, 35, 36, 93, 132

Barclay, David, 83

Barclay, Robert, 8, 14, 18, 75, 83–86, 92–93, 98, 103, 105–106, 115, 169–170, 172–174, 176, 211, 230

Barnard, Hannah, 173, 174, 176, 179, 181, 191–192, 194

Barney, Sarah, 124

Barth, Karl, 29, 31–32, 55, 78

Bellers, John, 96–98, 127, 130

Benezet, Anthony, 123–132, 136, 142–143, 147, 150, 156, 159, 168, 171, 237

Benezet, John Stephen, 123

Benson, Lewis, 28, 36

Bettle, Samuel, 183, 212

Biblical Theology Movement, 27, 31–32, 68, 77–79

Birkel, Michael, 15, 17–19, 78, 86, 120–122, 198

Bock, Paul, 78

Bohemia, 226–227

Boulding, Kenneth, 9

Brendlinger, Irv, 127

Briggflatts Meeting House, 25–27

Brinton, Howard, 27, 34

Bristol, England, 14, 75, 89, 104, 115, 125

British Isles, 101, 151, 159, 201, 226

Brookes, George, 127

Brookfield, New York, 222

Brooklyn, New York, 180

Brown, Moses, 130

Brown, William, 150

Buber, Martin, 27

Bunyan, John, 42

H

Haiti, 226, 227

Harvard, 79

Heller, Mike, 120

Hempstead, Long Island, New York, 180

Henry, Patrick, 126

Hepburn, John, 107, 119, 189

hermeneutics, 60–61

Hicks, Elias, 179–200, 204, 208, 210, 224, 227, 227–229, 233–235, 237

Hicksite Friends, 8–9, 215, 228–229, 233, 239

Hicksite-Orthodox Separation, 169, 229. See also Great Separation, the

Holland, 132

Hooten, Elizabeth, 101

Howgill, Francis, 40–41, 44–45, 55, 106, 230

Huff, Peter A., 104

Hungary, 226

Hunt, John, 149

Huss, John, 123

Huxley, Aldous, 28

I

Indiana, 8–9, 234

Indiana Yearly Meeting, 234

Ingle, Larry, 26, 229

Ireland, 132, 135, 159, 164, 171, 173, 201, 205, 207, 209–210, 226

Italy, 125, 226, 228

J

James, William, 56

Japanese American, 19, 79

Jefferson, Thomas, 170, 184

Jericho Monthly Meeting, 180, 182–183, 197, 198, 211, 228, 234

Jericho, New York, 180

Jones, Rufus, 27, 28, 34, 36, 208, 233

Jones, T. Canby, 35, 37, 47, 93

K

Kelly, Thomas, 9, 16, 28

King, Martin Luther, Jr., 37

Kirkridge, Pennsylvania, 9

Kolp, Alan, 16, 76–77, 123

L

Lamborn, George, 9

Lamb's War, 35–36, 47, 93–94, 96, 105, 161, 235–236

Lancashire, England, 25, 40, 70

Lancaster County, Pennsylvania, 9

Lancaster Prison, 25

Lay, Benjamin, 105, 114–118

Lay, Sarah, 115, 116, 118

Lichfield, England, 13, 75

Limoges, France, 224

Liverpool, England, 114, 209

Locke, John, 36, 103–105, 176

Lollards, 36

W

Wales, 25, 201, 209

War-Nation-Church Study Group, 37–38

War of 1812, 186

Waterford, Ireland, 207

Webb, Benjamin, 234

Wesley, John, 126, 170

Westbury, Long Island, New York, 180

Westbury Monthly Meeting, 180, 197

Westmorland, England, 25, 40, 43

Westtown, Pennsylvania, 210, 216

Westtown School, 211, 215

White, Dorothy, 18

Whitehead, Alfred North, 26

White, Joseph, 150

Whitman, Walt, 181

Wilberforce, William, 170

Williams, Walter, 174

Willis, Phebe, 182

Willis, Thomas, 182

Wilmington, Delaware, 147, 181, 182, 186

Wilmington Monthly Meeting, 181, 234

Wilson, Christopher, 149–150

Woodcock, Samuel, 171, 173

Woolman, John, 15–16, 17–18, 118–123, 130, 132, 136, 142–151, 156–157, 159, 168, 171, 190, 198, 212, 215, 217, 236–237

World War II, 19, 34, 79

Wright, G. Ernest, 10, 31, 32, 78

Y

Yearly Meeting of Ireland, 173, 210

Yoder, John Howard, 38–39, 76

Yorkshire, England, 25, 40, 135

Young, Rebecca, 225

Z

Zinzendorf, Count Nikolaus von, 124

288

CPSIA information can be obtained
at www.ICGtesting.com
Printed in the USA
FSOW01n1640150716
22789FS

9 781594 980374